Public Expenditure and Economic Growth of India and Tanzania

About the Authors:

Shri Prakash holds Master's and Ph.D. degrees in Economics. He is currently Professor of Eminence and former Dean Research, Birla Institute of Management Technology (BIMTECH). He has more than 50 years of teaching and research experience. He has authored 12 books and published more than 200 research papers in national and international journals of repute. He has chaired numerous sessions at national and international conferences in India and abroad; has been consultant to World Bank, UNESCO, UNICEF, and full time consultant to UGC; and has guided 31 MPhil and PhD scholars. He has been visiting Professor at Karl Marx (now Budapest) University, Institute of Econometrics and Statistics, University of Lodge, Poland. He was conferred Kautaliya Award for his contribution to teaching and research in Economics.

Richard Fue Kiangi holds Master's degree in Economics from the University of Groningen (Netherlands) and Ph.D. degree in Management from Mohanlal Sukhadia (MLS), Udaipur. He is a lecturer in economics and related disciplines at the Institute of Finance Management, Tanzania and also works as the visiting lecturer at the Institute of Tax Administration (ITA), Tanzania. He has over 10 years of teaching and research experience: he has also conducted research at BIMTECH. He has authored four research papers and presented several papers at national and international conferences. His areas of specialisation are: economic growth, econometrics and public sector economics particularly public expenditure.

Sudhi Sharma holds an MBA from Uttar Pradesh Technical University (UPTU), Lucknow, and Ph.D. in management from MLS University Udaipur. She has over 8 years of teaching and research experience. She worked as Assistant Professor at 3 reputed management institutes of Kanpur, Gurgaon and Noida, and has also worked as Senior Research Analyst/Associate at BIMTECH, Greater Noida. She is currently Joint Secretary, Northern Region, Input Output Research Association, India. She has published and presented 16 research papers in reputed journals and at national and international conferences. Her areas of specialisation are: finance, econometrics and financial econometrics.

Public Expenditure and Economic Growth of India and Tanzania

Shri Prakash
Richard Fue Kiangi
Sudhi Sharma

ACADEMIC FOUNDATION
NEW DELHI

www.academicfoundation.org

First published in 2017
by

ACADEMIC FOUNDATION
4772-73 / 23 Bharat Ram Road, (23 Ansari Road),
Darya Ganj, New Delhi - 110 002 (India).
Phones : 23245001 / 02 / 03 / 04.
Fax : +91-11-23245005.
E-mail : booksaf@gmail.com
www.academicfoundation.org

The book is in the series of publications of books by BIMTECH Faculty.

Cataloging in Publication Data--DK
Courtesy: D.K. Agencies (P) Ltd. <docinfo@dkagencies.com>

Prakash, Shri, 1938- **author.**
Public expenditure and economic growth of India and Tanzania / Shri Prakash, Richard Fue Kiangi, Sudhi Sharma.
pages cm
Includes bibliographical references.
ISBN 9789332704022

1. Expenditures, Public--India. 2. Expenditures, Public--Tanzania. 3. Economic development--India. 4. Economic development--Tanzania. 5. Finance, Public--India. 6. Finance, Public--Tanzania. I. Kiangi, Richard Fue, author. II. Sharma, Sudhi, author. III. Title.

HJ1331.P73 2017 DDC 336.390954 23

Typeset, printed and bound by The Book Mint, New Delhi.
www.thebookmint.in

CONTENTS

LIST OF TABLES AND FIGURES

TABLES

FIGURES

Foreword

Pursuit of excellence in academics and adherence to the ethical values have been the driving forces of Birla Institute of Management Technology (BIMTECH) right from its inception in 1988 and these still remain the part of its ethos. Academic excellence comprises mainly the attainment and maintenance of the highest standard in teaching and conduct of innovative and original research for filling up gaps in knowledge in relevant areas. It is generally thought that the basic objective of business schools is the preparation of future managers, who are well endowed with the advance knowledge of management science and who are equipped with versatile skills in the application of concepts and methods to data and information to find solutions to current and emerging business problems to improve current practices in the business world. Therefore, research is and should be an inseparable part of the academic profile of business schools. However, not many business schools attach importance to research. But the management of BIMTECH differed and still differs with this perception. Enrichment of teaching with the new knowledge is as much important as the dissemination of currently prevalent knowledge. It is the research accomplishments of the teachers of the educational institutions which fulfills this need. Learning and teaching of the advance knowledge of management is preceded by the generation of new knowledge and this is almost impossible without research. Therefore, BIMTECH established its Center of Research Studies in 2003 to launch PhD programme. Besides, BIMTECH encourages its faculty members to conduct and guide research, publish their research outcomes as research papers and books. Faculty is also encouraged to participate and present their research papers in national and international conferences. This is backed up by BIMTECH's programme of publication. It regularly publishes two journals and supports the publication of books authored or edited by the members of its faculty. This book is also a part of this programme of BIMTECH.

The topic and the subject matter of the book are interesting because it deals with public expenditure, the most important component of public finance, and its relation with the growth of the economy. Generally it is thought that the public expenditure plays the pivotal role practically in every field of economic activity in centrally planned socialist countries. But does this hold true for the emerging market economies which have been implementing the programmes of liberalisation, privatisation and globalisation for more than two/three decades? In other words, does public expenditure play any role in the growth of non-planned economies moving on to the capitalist path? Is public expenditure an important component of growth and welfare universally? I trust partial, if not complete, answers to such questions can be found in this book. This book fills up a few theoretically, methodologically and empirically empty boxes. It will not be an exacerbation or misplaced to designate the book as the Econometrics of Public Expenditure. So far as I know, no book is available on this subject which is based on in-depth research. Another feature of the book is the comparative analysis of economic growth and public expenditure of India and Tanzania. There is hardly any book which addresses comparative development of two developing countries though there are several books on the study of comparative development of developed capitalist economies.

In view of the above, I hope that the readers will find the book a stimulating reading experience. I appreciate, commend and congratulate the two young and upcoming scholars for their achievement of authoring the book when they were busy in completing their PhD dissertation at BIMTECH.

— Harivansh Chaturvedi
Director,
BIMTECH

Preface

Writing a book on any subject is a herculean task since the work is spread over the years. The job becomes all the more difficult if your co-authors are engaged in researching for PhD degree under your own guidance. The task becomes even more arduous if one the co-authors is researching in an area which is not even partially related to the specialised subject of inter-relations between public expenditure and economic growth of two different countries like India and Tanzania. However, my co-authors stuck to the task of completing their part of the work relating to the book very boldly and nonchalantly with conviction and dedication; they also displayed unflinching determination not to compromise with academic standard required for the book based largely on research.

My job became all the more difficult when Richard Fue Kiangi left for Tanzania after submitting his PhD thesis and Sudhi Sharma also got totally engrossed in the completion of her PhD thesis. The text of the book was prepared nearly two years ago, so it has to be thoroughly revised and updated. All the same, the book in hand is an outcome of the dedicated endeavours of all three authors. All the authors shared their workload of joint authorship.

Richard prepared the first draft of the chapters second and sixth; he also completed data analysis of chapter six. Sudhi Sharma prepared the first draft of chapters fourth and fifth and completed the analysis of results derived from the application of growth curves to the data of Indian economy. The data analysis of the seventh chapter was jointly done by Kiangi and Sharma. Shri Prakash wrote the first and third chapters and completed the updating and editing of the text of all the chapters of the book. It is possible that, despite the best efforts of the authors, some errors of omission and commission still remain for which the senior author takes the entire responsibility. Suggestions for improvement will always be welcome from all.

There is no fun in writing a book on any subject if it is repetitive or imitative. The excitement and pleasure lies in composing something imaginative, innovative and original, which also makes the book different from the ones already available. However, no book can ever be totally free from the influence of the peers, pioneers and their contribution to the stock of knowledge in the chosen area of research. This book is also no exception to the general rule. Authors also do not claim that this book is totally different from other books available in the market on the subject of public finance. However, to the best of our knowledge, there is hardly any book which deals exclusively either with public expenditure, or inter-dependence of public expenditure and economic growth alone. The book that comes nearest to the main theme and thrust of this book is *Expenditure on Education: Theory, Growth and Models*, by Shri Prakash and Sumitra Choudhary, National University of Educational Planning and Administration (NIEPA), New Delhi. Almost all the chapters embody the outcomes of in-depth research by the authors on the main theme of the book. Preliminary version of the last chapter of the book was also presented at the Second International Conference on Finance at Bali, Indonesia.

An attempt has been made to partially meet the basic requirements of the text book on Public Finance/Economics, which is taught at all the universities of the world. It is hoped that the researchers in this field, especially those engaged in research relating to India and Tanzania, will also find some helpful material relevant for their investigation. An attempt has been made to empirically and logically examine the implications of changes in public expenditure and GDP (gross domestic product)in the course of economic growth for all the components of public finance or vice versa. Therefore, despite the focus of investigation is on inter-relations between the growth of public expenditure and the growth of GDP, analysis of data goes much beyond this for discovering repercussions of changing public expenditure and GDP for public revenue, public borrowings, and fiscal deficit. But the taste of the pudding is in the eating. Great poet Tulsi Das wrote, "*Nij kavitaya kah lage na pyara, ati saras ho ya ati feeka*" (Every one likes one's own compostion irrespective of its being very lilting and sonorous or dull and monotonous). Therefore, it is for the readers to judge the book.

No attempt of this nature can be successful without the help and cooperation of several persons. This is true in this case also. Authors are extremely thankful to Dr Amit Sharma, Associate Prof BIMTECH, for his useful suggestions relating to some of the ideas in the nebulous and formative stage of the book. Mr Gautam Negi and Mr Ramdhani Khalid, Research Scholars at BIMTECH, also provided some useful inputs. Authors thank them with all the sincerity at their command.

Authors express their heartfelt thanks to Dr Harivansh Chaturvedi, Director, BIMTECH, for his continuous encouragement and unstinted support for the completion of this project. It would have been difficult to complete the book without his patient support for this endeavour. Authors consider him to be a part of the team which completed this book. Authors are also thankful to Prof Godwin Mjema, the Rector, and Prof Tadeo Satta, the Deputy Rector Research and Consultancy, Institute of Finance Management, Dar-es-Saalam for their encouragement and support to Mr Kiangi, one of the authors of the book.

Authors are extremely thankful to Mr Ramadhani Khalid, IFM and Scholar at BIMTECH, for the assistance he has rendered in the preparation of references.

Last but not the least, our thanks go to Mr Sanu Kapila and Ms Sona Kapila without whose patience and cooperation the completion of the revised text and timely publication would have not been possible.

—Shri Prakash, Richard Fue Kiangi and Sudhi Sharma

1

Basic Concepts of Public Finance

Introduction

Adam Smith, founder of modern economics, transformed the subject matter, nature and scope of the discipline now called 'Economics' by his book *An Essay on Nature and Causes of Wealth of Nations* (1776). Economics was known as 'Homestatis' in ancient times. It dealt with the nature and management of finances of the households. Thus the ancient concept of economics was essentially micro in nature and scope. Then, the subject went through a metamorphosis in the late middle ages when it was transformed and came to be known as 'Political Economy'. The subject matter of political economy was macro and its micro trappings were given up. It was a 380 degree change in the subject matter, scope and nature of economics. The name 'political economy' conforms to the nature and scope of the subject matter. It focused on the nature, sources, magnitude and disposal of finances of the state. In short, political economy dealt with 'public' or 'state finance'. But the subject matter of public finance was again transformed radically with the emergence of planned socialist economic systems in which state acquired monopoly over ownership, control and use of almost all the resources of the country. Market, private ownership of property and productive resources were replaced by state ownership, right to decide the level and pattern of utilisation of all resources of the state, which the government could mobilise.

The focus of this book is investigation of the nature and magnitudes of inter-relations between public finance in general and public expenditure in particular with economic growth of India and Tanzania.

This chapter explains and elaborates basic concepts relating to public finance and economic growth.

The concepts discussed in the chapter are: public finance; public budget and budgeting; types of budgets, fiscal policy; public expenditure; public revenue; fiscal deficit; public debt/borrowings; progress; growth and development; financial year; state; Government and its role and functions in the management and nurturing of economic growth, risk and its taxonomy.

Public Finance

Public finance comprises two terms each of which has a technical connotation: public and finance. Both these terms are explained one by one individually as well as jointly.

Public

The word 'public' has several connotations. 'Public' refers to common people in common parlance. This is the commonly understood sense in which the word 'public' is used. In literal sense, word 'public' is used as an adjective of anything which pertains to material goods, entity or people. Some of the terms which are qualified by adjective 'public' are public property, public agency, public enterprises, public choice, public good, and public sector. These are examples of such usage of the term 'public'. All these terms connote the sense of 'belongingness to the government'. In technical sense, public connotes government; government represents people of the country or region. Thus, the term public stands for the state and its government.

Money and Finance

Money

The term 'money' is used both in narrow and broad sense; it refers to what operates as money in the economy as well as monetary policy. Money is a 'medium of exchange and store of value'. Money may comprise physical objects, that is, notes and coin; or of book or computer entries, that is, bank deposits. Money was initially a physical substance such as 'gold or silver', which was valued for its own sake before it came to be used as coinage. Coins and notes are now usually tokens, with intrinsic value.

Money is also the verbal shorthand for 'monetary policy'. Thus, 'cheap money' means that loans are cheap and easily available; 'tight' or 'dear money' means that loans are expensive and hard to obtain. Money also denotes wealth in general.

Money is a part of financial resources. But finance is much more than money. It offers the means of acquisition of desired goods, services and assets/objects available currently or in future. Finance performs functions similar to the function of medium of exchange performed by money. But finance is not currency and coins alone.

Money does not perform the function of medium of exchange alone. Crowther, in fact, defined money as follows: "Money is a matter of functions four, a measure, medium, value and store." Medium of exchange is something which is accepted universally in exchange of goods, services, capital assets and wealth. Thus, money requires two or more parties to be involved for performing the role of exchange. But anything accepted as money is capable of measuring the worth of goods and services offered for sale and accepted for purchase by the parties to the bargain. Money thus, serves the purpose of evaluation of value of goods and services and the valuation is fairly stable. Thus, the function of measure includes the function of value also. Therefore, inclusion of value in Crowther's definition is redundant. Money is also the means of storing the values of the objectives without any decay or decline with the passage of time. A coin or note of ₹ 5 will embody the same value at all times. Money comprises coins and currency notes. These are the legal tenders which no one can refuse to accept as the price of goods, services and assets.

Money can also be used as a token of love or respect by giving it as a gift to some loved one or for discharging legal or social obligations. Fines, fees, taxes, dowry and gifts are examples of such functions performed by money in modern societies. Money also represents liquidity in the form of cash.

Finance

But finance is more than currency notes or coins. Finance comprises of money/cash and claims and payments' liabilities of an entity. Thus, finance includes inflow of money as income and outflows of money as expenditure and values of physical and financial assets. Financial assets are the source of income to the owners, while liabilities refer to claims which have to be honored by the owners of liabilities. Entity pertaining to finance may be an individual, family/household, institution, enterprise or the government. Thus concept of finance is very broad and diverse. The reason is that finance, including cash/money is involved in operations and transactions in every walk of life of all entities. Besides, cash or money is required and used by individuals, households, institutions, corporate houses and the government. Cash or money is the most important form of finance.

Finance refers to different forms of money. Currency is defined as narrow money and represented by M1. Some financial instruments are defined as broad money. Credit created by banks on the basis of deposits represents broad money which is denoted by M2. All choices, decisions and operations, involving the use and claims or entitlement over money, real or promissory, fall within the purview of finance. Besides, the term 'finance' is used in widely different contexts. Examples of these are households' finance, corporate finance, cooperative societies' finance, public finance and Finance Act. Finance Act deals with rules of procedures and regulations governing different facets and operations dealing with public finance.

Market

In common parlance market is a place where goods and services are offered for sale and purchased at mutually agreed prices at specified point in time. It requires the physical presence of the buyers and sellers at the same time and place for the performance of the transactions involving sale and purchase. But more transactions take place without the gathering of buyers and sellers physically through telephonic communication, written mail or letters. Therefore, market is that situation in which transactions involving sales and purchases of goods, services, factors of production and other income yielding assets take place at any time.

Market stands for a place/situation in which trading is carried out. Thus shares are traded at the stock exchange, corn is traded at *mandis*, and workers are hired at labour market. In many cases most of the trade is nowadays done by telephone calls or electronically. A stock exchange is often an institution rather than a physical place. In view of this, market may be defined as that state or situation in which two or more persons, groups or institutions carry out sales and purchase operations. Market of commodity futures, foreign exchange, and gold and other metals, oil etc., are also important.

Market was originally a physical location and it still is for some goods. Examples are markets of such goods as cattle, fish or vegetable. In other cases market is a network of dealers linked by telephone and computer where common trading rules and conventions are followed. Market facilitates trade in goods as is the case in commodity, securities and bond and capital markets. Spot markets handle trade in goods or services for immediate delivery. Markets also exist for goods, services, or assets for future delivery, that is, trade in forward or futures contracts, and derivatives. Examples are options and forward/contract market indices.

Money Market

A market in which money is sold and purchased at the negotiated or prevailing price is defined as money market. Foreign exchange market is a money market in which the currencies of different countries are sold and purchased. National currencies are also sold and purchased like goods and services at the prices prevailing in the market at the given point in time. The price at which a national currency is sold and purchased is known as exchange rate. Exchange rate has also got a 'futures market' like the future markets of goods like oil, gold, silver, copper, foodgrains, other agricultural goods, and shares of companies.

Money market is the market for very short-term loans. Transaction costs of lending money for very short periods, for example overnight are quite high relative to the interest that can be earned. Consequently, transactions in the money market are usually for large amounts, and the participants are mainly banks and other financial institutions such as 'Discount Houses', though large firms and a few exceptionally rich individuals also participate.

Demand for and Supply of Money

Supply of money is the total amount of money in circulation in an economy. It means that the stock of money is not the part of current supply. Stock of money refers to the amounts kept idle by individuals or institutions. Idle money does not perform any useful function except that a part or its total amount may be drawn to meet the contingency or emergency needs. Some part may also be kept idle for purposes of speculative use.

Quantum of money in supply may be the country's own money, supplied by its banking system, or foreign money, used in preference to domestic money. But there is no single accepted definition of what constitutes money. Notes and coins are 'legal tender' and have to be included in any definition. Bank deposits which are repayable on demand cannot be excluded from money supply. But there are various types of deposits in banks and non-bank financial intermediaries such as building societies, and various forms of highly liquid security, which can be included or excluded in various ways from supply.

Demand for money is embodied in total volume of sales and purchases which have been made during the financial year. This may symbolically be shown by DM=PQ, where P is average general price level and Q shows the quantities of goods, services and assets involved in financial transactions.

Money Multiplier

The rate at which an increase in money supply changes national income is defined as money multiplier. In the 'IS-LM' model an increase in money supply shifts the LM curve and increases national income. Money supply has at most a temporary effect on output and only has a lasting effect on the price level in most of the economic models.

Financial Markets

Financial markets deal in the trading of financial assets. Therefore, markets in which financial assets are sold and purchased on the spot are called sopt markets; and markets in which contracts of future sales and purchases are finalised are called futures or forward markets. These markets include 'stock exchanges' for the trading of companies' shares and government debt/bonds. Financial markets also include the money market for trading short-term loans, the foreign exchange market for trading currencies, and a number of specialised markets for trading financial derivatives. Most financial markets now operate minute-by–minute *via* computers and telephone linkages rather than traders meeting in person at a given time and place. But many participants still prefer to be near to other major market participants, which is why financial markets tend to be concentrated in large business centres such as Frankfurt, London, New York, Paris, Mumbai, Delhi and Kolkata.

Financial Sector

Financial sector stands for that part or segment of the national economy which is concerned mainly with lending and borrowing for long or short terms. Financial sector includes banks and non-banking financial institutions which act as intermediaries such as building societies (UK) or saving and loan associations (US) or cooperative credit societies of India as well as merchant banks, insurance companies, pension and provident funds and a range of financial managers and advisers. It also deals with certain very distinct facets of financial operations in the national economy. Some of these are listed hereunder.

Financial Futures

Financial futures refer to 'futures' contracts in currencies, interest rates, or stock indices'. Futures' contracts like forward contracts commit both sides to a transaction on a future date at a pre-agreed price. Future contracts are traded in futures' markets on organised exchanges. These contracts can be used either for 'hedging to reduce the risks traders are exposed to, or for 'speculation relating to taking an extra risk for the sake of expected profits. Financial futures are traded in the UK on the London International Financial Futures and Options Exchange.

Financial Ratios

Financial ratios like five economic ratios between various items in a company's accounts and the market value of its shares play an important analytical role. Most important of these ratios are the 'price–earnings (P/E) ratio' that denotes the ratio of the market price to earnings per share, and 'price-dividend' (P/D) ratio which shows the ratio of the market price to the latest dividend paid per share. These ratios are used in comparing the merits of investing in different companies. Debt-equity ratio, profit per unit of sales, return per unit of investment etc., are some other important ratios.

Financial Repression

Financial repression and interest rate are two important policy instruments of controlling inflation in an economy. Financial repression stands for the imposition of liquidity constraints through allocation of loans by administrative means rather than relying on market forces. Financial repression may be adopted for influencing the distribution of investment in the economy or for facilitating extortion by those responsible for allocating funds.

Public Finance

Finance and public finance are scientific subjects. Finance has come to denote the subject-matter of non-public corporate finance. Finance also refers to financial resources. Therefore, public finance in literal sense refers to financial resources and liabilities of the government and public agencies or bodies. But public finance in a more technical sense refers to mobiliation and utilisation of financial resources by public authority or government for public purposes. Public finance as a scientific discipline is an important branch of economics. Public economics has now encompassed public finance. Financial economics and financial econometrics have now emerged as a distinct field of specialisation. Financial economics is the field of economics that analyses the allocation of resources between consumption and financial assets on the one hand, and the equilibrium consequences of individual and macro choices on the other. Financial economics also analyses behaviour of financial institutions, including banks and investment companies.

Black et al. (2012) defines 'public finance' as "a branch of economics concerned with the study of financing of government. This includes taxation, spending by public bodies on real goods and services, provision of transfer incomes by the government, government property incomes, government borrowings and debts and the financial relations between various levels of government" (p.330). Public finance, in fact, deals with the theory and practice of raising revenue/income for the government on the one hand and the theory and practice of financing public expenditure for satisfying public needs/wants on the other. Public wants or needs depend on the political system, structure and stage of economic growth of the country. Political system play the pivotal role in determining the roles and functions of the government. Concerns and policy of democratic polity about the people, their welfare and economic growth differ from those of autocratic or dictatorial political system. This directly affects the nature and scope of public finance. Similarly, capitalist market based economic structure encompasses different public policy than the socialist planned economy. The thrust of economic and fiscal policies of developed and developing economies also differ in nature, thrust and scope. For example, classical school of thought trusted the effectiveness and efficacy of the market forces to be benevolent. Therefore, classical economists considered government intervention in economic affairs as unnecessary and unwarranted. Limited role envisaged for the government was treated as a necessary evil which had to be tolerated. As against this, socialist school of thought considered public intervention necessary to eliminate the imperfections and ill-effects of free market operations. Therefore, government has had pervasive role in economic affairs in the planned socialist economies irrespective of their development status.

Therefore, theory of public finance comprises theories of (i) taxation, (ii) public expenditure, (iii) public debt, and (iv) fiscal policy. Besides, the theory of public finance has to lean on the theories of social welfare and economic growth since fiscal policy has also to focus on these two objectives of growth. Consequently, theory of public finance has varied shades and streams of thoughts which are basically offshoots of the theory of state, role and functions of its government and theories of welfare and growth. Theory of growth is now required to focus on inclusive growth. Hence, fiscal policy has now been converted into policy of inclusive growth. Consequently, fiscal policy is now required to look at inclusive finance as one of the outcomes of policy. But the role and functions of the government basically depend on the political system and nature and structure of economy and its system.

Public finance basically relates to streams of in and outflows of income/cash in and out of public exchequer. Outflows occur for financing public expenditure. Current flows are the part of public finance. Besides in and outflows of resources, stock of cash/money, values of financial and physical assets and payments' liabilities of the government at any time are also included in finances of the government at any given point in time. Public finances also include financial stock. Stock of money and assets are accumulated through time; increase or decrease in stock of financial resources refers to the difference between inflows and outflows of money and assets and the stock brought forward from the preceding periods. Therefore, 'Theory of Finance' in general and 'Public Finance' in particular deals with choices and decisions relating to the acquisition and utilisation of financial resources including money value of physical and financial assets and liabilities.

Financial resources of the government represent an important operational side of the government. But operations of the government revolve round its functions and responsibilities. Role and functions of the government, however, depend largely on political ideology, political system and stage of development and structure of the economy. Topical problems and goals and objectives of the government also influence public actions. Role and functions of the government in a capitalist economy differ greatly from those in a socialist economy. Level and stage of economic growth may also affect policy decisions of the day. Fiscal policy of the developing economies generally focuses both on welfare and growth. Requirement of financial and physical resources for the discharge of responsibilities and performance of pre-determined functions of government determine the expenditure and revenue needs of the government. This in turn determines the actions and interventions of public policy in economic affairs of the country. Implementation of policy decisions involves financial transactions. Transactions result in inflows of income from different streams into public exchequer and outflows of resources involved in public expenditure. Liabilities represent responsibility for payment to discharge the same. Public debt instruments, interest payments and expenditure on ongoing projects and programmes of the government fall in the category of financial liabilities. As against liabilities, financial assets represent liquid or easy to transform wealth into cash/money. Financial assets constitute financial wealth of the country and represent streams of income at the given point in time and/or through time. Liquid cash and other financial assets of public institutions and public enterprises are also a part of public finance. Bonds and securities, loan papers, bank deposits, shares and debentures held by the government are the income yielding financial assets.

Financial (Resources)

Adjective 'financial' is often used in cases where finance or instruments of finance are involved. But the term 'financial' is used in diverse contexts. Some examples are financial account, financial assets, financial liabilities, financial crisis, financial regulation, financial deregulation, financial economics, financial econometrics, financial futures, financial innovations, financial intermediation and intermediaries, financial markets, financial health of the households, governments and companies finances, financial ratios, financial repression, financial security, financial services act, and financial year.

Assets

What is the meaning of asset and what differentiates financial from physical assets? According to Black et al. (2012) assets refer to possessions of value both real and financial. Real assets include land, buildings, and/or machinery owned. Financial assets include cash, securities and credit extended to customers.

The dictionary meaning of assets emphasises two aspects: (i) possession; and (ii) value. Possession can however be actual, notional or virtual. Virtual possession is like virtual enterprise and virtual capital. Notional possession refers to that state of ownership when the owner either does not have the right of use or the entity under consideration has only 'usurfractory' rights without the right to ownership. Similarly value may refer to market price, or owner's perceptional value or it may refer to book value or even virtual value.

Assets are owned and operated widely across the socio-economic spectra. The connotations of the 'term assets' therefore differ according to the context.

Financial Assets

Financial assets refer to money and claims as distinct from physical assets such as land, buildings, or equipment. Financial assets include money, securities constituting a claim to receive money, such as bills or bonds, and shares giving indirect ownership of the physical and financial assets of companies. The claims held as financial assets include the obligation of individuals, companies, and government, domestic and foreign to make payment on due date or on demand to the elements. Financial assets include shares in financial institutions, and derivatives such as 'options'.

According to Black et al. (2012) 'money and claims, as distinct from physical assets like land, machinery and equipment, are the part of financial assets'. Financial assets include money, securities, constituting a claim to receive money such as bills or bonds and shares.' Thus, financial assets have market value, present value, future value and discounted value. If payment of an asset falls due on some future date and it is en-cashed before that date, it will fetch its discounted value which is less than its value on due date.

Assets of Companies

Any possession which is capable of yielding streams of income over the years may be defined as an asset. But assets convey meanings distinctly different from those for other entities. The term 'asset' is also used in a metaphysical and usually favourable sense to describe things that cannot actually be owned. This is evident from the phrase that 'a company's best assets are the skills and loyalty of its employees'. Assets are also not always concrete material objects which may not yield immediate and direct returns. Brand Value or reputation or goodwill represents a non-monetary and non-material asset.

The assets' side of a company's balance sheet includes both real and financial assets. Assets are the credit side of a company's balance sheet. Management of companies' assets is a specialised job. Management of assets may also refer to managing resources for others for a fee. Portfolio of assets consists of real and/or financial assets. But 'asset striping' refers to selling off the assets of the companies.

Public Assets

Public assets are real as well as financial. Loans advanced to other governments, organisations, public enterprises, and interest receivable on debt advanced to others, bonds and securities of other country's governments held by the national government, money invested in different lines of production including investment in bonds of other governments and their organisations, amount of money expected to be received in the liquidation of loans advanced to other government all represent public assets.

Budget

Budget and budgeting are commonly practiced by most of the entities of real life. Each household prepares a plan and programmes of allocation of income among different lines of expenditure during a specified period of time, normally a month. Expenditure is incurred for satisfying needs/wants of the members of family. This plan or programme is called family budget. Thus the budget of household/family focuses on allocation of expected income among different items envisaged to be required by the family during the time horizon of the budget. Households' weekly/monthly incomes and amounts of expenditure on different items are generally known approximately if not exactly. Consequently, family budgets encompass very little uncertainty. However, incessant inflation or persistent recession generates uncertainty about the quantities of some if not all the goods to be purchased by households. Households' budgets are informal; so family budgets may or may not be made in written form.

Public and private entities, like the households, prepare their budgets in advance for allocating their expected income from all sources among different projects and programs planned or expected to be taken up for implementation during the budget period. Expenditure is also incurred on on-going projects which were started in the past but could not be completed. Some expenditure is also incurred on repairs and maintenance of buildings, machinery and equipment.

Budget period is defined as budget's horizon or just as horizon. But budgetary expenditure of public and private entities like the households' budgetary expenditure may also be classified into two parts: committed and discretionary. Total wages and salaries of all workers and employees current and planned to be in employment during the budget horizon, maintenance and repair of existing physical assets, payment of interest on loans and liquidation of loans payment of which is due represent the committed part of public expenditure. Such public expenses are known. But expenditure on initiation of new/planned programs and projects pertaining to welfare and growth displays discretionary part of allocation of income/revenue.

Expenditure of all public and private entities is guided and governed by their respective budgets. Budget itself is guided by fiscal policy designed for realizing objectives of welfare and growth.

Budgets of institutions and public bodies are prepared annually in advance. Therefore, budgeting and budget involve two time periods: (i) period of preparation of budget; and (ii) period of implementation of budget. Involvement of two time periods creates a certain degree of uncertainty both about the budgeted income and budgeted expenditure. Consequently, actual public income and expenditure generally diverge from the budgeted amounts by smaller or larger margins. Budgets of institutions, organisations and corporate houses and public entities are formal written documents. These written documents are made available for public (stakeholders) debate before finalisation. But public budgets are subject to scrutiny at different levels before their finalisation.

Public budgets are an inseparable part of public finance. Governments of all layers and levels prepare their annual budgets regularly. Public budget after being finalised and approved acts as the guide post of all decisions and operations of the government.

Technical Concept of Budget

Does the above connotation of public budget coincide with technical concept of budget in general and public budget in particular? According to Black et al. (2012), 'budget' is "a statement of a government's planned receipts and expenditures for some future period, normally a year. This is usually accompanied by a statement of actual receipts and expenditures for previous period. The annual budget statement is a statement of the government's financial plan made by the Minister of Finance with the approval of parliament." According to this definition, the term 'budget' is restricted to government or public budget. Therefore, this is not a generic definition of 'budget' per say.

The following are the main features of 'public budget' that are inferred from the above definition.

First, budget is a statement of income and expenditure which the government has planned to raise or expect to receive and intend to spend in the coming financial year.

Secondly, budgetary statement is extremely detailed with regard to allocation and expenditure on different items. Therefore, it is not a simple one or two page statement. It's contents are filled up with minute details and technical terms.

Thirdly, budget is accompanied by the statement of preceding period's performance with regard to receipt of income from different sources and incurring of expenditure on different lines. Statement of previous period's performance highlights the broad features of preceding budget, its various achievements and shortfalls of revenue receipts from taxation and other sources on the one hand and excess or shortfall of public expenditure in specified fields of government activities on the other. The statement of receipts and expenditure is generally accompanied by the targets set and achieved in different fields of activities of the government. Targets are mostly stated both in financial and physical terms. For example, x number of bridges over the roads covering an area of y acres shall be constructed during the financial year. Total amount of expenditure expected to be incurred on the construction of these bridges will be z. These targets are contrasted with actual accomplishments and shortfalls of previous year. For example z-r amount was actually incurred on the construction of bridges which made achieved target fall short in physical terms by p km/acres because of q factors. Adherence and compliance with, and hence, achievement of budgeted monetary and physical targets is important. Completed targets represent evidence of government's success or failure in various fields of activities. These parameters are often used for evaluating budgetary performance.

Fourthly, public budgets perform the following important functions:

(i) Budgets set the targets of fiscal deficit and public borrowings. The objective of details furnished by the budget is to highlight the nature and directions of government's past fiscal and monetary policies in different fields or areas of the economy. Besides, report of past performance puts current budgetary proposals in the context of the policy framework and future perspective.

(ii) Certain proportion of total budgeted expenditure is earmarked for schemes, projects and programs initiated in previous budget(s) but which are to continue in the coming financial year. For example, provision of 100 days employment for one adult of each family under Mahatma Gandhi National Rural Employment Guarantee Act (NREGA).

(iii) Areas of bottlenecks and constraints which accounts for achievements falling short of targets in the preceding period are identified for taking corrective measures in the coming financial year.

(iv) Intents and purposes of financial policy in the coming financial year are made explicitly clear by the budgetary details.

(v) Evaluation of performance of preceding year's budget in terms of full or partial realisation of targets enables the government to identify: (a) loopholes in policy formulation, (b) leakages and seepages in its implementation, and (c) gaps in the design and process of implementation.

(vi) Statements in the budget highlight the changes in regulatory provisions and mechanism, if any in financial laws of the country. These rules and laws are proposed in the budget for implementation by the regulatory authority. Laws of taxation included in each budget are an example of this. Thus, budget makes the implementation and enforcement of compliance easier than what would have been the case if the budget statement is not sufficiently detailed.

However, above definition of public budget is in a static framework. Budgets are instruments of formulation and implementation of fiscal policy by means of budgetary tools. Each budget is short run view of fiscal policy. Fiscal policy and hence public budgets focus on stabilisation in the short run. Occurrence of trade cycles necessitates use of fiscal instruments for stabilisation. For example, world-wide economic slow-down in 2008 induced governments of almost all the countries of the world to announce and implement rehabilitation packages for the reversal of slow-down. Euro-zone debt crisis still continues and member countries of EU are actively pursuing policies of stabilisation and revival of the economies of Greece, Spain, and Portugal.

Besides the short run objective of stabilisation, fiscal policy and public budget focus on growth of the economy and welfare of the people in the long run. Long run is nothing but an agglomeration of several short runs. So, the budget of each financial year is linked to the long run policy objectives of growth and welfare. Currently growth with equity and justice encompasses inclusiveness in general and financial inclusiveness in particular.

In the planned developing economies like those of India and Tanzania, each five year plan has five budget cycles of one year each. Budgets are organically synthesised into an integrated whole so as to facilitate implementation and completion of projects and programs of economic growth and social development included in the corresponding plan of economic growth and social development.

Nature and Concept of Public Budget and Process of Budgeting

Public budget and process of budgeting cannot be understood without proper explanation of intricate technical concepts and theories involved in the complex task of budgeting and budget making. Ubiquitous nature of budget and budgeting is obvious from the following:

Concept of 'budget' cannot be rigid and steel-framed. it has to be extremely flexible and malleable. The reason is that each layer and level of government and government organisations has to have a budget. One single rigid budget may fail to embody objectives of all entities of the government and other public organisations within a steely frame. In fact, government and its other entities have some or the other form of budget as the guide of their financial operations.

Governments ranging from local/village panchayat or municipal committee to provincial/county government and from provincial to central government require budgeting and budget. Even micro level government organisation, departments within directorates and directorates within ministries, and ministries within the central government require budget anfd knowledge of budgeting.

From households to schools/colleges and universities, private commercial and industrial establishments need some kind of the budget in order to keep the expenditures on operations according to the limits determined by the relevant authority.

Income or revenue constraint, once determined or imposed from the above, cannot be flouted in budgeting by any government or their units. This is the universal norm. Above consideration warrants the concept of budget and the process of budgeting to be defined in an extremely flexible manner so as to make it suit every requirement.

Concept of budget and process of budget making are like the tailor and tailoring. Tailor keeps in mind every customer's size, physical structure, taste and preference according to the fashion of the times so as to satisfy want or requirement of each and every one. Similarly, budget of an entity has to be tailor-made to suit its objectives and requirements which vary through time, nature and structure of the economy for which budget is to be made. Concept of the budget, especially the national budget, has been evolved, molded, twisted and tuned according to the needs of the time and the country or the entity of budgeting. But it does not mean that there is no general principle of budgeting. The general principle furnishes guidelines for making national budget and the budgets of other levels of government. Basic criteria for the budgeting are stated hereunder.

Public Revenue

Budgeting focuses largely on the allocation of public resources for utilisation for different public purposes. Resource allocation is based on public revenue or government's income. Public revenue also denotes public income. Public revenue refers to total receipts of the government during the specified period from all sources. Following are the major sources of public revenue or government's income: (i) annual yield or return received from physical public assets; (ii) returns from public financial assets. It includes interest receipts on loans advanced by the government; (iii) public borrowings; (iv) receipts from taxation; it is known as tax revenue; (v) fees, fines and penalties, (vi) fiscal deficit. Therefore, understanding of pubic revenue necessitates the knowledge of its components.

Taxation

Taxation, public expenditure and public borrowings are important instruments of fiscal policy. Public budgets are the major instruments of implementing fiscal policy. Consequently, proposals relating to taxation, public expenditure and public borrowings are important elements of annual budgets.

The process of levying of taxes on the people and their organisations is known as taxation. Payment is mandatory for those who are taxed. Psychological and financial impact of taxes falls on those who are taxed, irrespective of whether the tax is direct or indirect. But the incidence has to be borne by one who makes the final payment to the government. Both the impact and incidence of direct taxes fall on those entities which are taxed. But only the impact of indirect taxes is borne by the taxed entities, because they shift the burden of final payment and hence the incidence of tax to someone else. For example, sales tax or VAT is levied on sales outlets but they pass the burden of payment to the buyers.

Tax revenue probably constitutes the largest proportion of public revenue; tax revenue may also account for an extremely large proportion of GDP. But tax revenue as the proportion of GDP generally varies sharply between the countries. Tax revenue as proportion of GDP varied from 20 per cent for Turkey to 50 per cent for Sweden in 1981 among the countries of OECD. Besides, tax revenue as a proportion of total public revenue also varies between different taxes. For example, revenue from income tax accounted for only 13 per cent of total public revenue of France in 1981 while it accounted for 61 per cent if total revenue of New Zeland. Tax revenue as a proportion of GDP of developing economies may even be higher than that of developed economies. The reason is that the per capita income of developing countries is relatively quite low which makes their savings rate also low. Therefore, the governments of developing economies attempt to mobilise resources more by taxation than by other means. The developing economies rely more on indirect than direct taxes for obvious reasons. Indirect taxes may also be a factor of inflation in the economy. For example, one estimate shows that 30 per cent of total inflationary pressure in Indian economy arises from indirect taxes on goods and services. Taxation is not only the means of raising revenue; it performs other important economic functions also. Taxation may be used as an instrument of re-distribution of income and wealth in the country. Heavier taxation of the rich than poor, coupled with transfer payments performs this role. Taxation may also influence the people to change their purchase behaviour and pattern of consumption. For example, if heavy import duties are levied on say imported cars, then more people will buy domestically manufactured cars (Bowen, 1996).

Public Expenditure

Public expenditure refers to the spending by the government at various levels of governance; level of government spending varies from local to state, from state to the nation. This is from bottom up description. Top down description moves from national government's spending to the spending of the state governments, and from state government's spending to the spending of the local self governments. Spending of public funds also moves from government to departments of the government and from departments to the departmental enterprises. But spending of the public funds is guided and governed by the budgetary allocation of public revenue.

Payments by the central government to the state and local governments, public enterprises and other institutions are deducted from the sum total expenditure incurred by all above public entities in order to obtain net public expenditure. Public spending is done on real goods and services in the form of payments to the sellers/suppliers of these to the public agencies and different layers of government, public services like public administration, defence, police, administration of law and order, justice, health, and education.

Expenses on all these heads and items are in the nature of maintenance and recurrent expenditure. In addition to the above, public spending focuses on the promotion of growth and welfare. Expenditure on growth involves investment in productive ventures like social and physical infrastructure, grants and subsidies to the industries producing public goods, utilities, and industries which are considered to promote national growth and which somehow fail to attract adequate private investment. Transfer payments like pension, provident fund, unemployment allowance, payments to the disabled and aged etc., fall in the category of welfare expenditure. Public expenditure like taxation may also be used as an instrument of reduction of poverty and economic inequalities in the society. Payments of interest on public debt and redemption of debt on maturity fall in the category of their own (Black et al. 2012: 177).

Public Debt and Borrowings

Flow and stock have to be distinguished in the context of public debt and public borrowings. Public debt refers to the sum total of all public borrowings cumulatively accumulated over the years minus the debts and interest thereon already redeemed and liquidated. The stock of domestic and foreign debts represents the borrowings of all public bodies over the years that have been contracted and taken from the people and institutions/organisations of the country, foreign governments and international agencies like IBRD, IMF, and Asian Development Bank. Governments borrow from domestic and international financial markets. Burden of [public debt on national governments of India and Tanzania is quite heavy. Year on year borrowings of the governments lies at the base of public debt stock at any point in time. Management of public debt is quite a complex and intricate task.

Fiscal Deficit

Fiscal deficit has emerged as an important source of public funding now a days. It refers to the difference between total public income from all sources, including public borrowings, and public spending on all items and directions during the financial year. It represents the sum total of deficits of all layers and levels of the government and its agencies/bodies including public enterprises. It is generally covered by additional money supply by means of printing of currency notes.

Fiscal Policy

Fiscal policy refers to all financial and monetary measures undertaken or planned to be undertaken by the government (i) for raising resources, (ii) allocating the available public resources among the specified lines and items of public spending, and (iii) public spending according to the level and pattern of allocation during the given financial year. Fiscal policy is implemented by the changes in rates of taxation, introduction or withdrawal of existing tax(es) or levies, change in the rules regarding liability to tax, changes in the level and pattern of public spending, procedures governing public and private investment which furnish incentives for investment in some lines of production and prohibit or restrict investment in lines of production, changing the rules governing transfer payments and subsidies. Supply of money and measures to exercise control over liquidity in the economy are important tools of fiscal policy. Fiscal policy is operated with a view to alter the course of economic and business operations.

Risk and Taxonomy of Risk

Risk is a very commonly used word in common parlance. For example, people may often be heard saying that it is risky to go out in inclement weather. But risk is associated with uncertainty and the possibility of coming in harm's way in one or the other form. Inclement weather may adversely affect health. Similarly, risk arising from uncertainty about the behaviour of the market in future involves financial risks for investors and risk of over or under production for producers. Wherever and whenever there is no uncertainty, there is no risk involved in decisions and actions and outcomes emanating from them. Outcomes are, more or less, certain in uncertainty-less state. Thus, risks arise from uncertainty. Therefore, for the understanding of risk, connotation and implications of 'uncertainty' are to be understood.

Uncertainty refers to outcomes of such actions, events or occurrences involving change as cannot be foreseen or foretold in advance. It means that risk refers to uncertainty of outcomes. But an action which has only one single possible outcome will involve no uncertainty and hence risk. Uncertainty relates to multiplicity of outcomes none of which can be foreseen with certainty and even calculus cannot be associated with the same. It means that the occurrence of a given outcome is so uncertain that it cannot be predicted.

Certainty of a given outcome of an action or occurrence means that the outcome will definitely materialise; there is not even an iota of doubt about its occurrence. It means that the probability of the failure of materialisation of the given outcome of the specified action is zero on the evidence available at the given point in time. As against this, the probability of materialisation of the said outcome is unit. For example, if a person jumps from 50th floor of a building without protective gear, his/her survival is uncertain. Besides, past observations of the outcome of similar events point towards the fact that there are more chances of his death than survival. In this case, outcome of this jump is uncertain and there exists no absolute certainty of survival or death. But there are more chances of his/her death than survival. Therefore, the probability of survival is extremely low. Similarly, if an athlete has won ten out of 20 races of 100 meters, his/her winning the race in a particular competition cannot be foretold with perfect certainty. His/her winning or losing carries equal degree of uncertainty attached to it. Past evidence suggests that the probability of his/her win is 0.5.

As against the above examples, occurrence of certain events may, however, be foreseen and foretold or forecasted. For example, all human beings are mortal. Therefore, whosoever is born is certain to die. But the important questions in this regard are 'death will occur (i) when, (ii) where, and (iii) in what circumstances'. None of these questions can be answered with any degree of certainty. Obviously, answers to all three questions are uncertain in character.

An important aspect of the word 'risk' is that its connotation is negative, unwanted or undesired aspect(s) of expected outcome(s). For example one does not talk about risk of profit. But one talks about risk of loss. Similarly, one talks about risk of accident in cloudy, inclement weather and unruly traffic conditions. As against this, uncertainty connotes possibilities of success and failure, materialisation and non-materialisation of the stipulated outcome(s). Generally, risk is referred in terms of more or less chances in favour or against the occurrence of an event or materialisation of outcome of an action.

Generic Definiton of Risk

Risk, may be defined in generic terms as follows: Risk refers to unwanted and negative facets of outcomes of action or occurrence of events. Human behaviour in most of the cases involves uncertainty and hence risk. Risk and uncertainty are, in fact, intrinsic and integral part of each other. Almost all decisions involving financial and economic variables have a multitude of possible outcomes none of which is absolutely certain to materialise. Hence, all decisions and actions, which have two or more possible outcomes, embody uncertainty and hence, risk that certain outcome does or does not materialise. Risk is a negative term. It connotes possible loss, or non-fulfillment of expectation, falling short of planned target(s), etc. But the terms risk and uncertainty are often used inter-changeably, though these are very different in nature and meaning since the terms refer to distinctly different phenomenon/outcome.

'Uncertainty arises if future is unknown' and no objective or subjective probabilities are attached to alternative outcomes. But probability calculus may be associated with uncertanity and risk. Thus, the foundation of a large part of risk analysis lies in probability theory' (Liserllyn 1999). Analysis of risk has historically, by and large, focused on the corporate establishments and investors. Analysis of risk has dominated the area of finance. But it is relevant to all spheres of human behaviour since risk and uncertainty are not an essential attribute of financial decisions and actions alone. But what is 'action'? Action may refer to sports, events, growth of demand in the market, rise or fall in equity prices at a particular point in time. Risk of falling short of pre-determined targets is another example.

According to Black et al. (2012: 356), risk is "a form of uncertainty where, while the actual outcome of an action is not known, probabilities can be assigned to each of the possible outcomes. This permits application of the expected utility function to represent preferences over alternatives. The variance of the distribution of frequency function of possible outcomes is often used as a measure of risk, particularly in financial theory." The variance, according to the formula, is given either by (npq), or (pq/n), where n is number of observations, p is probability of occurrence of a particular outcome and q is the probability of its non-occurrence. Value of variance can determine the risk of particular option since its shows the average of squared deviations of mean of probable success in n trials.

This concept of risk and its measurement is a bit ambiguous, if someone is interested in estimating the risk of a specific action under the given state. For example, if one is interested in investing a given sum of dollars in Washington Equity Market, one is interested in knowing the risk of loss attached to the script under consideration for investment. How is the variance of the frequency distribution function helpful to him/her in taking this decision? This reminds of Alfred Marshall's comment on Fisher's Rate of Returns formula in the context of capital/investment theory. Marshall said 'it is too abstract and too mathematical to be of any use in the market place' (*Principles of Economics*, Appendix V). The probability calculus involved in the above definition is even more abstract, mathematical and complex than the concept and measure of rate of return on investment. If the person is new to stock market or s/he never invested in the given equity in the past, s/he will have no frequency distribution of probabilities based on his/her own observations/experience. But in such cases data from the stock exchange can be obtained. But how many common people know and are adapt in probability calculus? Does an investor go to the market with past data and laptop/calculator to do all these calculations before investment? Even if one has the laptop/calculator, s/he should be well versed in the theories of probability and mathematical expectation. Do all investors have the requisite knowledge for this? In our opinion, mathematical expectation of the occurrence of an outcome is a much better index of risk than variance: $E(X)=\Sigma pjXj$, where j is a given outcome from m possible outcomes, pj is probability of materialisation of j-th outcome and Xj is the value of gain associated with j. If this is considered in the context of real life investment decisions, then the decision making unit (DMU) has to consider all options at its disposal and degree of risk of non-materialisation of specific outcomes. For example, if a DMU finds that 1 out of 100 times the case of non occurrence was observed, then probability of occurrence will be as low as p= (1/100)=0.01, and probability of non occurrence will be q-=0.999. If the loss attached to this probable outcome is $1000, variance npq=0.001x0.999x100=0.0099. But the expected value of loss shall be: 0.999x1000=$999 only. The message is then to compare the gain of $1000 with the probable loss of $999 involved in investment. Gain from investment does not overwhelmingly outweigh the loss. The example highlights the fact that the investor should choose such an equity which involves much greater return than loss.

Above discussion necessitates explanation of the concepts of 'risk aversion' and 'risk bearing' propensities.

Risk bearing involves the comparison of pay-off from taking the risk against the possible pay-off/loss of risk aversion. Risk bearing refers to the state in which responsibility of risk of loss is accepted or shared with others by a DMU (decision making unit). Such decision making units are defined as risk seekers who are ready and willing to bear the risk. Obviously, risk bearer is one who takes the responsibility of payment of loss, if expected outcome does not materialise. Risk bearers prefer risky to non-risky options provided that the expected returns from such option are much higher than those embodied in lower risk options. The psychological horizon of risk bearers, backed as it is generally with the capacity to bear the impact of loss, prompts them to seek relatively high returns even though there is higher risk of loss. Off course, the differential degrees of risk attached to each option is compared and contrasted with other less risky or without risk options or assets with low but reasonable returns. According to Black et al. (2012), 'risk bearing' refers to "Having or sharing responsibility for accepting the losses, if projects go wrong. Most economic activities are capable of resulting in losses under certain circumstances, however good the expected results may be." Somebody has to bear the risk of meeting the losses. It is important to understand that risk is an abstract noun. Hence, bearing of risk needs its bearer. Somebody has to accept the bearing of risk of payment for losses resulting from the outcome of investment in risky option chosen by the risk bearer.

But risk bearers may be more than one. First bearer of risk of any project is management of a private firm or equity-holders in a company. If the issues are sufficiently bad, other people connected with the firm are also at risk, including creditors, tax authorities, customers who have paid deposits on goods and workers left unpaid when a business collapses. Another aspect of profit and loss associated with risk is that gain of one is the loss of another. But the main context of the book and its chapters are the expenditure decisions of the Governments of India and Tanzania. Therefore, risk bearers of faulty decisions or inappropriate implementation of policies are also the government and functionaries of these countries.

Most of the economic activities and decisions involving the use of financial resources embody risk of loss under specific set of circumstances. But degree of risk and amount of loss or gain associated, differ from case to case. Each case is guided and governed by specific set of circumstances. Risk averting decision units are converse of risk seeking decision units. As against risk seeker decision units, risk averting units prefer to have risk less options even though expected gain may be lower than that of risky options. But there is no water tight division between risk averters and risk bearers. Risk bearers also have financial and other constraints. These constraints limit the nature of risky options one chooses and the quantum of money at stake that constitute important parameters to guide choice of risky options. Risk averters may also not be totally averse to take risks. But such DMUs are generally cautious in decision making and they generally opt out of highly risky options. Minor risks may be right for several of them.

Overview of the Chapter

The chapter has discussed the following concepts which are essentially needed for understanding public finance; public budget and budgeting; types of budgets, fiscal policy; public expenditure; public revenue; fiscal deficit; public debt/borrowings; progress; growth and development; financial year; state; government and its role and functions in economic growth, risk and its taxonomy.

The words 'public and finance' have been articulated to distinguish their technical meanings from common usage. Connotations of such terns as tax and taxation, and budget and budgeting are distinguished clearly. Concepts of public revenue, public expenditure and public borrowings are explained adequately. The chapter has also briefly described the markets of financial assets and instruments such as stock market, spot and future/forward and contract markets. Thus, the chapter has prepared the ground for readers' understanding even if they are not familiar with the basic concepts of public finance.

2

Theory of State and Public Finances

Introduction: Theory of State as Base of Governance

The concept and theory of state have been evolved since the inception of civilisation. Naturally, different concepts and theories of state were formulated in different ages and stages of development of the society, economy and its polity. The changing concepts and theories of state ascribed differential powers, functions and roles to the state and its government in socio-economic and political spheres. But each state has had a government. The government is an apex political institution of the state. The state uses its government as an instrument of governing the national polity, its economic and social systems. Government also establishes numerous institutions and public bodies/agencies under its ownership, control and regulation as tools of governance and administration. Government's main function is to formulate rules and regulations, to govern and guide its own and its agencies' operations and activities. These rules and regulations furnish legal framework for administration of justice, maintenance of peace, law and order in the society and guide and govern economic operations and business activities. Besides, each government has foreign and defence policies. Some policies may be designed for application of corrective measures to such facts or aspects which result either from autonomous malfunctioning of the market or from distortions resulting from the manipulations of market forces by vested interests to gain undue advantage. Examples of such manipulations are insider's trading in stock markets, formation of cartel in oligopolistic markets or use of entry preventing measures by corporate entities, or getting undue advantage through contacts based either on cash or otherwise. But most of the public policies are designed and formulated to realise the pre-determined goals and objectives of the government at present. Each public institution has a set of rules and regulations to guide and govern its decisions and their implementation. Each institution has its own operational mechanism(s) also for the implementation of its decisions.

The government and systems and institutions created by it do not function on their own; government creates administrative machinery for this purpose. Administration functions through elaborate administrative structures, manned, managed and operated by civil servants. Economy and its systems operate in accordance with the rules of procedure and operational mechanisms in place; such rules are the important tools of governance of society and its economy.

Performance of designated functions and discharge of assigned responsibilities require financial and non-financial resources. The government uses fiscal policy to raise revenue so as to spend it on requisite real goods, services and assets on the one hand, and several other lines of public expenditure on the other. If public revenue does not suffice to meet expenditure needs of the government, public debt and fiscal deficit may be explored and exploited by the government as additional sources to obtain public income/revenue. Thus public finances and fiscal policy associated with the same are embedded in the theory of government. Theory and ideology of the government determine the roles and functions of the state.

The ascribed powers, roles and functions of the state directly guide, govern and even determine the nature, reach and expanse of fiscal and monetary policies. Fiscal and monetary policies shape, direct and fix the nature, composition and coverage of population by public finances. Therefore, the theory of public finance and its constituent elements directly depend upon the number and nature of roles and functions of the state and its government. But the roles and functions of the government also depend on theoretical paradigm and political ideology which the government subscribes to. Larger the roles and more varied the functions of the government, greater is the size and larger is the population coverage by public finances. This accounts for the differentials of size, components and structure of public finances during different stages of political, social and economic development in different phases and stages of evolution of civilisation. Therefore, the theory of state lies at the base of the functioning of the government of the day.

Components of Public Finance

Public finances comprise several components. But public revenue, public debt, and public expenditure are the major components of public finances. Proportionate shares of public revenue, public debt and public expenditure in total finances of the state reflect the financial structure. Besides the relation between roles and functions of the state and the theory and ideology of the government of the day, public finances are directly related to GDP (gross domestic product) of the country. Generally greater the GDP, greater is the size of public finances. As the economy of the state moves from lower to higher stages of economic growth, public finances as the proportion of GDP also tend to rise. But public revenue, public debt and fiscal deficit are generally related directly to public expenditure. This is a holistic and organic view of economy, its GDP and public finances. Main objective of the chapter is, however, to map out and briefly portray the evolution of theory of state and its relation with public finances in general and public expenditure in particular. The rest of the chapter attempts to recapitulate the evolving theory of the state and the resulting magnitude, direction and composition of public finances. Changes in size, composition and spread of public finances over space and population are associated with the changing roles and functions of the government in different stages and ages of evolution of civilisation.

Nature and Type of State, Government and its Economy

Nature and structure of government are reflected by the roles and functions performed and structure of the economy of the state. Ideology and theory pursued by the state determine its polity and roles and functions of its government. Nature and type of the political ideology and philosophy followed by state guide and even determine the nature and type of the political system in place.

Political system in its turn, shapes, governs and guides the economy of the country. Institutional set up, systems and structure of an economy depend upon the political system and type of government, which differ from time to time and country to country. Consequently, economic systems differ under different political dispensation.

Types of Economies

Following three types of economies exhaust almost all the national economies of the world: (i) Market Based Capitalist Economies which generally have democratic polity; their governments are democratically elected periodically by the people of the country; and (ii) Centrally Planned and Controlled Socialist Economies which are ruled by selected members of the ruling party; leaders either control the ruling political party, or are dictators, who have usurped power by political coup. In such systems, both polity and economy are subject to controls and rigid regulations.

However, there are different shades and hues of capitalism and socialism each of these shades has some distinguishing features to make it differ from others. Some economies have commercial capitalism. Structure of such economies is dominated by trade and commerce. Large proportion of total investment in the economy is accounted by commercial enterprises. Commerce and trade rather than industrial and agricultural production dominate the structure of such economies. But nothing can be traded without being produced. Trade and commerce also dominate crony capitalist economies, where middle-men and contractors rather than entrepreneurs, industrialists, farmers, and traders rule the roost. Decision or behaviour units/agents in such economies thrive on contacts and commissions earned through the mediatory services designed to get the decisions made by public servants/politicians in favour their clients. This leads to the domination of corrupt practices in the system.

Planned and socialist economies offer a striking contrast to capitalist economies. Such economies do not permit ownership of private property in any sphere of the economy, including means of production and production units, except labour/manpower. Public finances constitute the base of financing all production and distribution activities in such economies. Private consumption is also regulated in such economies which are totally or partially closed. People may consume only such goods and services which are produced within the country or are allowed to be imported and distributed by public organisations. All prices are generally administered some of which may be fixed at levels even lower than average cost of production. The cost-price gap is covered by the financial support provided by the government to production units. Prices are not determined to maximise profits of public enterprises. Public revenue and public expenditure play critical role in such economies. But taxation rates are on lower/moderate side. Level of living is often being deliberately kept low so as to mobilise larger proportion of resources for investment for accelerating growth. Public investment almost totally accounts for the growth of GDP in such economies.

Resources for financing public expenditure are usually mobilised from private sector (if it exists at all) and households through fees, fines other charges, and taxation (major source). Greater the public expenditure, greater tends to be the revenue mobilisation through public debt, taxation and surpluses generated by public enterprises. This involves effective transfer of resources/purchasing power from hands of the people, institutions, and producers to government; it reduces private consumption and has a crowding out effect on private savings and investment. Public revenue, especially revenue from taxation inflicts both monetary and real costs on consumers and producers. Indirect taxes on commodities and services also raise prices which may be inflationary on the one hand, and reduce peoples' purchasing power on the other. Producers are also adversely affected by price effect of taxation; increased prices result in reduction in demand which may induce producers to lower their margin over cost that they would have charged on cost plus pricing principle. This is largely the state in mixed planned economies.

Ideological predilections and experiences make people and analysts alike to formulate precepts and nurture views and thoughts about the state and its government. Effects of monetary and fiscal policies on growth, general living conditions of the people and their welfare also influences people's views and opinions about the government. The fiscal policies relate largely to policies of taxation and public expenditure. Taxes directly reduce the purchasing power in the hands of the people whereas public expenditure favourably influences growth of the economy and welfare of the people. The state, for example, irrespective of the nature of its government may supply such essential services as health care, education, transport, communication, water, electricity, gas, and other public and merit goods, which it produces under its monopoly but charges cost plus prices for earning surpluses. But average cost of production is unduly high due to inefficiency and absence of competition. It may adversely affect both growth and welfare.

There are planned mixed economies where both public and private enterprise coexist and operate in their well defined domains, which is fixed by law. Private enterprises in such economies operate under close watch and public control. In capitalist and planned mixed economies, role and functions of the market are manipulated and distorted in one or the other form. Both capitalist and intermediaries distort and manipulate the market in mixed economies for private gains. Even in centrally planned economies, powerful politicians and bureaucrats successfully manipulate policy formulation and decisions of implementation to derive individual benefits. Although the government is supposed to have many important roles and functions in the economy, yet it may also be associated directly or indirectly, willingly or unwillingly, consciously or unconsciously with some policy(ies)/operations having undesirable political, social and/or economic effects on the nation.

Policies and operations may relate to taxing activities which may require support, or imposing of quantity or other restrictions like banning of import, or consumption or production all of which adversely affect growth, though these may not be injurious either to health of the people or environment. Such policies may also relate to wasteful or unproductive public expenditure, withdrawal or reduction in subsidies which may adversely affect both growth and welfare of people. The government may indulge in splurge of public money even though money might have come from public debt, or carrying of unduly high burden of public debt for long periods. Inappropriate trade policies may also harm either growth or welfare or both. For example, import-bills far in excess of export earnings and general splurge of public money on populist programmes and decisions like exempting farmers and others from repayment of their debts for nurturing of or creating vote banks of the ruling clique in 1980s pushed India in economic crisis in 1990s. Similarly, Euro debt crisis and world-wide economic slow-down caused by sub-prime crisis of the US are only recent occurrences. If individuals, production or financial units become bankrupt, government can bail them out, but who should and would bail out the bankrupt government.

All states and their governments operate for correcting undesirable effects of autonomous as well as distorted and manipulated functioning of the market. This is objective is realized by enforcement of rules and regulations governing operations of decision units of the economy. Objectives of such rules, regulations and constraints which decision units in the market are supposed to follow are promotion of economic growth, stabilisation of the economy especially prices, and/ or promotion of welfare or some or all of the above.

Different Approaches to Theory of State

Theories and roles and functions of state have been changing since times immemorial. As society moved from less to more advance stage of civilisation, and hence, social, political and economic development, roles and functions assigned to or assumed by state and its government continuously increased in number, coverage and became more and more intricate, sophisticated, and complicated in nature. Increasing number of areas/fields of operations has also been shifting from individual to public domain or from public to individual domain with each successive level of growth. Besides, at each higher stage of social development and economic growth, inter-personal and inter-activity dependence are also intensified. For example, in the hunting age, there was no organised army of any society to defend itself from the aggression of other society. Each individual was a warrior and participated collectively in battles at the time of strife between two groups or societies. But in the age of settled agriculture, people engaged themselves in productive activities in times of peace but knew the use of weapons and became soldiers in times of aggression by other countries. As against this, Arab invaders or Greeks had organised armed forces (See, Smith 1776). In modern times, all countries of the world, big or small, developed or dev eloping have an organised army.

Government and its governance have acquired greater reach and intricacy due to expanse and complexity of inter-relations of different operations and activities of the government among themselves and their impact on individuals in the society and its economy in post industrial economies and newly industrialising and emerging market economies. These complexities and scope of public operations have been emanating from the polity and political systems which have also been changing radically from time to time. But the pace of change has been greatly accelerated over the past two centuries.

Evolving social philosophy, political and economic theory and political, social and economic systems have shaped and guided the roles and functions of the governments; these changes in turn shaped and guided the magnitude, composition and direction of public finances. Newer and newer sources of raising public revenue have been successfully explored and more and more items and lines of public expenditure have emerged in the course of political, social and economic development. Changing levels, composition and sources of public finances have affected the constituent elements and have also been affected by these constituent elements from time to time. The main source of the thoughts and theories of political thinkers, social philosophers and reformers are encompassed in different systems of philosophy, which have been changing like dress fashions partially because of advancement in knowledge, partially from successful experiences of past generations, and partly from perception based differences among thinkers, philosophers and theorists. Perceptions and thoughts are also guided by the conditions of the time and place of location of thought leaders and philosophers.

Thoughts and Theories of State and Government

Streams of thoughts about state, government and its roles and functions are broadly classified into two categories:

(i) Thoughts and theories relating to the concept and origin of state; and
(ii) Thoughts and theories relating to the roles and functions of the state and its government.

According to this classification, following approaches to concepts, theory, roles and functions of state and its government may be distinguished:

(i) Ideological and pragmatic approach to state and its roles and functions;
(ii) Macro and micro approach to state, its roles and functions;
(iii) Organic and mechanistic approach to state and its government.

Ideological and Pragmatic View of State and its Role and Functions

Ideology and pragmatism are two ends of the spectrum of human life. Ideology may prevail over pragmatism at times, while pragmatism may dominate pragmatism some times. Ideology plays a critical role in human life. Ideology, in fact, plays as critical role as pragmatism in most of the decisions made both at macro and micro levels. This also holds true for the state and its government. Historically once the state came into existence, two different streams of thought dominated political ideology relating to the concept of state: first, state and its government are the needs of the society; and secondly, principle of Divinity was invoked to postulate King as the embodiment of 'God's Will.

As God is perfect and God can do nothing wrong, state and its king, the derivatives and incarnation of God's will also be perfect. Hence, 'King doeth no Wrong' holds valid and King is above all laws of human society: 'Caesar and Caesar's wife' are above law. It is because all laws governing society, its polity and economy are made by the government and government transforms King's dictates into formal system of laws.

After the French and American Revolutions, the concept of 'liberty, equality and fraternity' came to prevail globally. Ideals of 'liberty, equality and fraternity' have become the ideological base of modern democracies. But political democracy remains incomplete without economic democracy. Economic democracy is the corner-stone of capitalism which gives maximum freedom of choice to individuals and limits the roles and functions of the state and its government. This is exemplified in Adam Smith's dictum: "*Laissez Fair*" which emphasises the axiom that individuals know their interests best. So, state should not interfere in social and economic affairs beyond the limited areas where individual action is inadequate to fulfil social needs/requirements. This distinction between social and individual needs arises from the differences between individual and collective/social circumstances. Individual's wants are conditioned, shaped and guided by economic and demographic status of the individuals; individual wants are satisfied by individual action by the use of personal resources. Individuals are allowed not only to pursue the occupations of their own choice but they are also allowed to own private property and other material resources. Collective or social wants depend upon level of economic growth of the society, population size and status of socio-economic infrastructure. Satisfaction of collective wants necessitates use of social resources and collective actions. Collective action may be based either on coercion or cooperation or competition. But satisfaction of collective wants involves mostly public action. Satisfaction and benefits accruing from the fulfilment of social wants are not confined to an individual as these are rather spread over large segments of society, social groups or even population as a whole. This philosophy and theory of state underlies the capitalist economies of the world. But market forces are allowed to operate freely and release signals for individuals to initiate necessary action in accordance with the state of the market.

As against the above, thinkers like Carlyle, William Morris, Engel and Marx highlighted the limitations of autonomously operating market mechanism and its ill effects on large segments of population in general and working classes in particular. This genre of philosophy became the root of Fabien socialism, or cooperatism. Ultimately it culminated in Communism and/State Socialism. Under a socialistic economy, state replaces individual as decision units and owner and user of all resources of the nation.

Theory and process of globalisation transcend boundaries of states for the derivation of economic benefits to the largest number of persons of the world. The economies under the process of globalisation go for replacement of state action by individual initiatives in most of the areas of the economy. So far so that even the collective wants like running of railways may be handed over to some corporate body having requisite knowledge, skills, expertise and resources for investment needed for owning and operating the system required for the satisfaction of such collective wants. For example, Indian railways were divided into zones and each zonal railway was owned and operated by a different organisation/company before independence. Martin Burn Company owned and operated Sahadra-Saharanpur meter-gauge railway till the end of 1960s. This company also owned and operated the systems of generation and distribution of electricity in different cities of India. British railways are also currently operating under private enterprises. Health and education services are other instances of public ownership and operation having been replaced to a large extent by private enterprises in India. PPP (public-private partnership) is new organism in vogue now.

Macro and Micro View of State and its Role and Functions

Rosen and Gayer (2008) classified approaches to the theory of state into two categories of (i) macro; and (ii) micro. Unit of decision-making and functionality tend to overlap in the classification in micro and macro categories. An important difference between micro and macro approaches lies in the view point from which the decision unit is looked at. An industry is micro from the view point of the economy while industry is macro from the view point of a company or firm. Similarly, a *Panchayat Samiti* (Village Committee is macro from the view point of individual villagers but it is micro from the view point of the state government. State government itself is micro decision unit from the view point of the central government. Main distinction between macro and micro approaches to states and their governments arises from their rights and powers on the one hand, and economic functions and responsibilities that states and their governments are supposed to perform, and units of decision making and accounting which bear the impact of decisions on the other. But a detailed discussion of the features of each of these two approaches is required for full understanding of the same.

Micro Approach

Micro approach is based on the impact of state and its government on resource allocation among different lines of expenditure and distribution of benefits of resource use among sectors, segments of population and individuals. Allocation and distribution of burden of mopping up of resources for public use have the following two aspects:

(i) First facet relates to the distribution of burden/cost among the different sections of population from whom resources are collected by the state through taxation, fines, fees etc.; and

(ii) Second facet of the raising of resources from the people relates to public debt.

Allocation and distribution of public resources among different uses and conferment of benefits on people have the following aspects:

(i) Allocation of public resources among the productive uses which relates to public investment in various lines of production;

(ii) Allocation of public resources for the provision of subsidies to such lines of production as may serve good public purpose and production of which may be adversely affected without subsidy or cost may be so high as makes its use unaffordable to the wanted segments of the economy. Subsidies to units producing fertilisers and power are Indian examples of this; and

(iii) Allocation of public resources for the conferment of benefits arising from the use of allocated resources, that is, public expenditure is an important aspect. Cash transfers which affect distribution of income and wealth among the sections of people in the society, and sectors of the economy. These roles and functions involve the disposal of public revenue and money raised from public debt or fiscal deficits. In other words, such functions of the state deal with the efficient allocation of public expenditure on the one hand, and efficient resource utilisation, that is, expenditure incurred by the government on a particular line is required to be used efficiently on the other.

Critical Evaluation

Efficiency and efficacy of policy of taxation have been taken for granted by Rosen and Gayer in the above description of micro approach. Besides above propositions make the approach moves from macro to micro units though the discussion relates to micro approach. They probably begin from macro perspective because policy decisions and their implementation are the twin functions of the state/government and state is the macro unit. Second reason of move from macro to micro appears to be the fact that micro units are directly involved and affected by macro decisions; it is these units who make sacrifices for providing resources to the state who collects revenue from these units and the beneficiaries from public expenditure are also some of these micro units. Total money/resources at the disposal of the government is also a macro aggregate but distribution of its benefits represents smaller quantities which are appropriated by individual units.

Macro Approach

As against micro approach to the state, macroeconomic functions of the state and its government deal with fiscal policy as a whole. Two main functions of fiscal policy are mobilisation of revenue or income for the government from all sources and disposal of the same for the realisation of pre-determined policy objectives. Fiscal policy is an instrument of the raising of public revenue and public borrowings on the one hand, and creation of fiscal deficit if revenue and public borrowings together fall short of requirement of public expenditure on the other. Both these functions are performed to fulfill the needs of public expenditure, which is the other leg of fiscal policyvon the other. All three operations are largely confined to the macro decisions of the government. Beside the fiscal policy, macro functions of the government also encompass formulation and implementation of commercial and trade policies of the government. Formulation and implementation of monetary policy falls within the purview of Central bank, which is generally an autonomous organisation created by the government for managing monetary resources of the economy. Central bank of a country is an autonomous and independent part of the government. But both the government and central bank have to coordinate the fiscal and monetary policies with a view to skirt the possibility of these policies running counter to each other. This is what had been happening during the United Progressive Alliance (UPA)-2 government in India in recent years. Whereas RBI was trying to control excess liquidity in the economy, Government of India was splurging money on non-productive populist programmes and projects; these projects and programmes were designed to win votes for the Congress Party and its allies rather than adding to productive capacity, capital stock or income flows into the country. Consequently, neither inflation could be controlled nor economic growth could be accelerated. Basic objectives of monetary and fiscal policies are maintenance of price stability, reduction of unemployment, reduction of poverty, achievement of higher economic growth, ensuring inclusiveness of growth and promotion of social welfare.

Rosen and Gayer also highlighted two major ideological views about the state and its government; these ideological concerns determine state's/government's functions in the economy. Ideological considerations also determine relationship between the state/government and its people. The ideology furnishes the framework for policy formulation and decisions to implement it.

Organic View and Mechanistic View of Government

These two approaches differentiate organic view of government from its mechanic view.

Organic View of Government

Organic view and perspective of state and its government highlight three different aspects of entities involved in analysis:

(i) Society is postulated as a natural organism;
(ii) Individual is conceived as part of social organism; and

(iii) State and its government are envisaged as the heart of the social organism.

All these three aspects of organic perspective of state are discussed briefly one by one.

Society as Natural Organism

The organic approach envisages society to have been an outcome of natural process of evolution. Man had learnt a lot from observation of fauna and flora, and other aspects in the behaviour of nature, their operations and inter-relations. Several animals live and move in herds. Similarly, men also moved in groups in search of animal for hunting when the place of their abode became barren of hunt. During early stage of agriculture age, humans moved from one to another landscape to find better and more fertile lands for cultivation. Men also learnt from operations of nature and several social laws were patterned on the laws of nature in early stages of evolution of civilisation (Shri Prakash 2010). Society may therefore be treated as a natural organism in this sense.

Individual as Part of Social Organism

Society cannot exist without its members. Just as individuals need society for their benefit society requires individuals for its existence and operation. But society is a macro entity as against individuals who constitute its micro components. But, individuals are integral part of social organism and individuals make society operational. Society exists for individuals; it is individuals who formulate the operational rules of society and implement the same. But individuals should not be treated as if they exist for society; society exists for individuals. Each community/society formulates such rules and conventions as are viewed to be the best at the given point of time and space. If conditions change and warrant the change in conventions and rules, it is individuals who will design and implement these desired changes in social fabric, its structure and rules of procedure.

Government as a Benevolent Institution

Like society, government cannot exist without people whom the government rules over. So, government is envisaged to be a benevolent entity, which operates for the promotion of well-being of its people. The government is, therefore, required to have a heart in place to feel and recognise the problems and needs of the people. Problems and needs of the people should be the guide-post for public decisions.

But there exist many conflicts of interest among the people belonging to different income, education, occupation, demographic and social groups. Besides, individuals do not have the full view of either economy or society due to which they may not think for long run in macro perspective. In our view, proponents of this thesis should have used the expression that the government should have "head and heart" rather than using the word 'heart' alone. Head has to play the central role in the formulation and implementation of public policies which are designed to benefit all members of the society. In other words, the government should strive to satisfy Pareto's optimality condition where no one's welfare may be increased without adversely affecting the welfare of someone else.

Followers of above ideology argue that there exists mutual interdependence among three facets of state and its government. Society or country, like human body, is viewed as an organic whole. All parts of this organism have to operate in unison, which requires that the functions of three components of the state/government have to synchronise both in time and space. State and its government are not like lifeless machine, which can be put apart by the owner or mechanic and put it together again and again. But the machine can also function only if all components are functional and discharge these functions together. Each part and component of a machine has to function. Similarly, each individual member of society plays a role assigned by the society/community. Good of an individual relates to what the individual does for the society. Government acts as the monitor of the entire society, but the society/community is ranked above the individual. This is like Jeff Kennedy's dictum "Do not ask what the country can do for you, but ask yourself what you can do for the country".

Plato (Republic) also considered activities of individuals as desirable only if the actions result into being a part of just society. Besides, the government/state sets the goals and objectives for society and its members to realise. However, objectives differ between states and through time. Plato's Republic focused on an ancient society goal of which was to reach the golden age in which human activity was guided by perfect rationality. Kautilaya, however, envisaged that an empire will always be confronted with internal strife and possibility of lawlessness and even of revolt against the state; he also envisaged eternal threat of possible foreign aggression. So, he postulated an elaborate administrative machinery to take comprehensive care of internal rule to prevail within the empire for which provisions of wide range of contingencies for the maintenance of law and order and administration of justice in a transparent, fair and efficient manner were made. Adequately armed and physically fit army was always kept in readiness to face external aggression that is why Chandra Gupta Maurya, whose minister and adviser Kautilaya was, succeeded in repulsing the invasion of Siliceous. Thus, presence of evil forces was envisaged to exist both internally and externally for which extensive and exhaustive administrative machinery has to be kept well oiled all the time. It is thus obvious that Plato was more Platonic or idealist, while Kautilaya was more pragmatic and realist in his formulations.

A few decades ago, the Iranian Leader Ayatollah Khomeini is reported to have stated that "Only a good society can create good believers." He argued that "Man is half-angel, half-devil." So the main goal of government is to deal with this devil part by means of laws and appropriate punishments for violations of laws to deter the wrong doers. So, the government and its society have to institute an in-built mechanism to keep the Angelic elements in humans performing in the interest of the state and society.

Mechanistic View of Government

Mechanistic view of the state looks at it and its government in a mechanistic way. Certain functions devolve on government as an autonomous but mechanistic flow from its concept of state and its government. Whereas the organic view flows as water in river in a natural way, mechanistic view is derived from the mechanism of ruling by the government over its people.

It addresses the questions of: (i) What are legitimate rights of the state and its government? and (ii) What are the duties and responsibilities which devolve from the right to rule?

Mechanistic view of the state and its government offers an alternative to Organic philosophy of state. According to this philosophy and theory it embodies, government is created by individuals to achieve their personal goals by better means and more efficient ways. Thus, the state and its government are deliberate and conscious creation of individuals' collective decision. The government is construed to be a trustee and its officers are trustees of the people. Government is constituted and its officers are appointed to confer benefits on society. Therefore, the prime obligation of government is the doing of good of the people, protection from internal disorder and violence, and defending against external aggression. These are primary duties of the government. Consequently, incurring expenditure on internal security, administration of justice and the raising and maintaining of armed forces are legitimate items of public expenditure. But the government is not envisaged to spend on growth and welfare beyond the above.

Thomas Hobbes, for example, opines that "Life of a man becomes solitary, poor, nasty, short and brutish" without government. Therefore, government is given the monopoly of coercive power for prevention of the eruption of anarchy in society. Somalia is a burning illustration of this postulate which has no effective government to prevent the prevalence of anarchy or lawlessness prevailing in that country. Their illegal activities have also extended over the seas from where they seize and rob ships with cargo; this reminds one about the late middle ages during mercantilist era when sea robbers ruled the high seas.

Adam Smith's philosophy and theory he formulated are based on his learning about society and its functions through different stages of evolution of civilisation. He took to heart ill social effects of too many government's interventions in the economy and social affairs in the past, especially during the mercantilist era and Physiocrats' France. The reasons behind Smith's thought were two-fold: both the above periods had pre-industrial societies and Smith gained lot of insights on hind sight about the social and economic ill effects of excessive interventions of the government in social and economic affairs. He considered polity and its political affairs to be the legitimate domain of the state and its government. Adam Smith naturally went a couple of steps beyond the above philosophy of state and its government. He opined that the state should limit itself only to: (i) defence against foreign aggression; (ii) administration of justice and maintenance of internal law and order; (iii) spending on public works. In other words, government should incur expenditure necessary for defence of the country, maintenance of law and order and administration of justice along with the provisions for public utilities like roads and supply of other public and merit goods, which the market cannot provide to the society, especially the needy.

Benefits of such expenditure accrue to large segments of society rather than being confined to an individual who will incur expenditure on such works or goods. However, Adam Smith did not include subjects like health and education in the list of merit and public goods because of which he did not put expenses on education in the purview of public expenditure. For example, he considers education system to be largely self-reliant, since educational institutions raise endowment and charge fees from the scholars which should suffice to defray their normal expenses. For example, he says, "The institutions for the education of the youth may, in the same manner, furnish a revenue sufficient for defraying their own expense".

But a careful study of Smith's book reveals that he goes beyond the above position. He has said that:

> The education of the common people require, perhaps, in a civilized and commercial society, the attention of the public more than that of people of some rank and fortune. People of some rank and fortune are generally eighteen or nineteen years of age before they enter upon that particular business, profession, or trade, by which they propose to distinguish themselves in the world. They have before that full time to acquire, or at least to fit themselves for afterwards acquiring, every accomplishment which can recommend them to the public esteem

> or render so accomplished, and are, in most cases, willing enough to lay out the expense which is necessary for that purpose. If they are not always properly educated, it is seldom from the want of expense laid out upon their education, but from the improper application of that expense. It is seldom from the want of masters but from the negligence and incapacity of the masters who are to be had and from the difficulty or rather from the impossibility which there is in the present state of things, of finding any better. The employments too in which people of some rank or fortune spend the greater part of their lives, are not, like those of the common people, simple and uniform. They are almost all of them extremely complicated and such as exercise the head more than the hands.... employment of people of some rank and fortune, besides, are seldom such that seldom harass them from morning to night...It is otherwise with common people. They have little time to spare for education. Their parents can scarce afford to maintain them even in infancy. As soon as they are able to work, they must apply to some trade by which they can earn their subsistence..... though the common people cannot...be so well instructed in....the most essential parts of education, however, to read, write and account, can be acquired at so early a period of life, that the greater part even of those who are to be bred to the lowest occupations, have time to acquire them before they can be employed. For a very small expense the public can facilitate, can encourage, and can even impose upon almost the whole body of the people the necessity of acquiring those most essential parts of education (pp.989-90).

It is thus obvious that Smith has advocated supply of that education called basic education in modern times free and compulsorily to all. Thus, public expenditure on basic education has been admitted by Smith as the public good.

Adam Smith included healthcare and education also in public or merit goods. Public and merit goods were included by Smith as part of public expenditure. This runs counter to the view expressed by Shri Prakash and Chowdhury (1995) relating to Smith's stand on public expenditure on education and health (Shri Prakash 1996: 989).

The strains and streams of thought about mechanistic philosophy and theory of state differed among thinkers and over space and time. Libertarians subscribed to the thought of limiting the role of state and its government in economic affairs. Adam Smith is one among such libertarians. He exclaims that: "Every man, as long he does not violate the laws of justice is free to pursue his own interest in his own way." The underlying thought is that the individual knows best what is good for him and how can it be achieved. So state should not do what the individual can do. Conversely, state should do what the individuals cannot do themselves. Thinkers of this strand doubt whether government has the ability to promote social welfare by entering such areas of economy where individuals excel in the market.

But social democrats believe that large scale government interventions in the economy are required for correcting distortions in economic structure and social ethos caused by mal-functioning of the market forces. Examples are the prevalence of economic inequality, especially the inequality that marks distribution of income and wealth in market based capitalist societies, wasteful expenditure by individuals on conspicuous goods and items of distinction which distorts the composition of national output and accentuate the inefficient use of scarce resources. However, such arguments miss the point that governments may as much be prone to incur public expenditure in wasteful manner and in accordance with distorted priorities and objectives. For example, construction of statutes of selected public figures which are marvel of architecture, grand in design and splendid in appearance. Numerous examples of this type may be cited. Taj mahal built in the memory of Queen Mumtaj Mahal by Shahjehan, the Mughal emperor is among seven wonders in the world. Contemporary democratic India is not free from this malady.

Regulatory framework and laws for the safety related provisions for workers at the work place, laws against racial and sexual discrimination etc. have to be enunciated and enforced by government. The government intervention is also advocated for the realisation of such macroeconomic objectives as price stability, reduction of unemployment, and imparting momentum to economic growth, or extricating economy out of the morass of recession.

Theories of Origin of State

Major strands of thoughts and streams of political philosophy, and social and economic theories, which deal with the origin of state, may broadly be classified into four main groups. These streams of thought explain why and how has state come into existence. These theories are briefly described hereunder.

Theory of State by Force

The theory of state formation by force explains that one powerful and strong person or a small group of persons took control of an area and forced all people within it to abide by his or group's dictates and accept to be ruled by him/them. Theorists believed that the state originated from use of force by more powerful over the weak. This is like Darwin's Theory of Survival of the Fittest in Jungle, where the strongest and the fittest emerged as the Ruler/King/Lord and the weak succumbed to the force and became the ruled. In this context, survival refers to the status in which people lived before being subjugated by the powerful and strong, who formed the state by force and subjugated people who failed to protect their autonomy. Force stands for armed force, or military power. Force or military power is not in the modern sense of the term. Force or power in primitive stage of civilisation may be owned by the leader of a group of people, who joined together with a view to become the ruler(s) of an area. There are examples when erstwhile bandits/dacoits declared themselves kings/emperors. There are also instances, when some-one entrusted with responsibility of ruling an area on behalf of emperor, revolted and declared himself King or Nawab. In such cases, armed forces under the control of such person were used to snatch a part of the kingdom from the real king/emperor. This practice became frequent in the middle age.

Powerful states, strong and powerful rulers thought that they owed it to their people to protect them from invasion from outside and disturbances from people or forces from within the state. Thus, defence against invasion and enforcement of law, order and justice emerged as main responsibilities of the state and its ruler. For the discharge of such duties revenue had to be raised from the people. Invasion from outside was not only threat to the people but it was a threat to the ruler himself. Besides, the ruler has also to maintain administrative paraphernalia of his court and courtiers, which often required relatively heavy public expenditure. So, revenue was needed to be raised from the public not only for meeting expenditure requirements of defence and internal law and order but also for administrative machinery of the king. Thus, roles and functions of the state were limited, and hence, limited public expenditure was incurred which was warranted by such extremely limited roles and functions of the government.

Theory of Evolution of State Through Stages of Civilisation

The theory of evolution argues that state emerged naturally out of the early primitive society, comprising nuclear/small families in which one person was the head. People of these ages have gained extensive observations about the behaviour of flora and fauna and they had gone through a variety of experiences; these varied experiences were great teachers and important source of learning. Experience gained and knowledge gained furnished inspiration and imparted motivation to experiment with several types of organisations, learnt about benefits and limitations of different types of cooperation, and division of labour etc. All these were used as the base of evolution of a different level of civilisation and styles of living together or separately. Consequently, society comprising nuclear families furnished the base of alternative and larger and more varied structure of societies. The societies over the years became a network of families called clan, then a tribe. Eventually from the concept of tribe emerged its practical counterpart concept and birth of the state. The concept of head of family/household and its practical applications were extended to cover all entities/families residing in a specific spatial unit. The size of spatial unit was also extended over a larger area in this process. The evolution of state in this conceptualisation is conceived to be consensual. Naturally, theory of evolution of state is based on consensus.

Before the emergence of Gupta Empire, Village Gantantars existed over an extensive area of India, especially North India. Samudra Gupta conquered all these Village Gantantars one after the other on the basis of strength of his armed forces. He did not encounter much resistance since these gantantars were small in size and did not maintain armed forces for their protection. Village Gantantars were democracies in practice and Head of each gantantatra ruled over the entire populace and area of its location. Ruler/head was selected/elected by consensus. Samudra Gupta consolidated all these units into a large Gupta Empire of Ancient India.

These gantantars had the following features: (i) each entity was small in population size and spread over small geographical area, (ii) Head was an elected member, (iii) decision-making was the prerogative of village council, who were democratically elected for specified period of time, and (iv) India had as many governments as the gantantars. Gantantar stands for peoples' rule or democracy. But consolidation of these village democracies into Gupta Empire replaced many by one ruler and one state. Gantantars were driven by peoples' will and governance focused on social welfare. Thus government formation by consensus was replaced by state formation by force.

Divine Right Theory of State/King

Divine right theory holds that the state was created by God and that God gives those of royal birth a "divine right" to rule. People of such society must, therefore, obey the ruler or divine king just as they obeyed God. This theory became the basis of most of the states in the world from early middle ages and it continued during 15th to the 18th centuries. However, the concept of divinity associated with King/Emperor was not confined to Europe alone. As the mythology goes, King Ram and Krishna were incarnations of Vishnu, the God. So theory of divinity or divine ruler prevailed in pre-historic India also.

The divine theory argues that the state arose out of a voluntary act of free choice of people. They reposed faith in King (Emperor) as the representative of God. But the state, king and his government arrived together on the stage in first instance and kingship became hereditary in due course.

Social Contract Theory

Last theory of state is social contract theory; it explains the reasons which prompted people to become members of society.

State emerged from society along with its government subsequently. Society or group of people entered into contract among themselves to create a state and its government in order to avoid chaos or anarchy, catastrophe, or free for all and possibly conflicts of interests. Thus creation of state and its government was required and aimed at institutionalisation of the system of state and its government. Social contract theory replaces selection by election of the ruler. This concept of the origin of state has been supported by numerous philosophers including John Locke, Hobbes and others. The theory lays stress on democratic base of the institution of King and Kingdom.

Concept of State in Retrospect

The evolution of the concepts of the state, king and governance resulted from the thoughts of a number of philosophers like Plato (437-347 BC), Aristotle (384-322 BCE), Thomas Hobbes (1588-1679), John Locke (1632-1704), Jean-Jacques Rousseau (1712-1778) and others. Plato is considered to be the first planner and founder of communist economy in ancient Greece over four hundred years before Christ. He is probably the founder of communism because of his pro-people leanings.

Plato was exiled from his first abode, though he justified the existence of state. His concept was that of a city state, probably because the primitive means of communication and transportation limited the scope of expansion of the boundaries of state during those days. This limited geographical expansion of state beyond the city. Many people believe that planning as a concept was also propounded by Plato. But planning was put on a higher pedestal by Karl Marx and his followers. Karl Marx, whose ideas formed the foundation of the cradles to nurture socialism. Plato, however, in his Republic laid the foundation of the concept of "Welfare State". Plato relied on large centralised state under the control of few people or totalitarianism. He propounded the theory that the State should be ruled by a few powerful and wealthy elites of society. He is called philosopher King. He opined that the state should take care of the society, maintain peace, order and security and provide public goods. These views of Plato have been nurtured by subsequent generations of philosophers, political thinkers and economists. Plato further argued that size of the government may differ between states, depending on the internal and external circumstances, that is, degree of law enforcement required within the state. Therefore, size of the government may directly be related to size of the population, number and nature of problems of law and order and geographical spread of the state Plato's concepts entailed seeds of public finances. Howsoever rich or wealthy the king himself may be, he cannot spend his own money forever on public affairs. So revenue has to be raised from people for meeting public expenditure needs. But size of the public expenditure and its composition will depend on the size of state and responsibilities of the king towards his kingdom and its people. From these concepts of state and its King emanated the idea of social divide into rulers and the ruled, rich and the poor, and elites and commoners.

Like Plato Aristotle also inferred the need for state as the means of protection and security of the people. Despite Aristotle's acknowledgement of goodness of planning and focus on humanity, he differed with Plato, his teacher. While Plato believed in large centralized state as the means to improve social welfare, Aristotle believed that there was no need for having massive centralized government to take control over everything and everyone and exercise control over ownership of property and decided which property/goods to be owned by the people and which by the government. Aristotle conceived the government as merely the means to maintain peace and provide security to the people. Aristotle, however, conceded that the state has to take care of welfare of the people, especially the poor whom state may provide financial means to begin small businesses Thus, thoughts of Plato and Aristotle together delineated the domain of state's roles and functions, especially as the final arbiter of public expenditure. Public revenue and public expenditure are inseparably woven together. Philosophers like Hobbes, Locke and Rousseau further enriched the thoughts of Plato and Aristotle by their own contribution. Origin of several streams of thoughts about polity, and government may thus be traced to Plato and Aristotle in full and some thoughts may be traced to them in embryonic and nebulous form.

Thomas Hobbes in his famous book *Leviathan* deliberated on the need for and nature of 'state'. He postulated that "human life without rule of law or government is like the life of every man against every man which would be nasty, poor, brutish, solitary and short". This assertion of Hobbes is validated by the example of Somalia, where no effective national government is in existence now and violence is widespread. It is, therefore, obvious that in the absence of state/ government, maintenance of law and order may be hay-wire; it shall validate Darwinian Theory of 'survival of the fittest' and 'prevalence of the Law of the Jungle' in which the stronger swallows the weaker. This may be avoided by formation of state that will protect such natural rights of people as right to life, right to liberty and property. Hobbes thus differed from Plato and Aristotle; he shifted focus from the Welfare State of, Plato and Aristotle to the 'Ruling State'. His main concern was governance for security from foreign aggression and maintenance of internal law and order. This naturally limited the size and expanse of public finances.

Locke's most important works on political theory are two treatises on Government, especially second Treatise on 'Civil Government'. Unlike Hobbes, Locke was against the contention that 'people were born in natural subjugation of their king'. He argued that 'the power of the king or any government is derived from the people who contract to obey their ruler in exchange of law and security. Individuals have the right to own property and this cannot be taken away from them without their consent'. According to John Lock, an individual is known by his personality; but personality is determined by ideas and thoughts that the individual subscribes to, holds and allows these thoughts and ideas to shape and guide his behaviour. But like Hobbes, Locke also emphasised that the main role of government is to protect people's life, liberty and property. If however the government fails to provide the desired protection to people, they have the right to oppose it and form a new government. Individuals have the right of ownership over their knowledge and thoughts, and hence, s/he is free to have the government of her or his choice. These views furnished justification for the American and French Revolutions and their guiding principle

'Liberty, Fraternity and Equality'. He insisted that the people have the right to own private property, and it shall not be the right of the state to redistribute property or wealth of the rich among the poor. John Locke's theory paved the way for democracy. However, such theories of state and roles and functions of the government limit the government's expenditure only to security from external invasion, maintenance of internal law and order, administration of justice and insurance of private right to property. Right to property implies that the government will prevent all from encroaching, misappropriating, and usurping of others' property and wealth. The state shall largely be restricted towards protecting people so as to ensure that they live in a peaceful environment; but the government has the right and responsibility for solving conflicts among individuals. This indicates importance of state in any economy though it has to be limited to the maintenance of peace and security. Consequently, size and composition of public expenditure shall only be limited to the discharge of such roles as are prescribed by above theories. Limits to expenditure will automatically limit public revenue.

Jean-Jacques Rousseau, a political philosopher of his times, subscribed to the view that small public spending on protection of the state and its property is legitimate. He asserted that "Man was born free and he is everywhere in chains." Chains that Rousseau talks about refer to fostering of industrial freedom and consequent chains of poverty and deprivation that entrapped large mass of the people in the industrial society of his times. Other chains that Rousseau was probably considering are inequality in distribution of income, violation of human rights, deprivation, distress, and so on. Rousseau also argued that all human beings are born inherently good 'Nobel Savage'. However, once the idea of private property was introduced in the stream of thoughts and it intruded into real world, class conflicts occurred between the haves and have-nots. Individuals, who possessed large amount of property, generally created government that would be in their best interest to protect their life and their possessions. This justified existence of government and public expenditure that will free such individuals from any chain, especially fear of loss of their wealth and source of income which clouds their thoughts and actions. The concept of fiscal deficit and theory of public debt had not emerged during the era of these theories. Consequently, public finances comprised only public revenue and public expenditure. Size of public revenue to be raised depended upon the public expenditure needs of the state for the fulfilment of its limited roles and functions. This in turn depended on the size of the kingdom in terms of population and geographical spread of the kingdom and partly upon the perception of the government about the danger of foreign aggression, possibilities of public disorders and style of governance in terms of efficiency, scale and display or conspicuous nature of all that was under the government including the life style of the Royal Family.

Mercantilism and Physioctrats' Orthodoxy

Above discussion has laid bare the ancient philosophical foundation of the institution of state and its government. These thoughts have been adapted, modified and even replaced by the modern political theory. Government was more concerned with the promotion of trade through exports and reduction of imports by means of controls and regulation during mercantilist era. Mercantilist's philosophy as pioneered by Jean-Baptise Colbert in the 16th and 17th centuries perceived that wealth and power of the state were best served by increasing exports to collect precious metals in return of exported goods. Trade was conceived as the major means of accumulation of wealth, especially in the form of gold and silver which were the then indicators and measures of wealth and prosperity of nations. As most of the countries did not have, gold, silver, diamond mines, which only some countries of the world were and are lucky to have got, trade was the main instrument of accumulation of precious metals like gold/silver and diamond. The fact that the countries then used gold and/or silver standard, value of these metals was naturally beyond their practical and productive uses. But these were the medium of exchange and standard of measure besides being the safe store of value. All these attributes are associated with the functions of money. The governments of those days have had practically total control over the economy. However, public spending was mainly accounted by defence, maintenance of law, order and justice and the promotion of production of goods for export. Promotion and protection of trade and trade routes was the highest priority of governments. This needed incurring of heavy public expenditure. Protection of international trade was reflected by measures of export promotion by means of a variety of incentives and inducements, and discouraging imports was done mainly by imposition of tariffs. This was designed to promote production of domestic import substitutes for securing of favourable balance of trade, balance of payments, and accumulation of reserves (gold and silver as foreign currency). State directly participated in economic activities some of which like mining of precious metals were in state sector.

Physiocrats shifted emphasis from trade to agriculture for acquiring 'Real Net Produit' from agriculture rather than earning precious metals from trade. They thought that agriculture alone produced net output/produit. Real net produce referred to output of real goods rather than value addition by transforming form, size, structure and shape of the materials as is done in manufacturing, or adding value by change of place as is done by transporting, change in ownership as is done by trading or sales and purchases. Agriculture alone could produce more output than what it used in production process (seeds, manures). But agriculture was dispersed over the entire landscape of which individual farmers were the owners. Farmers owned the farms, implements of cultivation/farming, and barns. Land, the real means of producing real net output, replaced metals as wealth. But farming was carried on by individuals by their own enterprise and private investment. It reduced the need for public expenditure for promoting growth of real output. But public revenue was needed for financing the expenses of the (i) kings and queens who lived an extremely luxurious life, (ii) courtiers and administrators, (iii) other support systems for protection against foreign invasion and internal uprising or disorders, and (iv) dispensation of justice etc. These were purely administrative rather than business or economic expenses.

Thus, unlike mercantilist, physiocrats were concerned more with the promotion of agriculture than trade. Even otherwise there was hardly any scope for trading in agricultural produce due to a variety of reasons; an important reason was that every country has had its own share of agricultural land which was used for meeting the food requirements of the populace rather than for exporting to other countries. Therefore, the government played the role of facilitating development of agricultural infrastructure which was needed for agricultural development. Infrastructure needed investment beyond the means of individual farmers such as irrigation, roads for transportation of produce from production to consumption centres fell within the purview of public expenditure. Thus, Physiocartic philosophy moved beyond the thoughts of earlier thinkers who limited the state's functions to defence, law and order, dispensation of justice. Physiocrats' thoughts were founded and led by Francois Quesnay in the 18th century. Their thoughts shifted Mercantilists' focus from trade to agriculture rather than limiting the roles of government to defence and law and order. A group of physiocrats raised their voice and protested against the excessive government controls and regulation of the economy between the late 16th and 18th centuries. They argued that 'The dead hand of the state would only corrupt the natural evolution of the economy'. This thought formed the base of their support to the so called '*laissez faire*'. They argued that business should follow the 'natural laws' of economics freely without government interference. Physiocrats may, therefore, be considered as the fore-runners of Adam Smith and other classical economists, who advocated policy of *laissez faire*. They also limited the scope of public expenditure on economic activities beyond administrative services and few promotional measures for development of agriculture.

Jacob Viner (1892-1970) referred to Physiocrats as one of the "pioneers and systematic exponents" of *laissez-faire*. Their thoughts are compatible with those of David Hume, Adam Smith and J.S. Mill. They, in fact, may either be thought of as mentors of Adam Smith et al., or as those who anticipated the dominant thoughts of future. Their philosophy, especially the philosophy of *laissez faire* was strongly supported by David Hume, Adam Smith and JS Mill. They also laid down the foundation of subsequent evolution of the theory of cost advantage as the base of international trade. Net produce represents surplus over cost, and larger the surplus greater shall be the cost advantage.

Classical Economic Thought on Government's Functions

Classical economics is widely regarded as the first school of modern economic thought. Major contributors to classical thoughts are Adam Smith (1723–1790), Thomas Malthus (1766–1834), David Ricardo (1772–1823), and John Stuart Mill (1806–1873). Classicists were opposed to mercantilist (i) theory of protection and promotion of trade; they espoused the cause of free trade in accordance with cost/comparative cost advantage, (ii) consideration of precious metals alone (which were used as, money during gold, silver standard) and interference in free operations of market mechanism. They also went beyond the Physiocrats to emphasise value addition not only by farming but also by manufacturing and trade. However, the classicists used philosophical framework of Plato, Aristotle, Hobbes, Quesnay and others to determine areas of state's role and functions within the framework of which they developed economic theories and laws, including those relating to public revenue and public expenditure. All classical economists advocated the policy of minimal government intervention in economic matters. Some thinkers also include economists like John Maynard Keynes, Karl Marx and his followers among the classical economists. However, Karl Marx focussed more on ill effects of autonomous working of the market forces in a capitalist economy rather than eulogising the virtues of the capitalist system. Marx and his followers articulated various ill economic effects of class conflict. Marx in fact perceived class conflict to be in-built in the processes of free market operations. Working of the market and its outcomes are influenced by the haves rather than have-nots. Profits of capitalist class and wages of labouring class together exhaust the total value-added. Greater the profits, lower shall be the wage bill. But the capitalist are and will always be interested in profit maximisation; the adage goes 'Profit is the only business of business.' Therefore, class conflicts arise from the interests of labour and capital being in juxtaposition to be harmonised and synthesised in complementary cooperation rather than competitive conflict. This runs counter to Smith's postulate that individual interests are in harmony. This assumption enabled him to advocate *laissez faire*. *Laissez faire*, the policy of minimum government interference in economy implies limiting the size and role of public finances. Minimum role of government minimises needs of public expenditure; this in turn reduces the need for raising public revenue to the minimum.

Adam Smith (1776), the pioneer of classical economic thought, in *Nature and Causes of Wealth of Nations* advocated the philosophy of '*laissez faire*'. Adam Smith argued that the economy of any state can work best if it is left to function on its own without government intervention. Public intervention is generally by means of taxation/tariffs, controls and regulations and other measures which tend to limit individual initiatives and entrepreneurs' exploration of opportunities for maximising profits. Adam Smith wrote, "in the economic market people who only intend to serve their self-interest are driven by an invisible hand to serve the public interest, which was no part of their original intention." The metaphor 'invisible hand' connotes the market mechanism operating autonomously to bring about the balance between demand and supply, and hence, price and cost. It is implicit that if short-run price is higher than cost, it is mitigated autonomously by the market; price in excess of cost yields higher profits which induces producers to raise supply in the long-run. This eliminates the impact of excess demand on price. So there is no need for state to intervene either by the instrument of taxation which raises cost to the producer and yields revenue to the government, or administrative control or regulation which leads to rise in public expenditure and may create shortages of supply. Thus, eschewing of all such measures limited the scope of government's role. Consequently, this theory denied a great deal of role to public finances in the operations of government relating to the economy. All the same, Smith's focus was welfare of the society as a whole and he visualised the free market or the forces of demand and supply to bestow benefits on all.

Freely operating market offers equal opportunities to all to maximise their gains according to the best of ability of each of them. Smith focused on the determination of economic functions of market with no or minimal government intervention which will promote individual interests of all. It is his concern with welfare that prompted him to use 'economic market rather than market' in his exposition of the role of the government.

Adam Smith stressed that the government intervention is justified only by the beneficial effect on efficiency of allocation of resources among different lines of production on the one hand, and reduction in the distributional inefficiencies of the market failures on the other. Inefficiency arises from the impact of externalities on efficiency which individuals may not be able to control, asymmetric information due to market imperfections, inadequate output of public goods, monopolies, and manipulation of market mechanism by few powerful operatives. He visualised a trade-off between efficiency and inefficiency of these two genres. Therefore, he limited the role and functions of state to three major activities: (i) protecting the society from internal violence, and protection from injustice or oppression for which the government has to maintain internal law and order machinery, (ii) protection of every member of the society from foreign invasion for which armed forces have to be maintained, and (iii) provision of public or quasi-public goods and services along with transfer payments. An interesting feature of Adam Smith's postulations is that before finalising his views on public expenditure on such objects as defence, law and order, administration of justice, education and health he extensively reviewed nature, composition and organisational aspects of government's roles and functions in different stages of evolution of civilisation and development of economy and its structure. He extensively discussed the means, ways and modes or modalities of discharge of public responsibilities for above mentioned subjects and the level and structure of public expenditure of the same. It gave him very wide historical perspective in which he formulated his concepts and theories (See, *Wealth of Nations*).

All functions except the ones listed above were considered beyond the scope of state. Expenditure on functions other than the listed ones was treated as unjust and wasteful. Public expenditure on above listed functions and activities related to their performance was considered as the part of expenditure on legitimate functions of the state. These activities by their very nature are difficult for individuals to perform. Public expenditure on aforementioned functions of the state also varied in practice between states according to geographical spread of the state and size of its population on the one hand, and it varied inter-temporally within the state according to expanded requirements and state's income on the other. Adam Smith is considered as Father of Modern Economics, especially in current era of Liberalisation, Privatisation and Globalisation. Today's size of national economies and their structures have undergone sea change; it has changed the size, direction and composition of public expenditure also since Smith's times. Views and thoughts about the roles and functions of state have also been transformed.

Malthusian thoughts on public expenditure may be inferred from his writings on population growth and differential legal framework affecting growth of population in different countries of Europe. Thomas Malthus in 'Principles of Population' opined that poverty and distress are inevitable consequences of unchecked population growth, which tends to outrun supply of food. He argued that population grows geometrically whereas output of food increases in arithmetic progression. Population doubles every 25 years, while doubling of food supply takes much greater time than this. This imbalance between the demand for food due to rapid population growth leads to excess demand over supply of food which leads to rise in price. Population of labour class increases more rapidly than their income; it combined with the practice of 'Iron Law of Wages' results in the accentuation of inequalities of income. This leads to petulance, misery, starvation, disease and death among the poor, especially the labour class. Increase in population without any checks leads to decrease in availability of food per person/hectare of land, hunger and starvation.

He studied population growth of different countries of Europe along with their laws relating to (i) compulsory military service which kept men away from women for prolonged periods; (ii) prohibition of marriages before the age of 18 and without employment; and (iii) free or restricted trade in food items, Enforcement of such social and economic laws entailed public expenditure much beyond that was envisaged by Smith (See Shri Prakash 2005). Malthus advocated the virtues of celibacy and recommended positive checks for controlling population growth. Implementation of these checks also involved government intervention for family planning, enforcement of marriage laws and laws governing food supply. All such public actions result in public expenditure more than what Smith's prudence visualised. Malthus criticised poor laws imposed by the British government because they led to higher population growth relative to food production. Malthus initially supported protectionist Corn Laws, which had involved imposition of taxes on imported wheat into Britain. But he changed his stand latter to support free trade as a way to reduce high prices of food for checking distress among the working classes in towns. High prices resulted from the corn-laws in Britain after the Napoleonic war. He argued that if traders were free to import cheaper food, problem of famine, distress and starvation could be eliminated. It may, therefore, be inferred that, although Malthus did not deliberate much on the roles of the state in the economy directly, his thoughts show that substantial government intervention is needed for formulating and implementing laws for population control. Enforcement of laws to control high population growth and initiate programmes which promote increased food production for the benefits of the society as a whole increased public expenditure. Incurring increased public expenditure needs increased revenue to finance it.

David Ricardo was an outstanding British political economist in classical mould. He authored *The Principles of Political Economy and Taxation*. The title of the book itself suggests that, unlike Adam Smith, Ricardo considered public finance, especially public revenue as an important part of economic analysis. Taxation is the most important instrument of raising revenue to finance public expenditure. So, taxation is an important part of public finance. He propounded the theory of comparative advantage of trade. The comparative advantage theory provided the basis of evolution of modern trade theory of factor endowment.

Like Adam Smith, Ricardo was also an opponent of protectionism. Like Malthus, Ricardo also opposed the "corn laws," which were intended to protect British landowners from foreign competition by guaranteeing them the high prices for their produce. He believed that protectionism led to economic stagnation. He argued that protectionism by more advanced nations led economies of less developed nations to stagnation. Thus he was able to anticipate current scenario when developing countries insist in negotiations at WTO that developed countries should not resort to protectionism but they should not expect exact reciprocal response from the developing countries which are in the early stages of industrialisation. Ricardo's ideas influenced later economists in the belief that protectionism is bad for economic growth. Although Ricardo is against government restrictions and regulation of the economy, he does not propose that government is not needed at all in the economy. His philosophy, by and large, supported the *laissez-faire*, as subscribed by Adam Smith, which assigns the government or state minimal roles and functions in social affairs in general and management of economy in particular. The government has to perform the roles of protecting people from internal and external violence, administration of justice, provision of public goods. Performance of these functions was then considered as the main determinants of size, composition and pattern of public revenue on which depended the level of public expenditure.

J.S. Mill (1833), like the earlier classicists, in 'Utilitarianism' defined what has been accepted as the minimum level of state interference in economic affairs. He pointed out that the size and structure of public expenditure and government intervention in the economy should be limited to the power to enforce contracts, ensure property rights, and conduct administration of justice. Power of enforcement of contract and right to property go a bit beyond the roles of government assigned in earlier thoughts. In return, state has the right to tax people in order to provide public goods such as transport, sanitation, public health and state supported education. It is thus obvious that J.S. Mill not only elaborated and explained the functions of state, that had been envisaged by his predecessors but he also added certain lines of public expenditure such as sanitation, public health and education in more forceful way than his predecessors. He also propounded the thesis that the market might be efficient in allocating resources but it does not distribute income among the people efficiently, making it necessary for the government to intervene in the economy. Thus, income redistribution to mitigate inequalities of income beyond a point falls within the purview of policies of taxation, while transport, health and education, and provision of other public goods were legitimatised by Mills as part of public expenditure. Expenditure on promotion of social welfare up to a point shall also be admissible as per his theorisation.

Advent of Welfare State

Experience of adverse and observation of even bitter effects of freely operating market in capitalist industrial societies over a period of time evoked bitter criticism of classical thoughts by philosophers and thinkers like William Morris, Ruskin Carlyle and others. These criticisms and dismissal of economics as a Dismal Science by contemporary thinkers made economists and political scientists to evaluate the status of their respective disciplines. Re-evaluation of the subject matter of economics induced economists to revise the conceptual framework of economic analysis in which state and the functions of the government were conceived and perceived by classical school. Nature and contents of economics as a science were severely tested and re-evaluated in retrospect against the facts of life. Severe ill consequences of industrialised capitalist economy in the form of social divide into the haves and have-nots, rich and the poor, and poverty, misery, deprivation and destitution of the workers in the midst of the enclaves of prosperity of erstwhile land lords turned contemporary industrialists persuaded not only philosophers and rational thinkers but economists also to challenge the philosophy of *laissez faire* and the concept of efficient functioning of Autonomous Market Mechanism in the free economy. In other words, failures and imperfections of the market in the attainment of gains of free market economies and certain socially desirable economic objectives envisaged by the economists came to lime-light. However, the changes in policy rather than concepts and theory were the centre of criticism.

This necessitated changes in philosophy and political and economic theory. Consequently, concept of 'Ruling State' was replaced by the concept of 'Welfare State'. Besides, causes and nature of national wealth as the content or subject matter of economics was replaced by the 'Study of Human Behaviour and Promotion of Well-being' of the people. This led to the enlargement of roles and functions of the state and its government in social and economic affairs. New policy paradigms resulted from extremely rapid expansion in the functions and roles of the state in various countries. This is mainly considered to be a reaction towards major distortions in economic structure that *laissez faire* based capitalism of the 18th and part of 19th century brought about.

Capitalism versus Welfarism/Fabian Socialism

The major challenge to classical economists came in the 19th century itself under Marxian thinking founded by Engel and Marx. It emanated from Karl Marx's *Das Capital* and jointly authored *Manifesto* by Engel and Marx. Critical evaluation of market based capitalism resulted in bitter criticism of capitalism under *laissez faire*, the system in which few individuals or industrialists exploited the working class for making huge profits at the expense of workers. The Marxian thinking strongly influenced socialist movement in Europe. Laski at London School of Economics emerged as an important thought leader in early 20th century, who influenced many scholars from the third world, who went there for further studies. V.K. Krishna Menon and Dr Ram Manohar Lohia from India may be cited as his distinguished disciples, who gained prominence as leaders of socialist thought in India. Jai Prakash Narain and J.B. Kripalani may also be cited as the luminaries among socialists of India. Julius Narere of Tanzania is also in this category. With socialist movements across the glove, nature and number of the roles and functions of the government were radically changed.

The objective sought to be attained by policy makers was not the maximisation of wealth of the nation or profits of producers. The force propelling Fabian socialism was to realise the objective of ensuring maximum good of maximum people. But establishment of

Fabian socialism was conceived to be based on consensus rather than force. The functions of the government under this dispensation were different from those under market based capitalism or centralised planning based socialism. This conception of the state was envisaged to lead to the creation of an egalitarian society, where everyone was deemed equal in social status and distribution of income and wealth was not greatly unequal. Under this system, focus was on ensuring equal opportunities to all rather than to make every one equal in economic terms. The state may control or regulate production and ownership of limited private property is compatible with the system of Fabian Socialism. But the economy remains under state's surveillance and regulation and large segment of the economy may be kept under state ownership.

The underlying assumption is that the state is required to maintain welfare of the entire population. This thought accelerated expansion in the roles and functions of the government. Hence, the theory of public finance, including public expenditure had to be more exhaustive and inclusive than the theory developed for capitalist economies. Theory of public expenditure occupies pre-eminence in the theory of public finance. Shri Prakash and Chowdhury (1995: 20) argued that understanding of the theory of public expenditure is needed for understanding the concept, meanings, scope and nature of public finance as a whole.

Planned Socialist Economy

Fabian Socialism could not gain much footage in the management of practical affairs of capitalist economies, adjustments made in the policy of *laissez faire* for inclusion of some additional roles and functions of the government and mobilisation of tax revenue for meeting additional public expenditure notwithstanding. Bolshevik Revolution in USSR in 1917 brought about a sea-change in contemporary political and economic thinking. An altogether new economic system emerged in the form of centralised planning under state socialism. Centrally planned socialist economies offered a real option and challenge to market based capitalism. Level of development attained by the UK, the US and other West European countries over centuries and that too through colonial exploitation of resources of third world countries in a couple of cases was achieved by the USSR in a couple of decades. The USSR and the US emerged two super powers of the world after the Second World War. Therefore, centralised socialist planning emerged as an option for numerous countries of the third world, including India and Tanzania, which got political independence during post Second World War era.

According to classicists, guiding principle of the state policy was to leave the individual free to pursue his self-interest in the best possible way that he could, because he knows better what is best for him than the state. Therefore an individual unit can be the best judge of its own economic interest, which the government cannot know precisely, and hence, it will not be able to decide correctly on behalf of such self-seeking entities. In such systems, the state was supposed to leave the economy under the control of the market. Thus, political philosophy and economic theory propounded by classicists are neither supportive of high level of public expenditure at any given time nor to its growth through time and across the states. But in a socialist economy, state controls all production units across sectors and throughout the length and breadth of the country. Therefore, the revenue raised by the government is available and used by the government for spending on growth, promotion of social welfare, administrative apparatus and its expansion. Defence, law and order, dispensation of justice, trade, transport, communication, industry, agriculture and miscellaneous all are covered by public expenditure. In such states, political class and bureaucratic hierarchy tend to multiply rapidly resulting in ever soaring public expenditure. This is anti-thesis of classical school of thought. Underlying philosophy is that what individuals can do, state does it better, what the market can achieve, executive fiats can deliver better. It is like 'King Doeth No Wrong' and individuals most of the time compromise macro productivity by diverting resources to most profitable rather than most socially desirable lines of production. This theorising missed the point that 'power corrupts, and absolute power corrupts absolutely.' Ever spreading wings of bureaucracy emerges as the ultimate authority in most spheres of life, which makes them immune to adherence to the ethical values, resulting in corruption even in high places. The practical experience of Post Second World War period stands testimony to the above adage; the result is that rather than maximum good of the maximum people, a few powerful individuals emerge as undisputed authority in their respective area, which they use for personal benefits. Power and Prosperity/Riches coincide in such cases.

Spread of process of economic development, based on industrialisation, over the nations in various parts of the world resulted in high level of economic inequality due to differences of development among the nations. But economic inequalities among different areas/regions and among different groups and economic classes and social strata may even be worse than the inter-national inequalities of development as a result of mal-distribution of wealth and income. Highly marked inequalities of income and wealth resulted from the denial of legitimate share to labour in the rising production and productivity throughout the world economy. Disproportionately large share has been appropriated by capitalist entrepreneurs from the productivity and growth gains, leaving measly returns to owners of human capital as a class. The working class was highly exploited by the few rich, which resulted in increased misery, poverty, ill-health and immisrisation of the vast majority of the masses. The realisation and recognition of these ill effects of capitalism resulted not only in the criticism of *laissez faire* as policy but it also led to the change in the definition, scope and nature of economics and its constituent part of public finance, including public expenditure. It then became difficult for economists, activists and governments to defend status quo and continue to adhere to the old philosophy and policy emanating from it. Thus, the ideology of Fabien socialism, Cooperatism and Welfarism emerged and resulted in the change of focus of political philosophy and theory of state, its functions and economic theory associated with public expenditure. This affected the nature, scope and structure of economics and public finance. The emergence of socialist states led to the transformation of the subject of public finance into public economics. Like public finance public economics has public expenditure as its hub.

Economists like Marshal, Pigou and Cannon incorporated welfare as a subject matter of economics to broadly define economics. Focus was then on maximisation of social welfare which entailed maximisation of satisfaction of the people and output of the economy rather than private profit. The objective of production was maximising growth rather than private profits in order to ensure the maximum good of maximum number of people. Consequently, structure of production moved in favour of mass consumption goods at the cost of luxury production.

Luxury and conspicuous goods were either excluded from production programmes or were heavily taxed. Imports of such goods were also either altogether prohibited or exorbitantly taxed. This resulted in mitigating inequalities of levels of consumption in the society. Both these dimensions of theory, entailing economic policies covering almost all economic facets of operations, resulted in exponential increase in public expenditure on regulation, control and tax administration on the one hand, and production of mass consumer goods, education, health, transport, etc. on the other in planned economies like the Indian and Tanzanian ones. Disposal of essential goods like food items through public distribution system at lower than market prices is another important item of public expenditure in such economies. The state functioned as the protector of the poor and the weak from economic exploitation on the one hand, and as caterer of their basic needs on the other. This led to rapid growth of public expenditure on subsidies, direct transfers and economic as against general administration. Consequently, public expenditure has been the main propellant of economic growth. For example, Shri Prakash (1989) found that current public expenditure and preceding year's public expenditure together accounted for more than two-thirds growth of GDP of Indian economy.

Arthur C. Pigou developed the theory and policy of welfare economics. He argued that an economic system was better if welfare of even one person was improved without jeopardising anyone else's welfare. This is, in fact, the restatement of Pareto's condition of welfare maximisation. The theory postulated public expenditure to focus on maximisation of social welfare. Welfare economics has emerged as distinct branch of economic analysis since then. In order to maximise social welfare, state was expected to invest public funds in socio-economic infrastructure like health, education, street lighting, social security and insurance, power supply, transport and communication, irrigation and other public or merit goods. These roles and functions were encompassed in the list of legitimate functions of the state.

The modified and extended theory and philosophy of the state's roles and functions and public expenditure started in the last quarter of the 19th century and continued till the end of the first quarter of the 20th century. The first quarter of the 20th century witnessed three important events (i) Breaking of First World War; (ii) Bolshevik Revolution in the USSR; and (iii) Entrapment of World Economy in Great Depression.

The socialist revolution in the USSR emphasised public ownership of all means of production except labour and reorganisation of production for accelerated maximal growth rather than private profits earned by few individuals. Maximisation of growth was sought to be achieved by maximising producer goods, including defence related items to secure country's borders from external aggression. Second priority was assigned to production of mass consumer goods like food, clothing, health, education, textiles, transport, communication and so on. But production of luxurious goods like cars, ac and high priced electronic goods was looked at with disdain. Production and distribution of goods and services by public enterprises resulted in massive growth in public expenditure. Thus, the theory addressed not only the determination of size but also composition and structure of public expenditure. Nothing is left implicit in this theory. The emergence of socialist revolution brought planning in its trail which was a tool to oversee the level of industrialisation and all aspects of economic development. With socialist movements, the roles of state encompassed both growth and welfare. All these initiatives led to an increase in the proportion of public expenditure in GDP and public revenue.

Great Depression and Irrelevance of Classical Thought

The Great Depression of late 1920s and early 1930s invalidated Say's Law of markets and ended the influence of classical theory including policy of *laissez faire*. This occurred because Great Depression inflicted heavy losses on industries which resulted either in closure or reduction in scale of operations and widespread unemployment. Prices crashed, profits vanished and unemployment became widespread across the globe. This accentuated poverty and deprivation as loss of earnings entailed in unemployment affected working classed more than the capitalists. Similarly, depression proved the inefficacy and ineffectiveness of Say's Law of Markets. According to the Say's law, 'supply creates its own demand, and hence, 'production is matched by consumption'. In other words, people produce and sell goods and services in order to buy things they want. Growth of output includes rise in employment, and hence, wages that confer purchasing power on employed. The fault in this law does not relate to logic but to negligence of lead and lag feature of the spending of money on purchases for consumption, generation of employment, production and consequent creation of incomes and output. Operation of Say's law ensures equilibrium at full employment. Thus, existence of demand recession and prevalence of widespread unemployment created a void between theory and facts. The Say's law was invalidated because of increased deficiency of demand (over-production) and widespread unemployment that occurred as a result of Great Depression.

Great depression paved the way for Keynesian Revolution in Economic Thinking and Theory. Keynes overturned Say's law by postulating a converse law that demand creates its own supply. Public expenditure was strongly established as the best instrument to pull up aggregate demand in order to attain full employment equilibrium. According to Keynes, public expenditure was an effective instrument to fill-up the income-consumption gap. He postulated that consumer behaviour may be analysed on the assumption that the marginal propensity to consume is invariably less than one and it tends to decrease with increasing income. Therefore, public investment is required to fill-up the income-consumption gap which is likely to be left uncovered by private investment that is guided solely by profits and governed by marginal efficiency of capital. Market based capitalism fails to cover the income-consumption gap, as had happened during the depression. Therefore, positive intervention in the market mechanism by the government with public investment is essential for stabilising and pushing the economy to full employment path. Keynes did not differentiate between productive and unproductive public expenditure as an instrument of generation of aggregate demand; it is encompassed in his dictum that even if no other work can be given, employ people to dig holes in roads and then fill those up.

However, negligence of structure of public expenditure which determines structure of aggregate demand may over a period of time result both in inadequacy of demand for some goods and excess/over-supply of other goods (Shri Prakash 1992). Besides, demand for essential goods, including food, grows less than proportionately than population and income. Keynes did not recognise this aspect, he did not carry less than one marginal propensity to consume and less than proportionate growth of consumption of food than income to its logical end as per prediction of Engel's Law. It is structural aspect of the economy that accounts for the existence of demand recession in the midst of high inflation in large number of sectors of the economy (Shri Prakash 1981). Hence, structure of public expenditure is as important as its level.

Extension of Keynes' Theory to Public Expenditure

Keynesian thoughts can be linked with two major theories of public expenditure: Wagner's Law and Wiseman-Peacock Hypothesis. Adolph Wagner (1883) propounded "The Law of increasing state activities". The law states that as an economy grows over a period of time, roles and functions of the state/government and its expenditure also increase. Shri Prakash and Chowdhury (1995) suggest that Wagner's law operates both at macro and micro levels and it applies both to aggregate expenditure as well as its individual components, irrespective of the items of expenditure. They also hypothesise that public expenditure is greatly upward flexible but it is highly downward sticky and rigid just like households' consumption expenditure.

The reason is that current expenditure depends partly on its level in preceding period(s) and partly upon its growth from the preceding to present level. Besides, expenditure on several items represents committed part of public expenditure. Current expenditure on incomplete but on-going projects and programmes of growth and welfare furnish an example of this genre. Then, several existing institutions of the government cannot be wished away and these need running/operational expenditure to be incurred. Prakash-Chowdhury also postulate that with the growth of GDP, capacity to mobilise revenue and raise public debt increases, which mitigates capacity limitation of public expenditure.

Wagner did not examine causes underlying growth of public expenditure. It is, therefore, hypothesised that the law will hold only if public expenditure grows less rapidly in future than national income despite the fact that it has increased more than proportionately in the past. It is a commonly observed fact that households cannot live beyond their income and wealth beyond a point. Similarly, states cannot spend beyond their means over long periods, without inviting crisis if not calamity or catastrophe or chaos. Recent debt crisis of some members of the European Union (EU) is a testimony to this. International Agencies' concern for Public Debt of certain developing economies, especially the least developed and lowest per capita income economies of the third world, also manifest limits to growth of public expenditure. Therefore, at the lower stages of development in the countries of third world, state has to incur expenditure on various public activities in order to fill-up the gaps in existing socio-economic infrastructure. But at no stage, these states can spend beyond a limit. In these countries, state has to overcome shortages of enterprise, human resources of requisite quality and capital. However, as the economy moves from lower to next higher stage(s) along its development path, several gaps would have been filled up and several deficiencies would have been made good. Growth of public expenditure (not absolute) may then slow down (Shri Prakash and Chowdhury 1995).

Shri Prakash and Chowdhury (1995) inferred on the basis of the study of data of 90 countries of the world covering long stretches of time periods that, on an average, expenditure on education increases by 10 per cent over a period of one decade. It implies 1 per cent annual growth of educational expenditure. They further inferred that expenditure on education tends to increase in arithmetic progression. Both these laws were generalised to cover total public expenditure. The private entrepreneurs may then crop up in adequate numbers with sufficient capital base to allow the state to hold its operations or even withdraw from some sectors of the economy at mature stages of growth of national economies. Because our study focuses on developing countries (India and Tanzania), expansion of public expenditure is envisaged to be necessary until the vicious circle of poverty has been converted into a virtuous circle of cumulative causation of growth.

Post Keynesian Thoughts

Wiseman-Peacock (1961) analysed public expenditure of the United Kingdom for the period from 1890 to 1955 on the basis of Wagner's law and found the law to be valid for UK. They postulated that public expenditure tends to increase sharply and in a step-wise manner rather than continuously and smoothly. This process is caused by expenditure needs for periodic occurrence of socio-political and economic disturbances, and/or natural disasters and calamities, which made public expenditure to exceed the revenue limits. This generates what is called 'displacement effect' by moving expenditure and taxation to higher level necessary for generating revenue to be used to overcome these disturbances. This is noteworthy that disasters, irrespective of their varied hues and shades, do not occur regularly and there is hardly any systematic pattern of their occurrences. Therefore, one needs to distinguish regular public expenditure from public expenditure on mitigation of disasters. Wiseman-Peacock fail to do so. They also did not show that after reaching a plateau in response to disaster, public expenditure declines to its earlier normal level. It implies that each disaster pushes the earlier plateau to next higher plateau. This substantiates Prakash-

Chowdhury thesis that public expenditure is downward rigidly sticky. Hence, if one particular plateau is scaled once by public expenditure, it is difficult to move down from it. It is like riding a tiger, you may mount it but it is not easy to dismount from the back of the tiger. Once public expenditure is incurred on one or more activities, it becomes difficult for government to move away from there. A part of the reason of this facet is the fact that once revenue has been raised either by imposition of a new tax, or rates of existing taxes have been hiked, governments are reluctant to withdraw or reduce the same. But revenue raised has to be spent on one or other line of expenditure. Although Wiseman-Peacock hypothesis is consistent with British data, its validity for other countries seems questionable. Even otherwise, the hypothesis needs validation in general framework.

In developing countries, where economic growth and development have been initiated, sustained and guided through public enterprises, public expenditure grows consistently under the impact of growth of planned investment. Therefore, rapid growth of public expenditure may be explained by systematic growth of public investment in economic development and resultant growth of GDP and public revenue. A general hypothesis about the growth of public expenditure in general and development expenditure in particular is that as a developing economy moves to a higher level of per capita income after the completion of one plan of development of a developing economy, public expenditure, especially public investment in each successive plan of development grows exponentially. The hypothesis may be tested with the data of planned developing economies. Another thesis is that even if a developing economy has adopted the policy of globalisation, liberalisation and privatisation it cannot move down from the plateau of public expenditure it has already scaled in the past.

Galbraith's "The Affluent Society" (1958) used the experiences of great depression and success of expansionary fiscal policy before the World War II to formulate his thesis. He backed the Keynes' view that 'in the event of insufficient demand, public expenditure should be increased and tax should be cut'. Reduction in tax rates will release more purchasing power in the hands of the people, which they will use to finance consumption and/or investment. This will stimulate consumption multiplier to raise growth (Shri Prakash and Sharma 2013: 14). Galbraith was in favour of Keynes's work of so called 'The End of Laissez-Faire' because he believed that free market economy, as advocated by the former classicists (alongside Adam Smith), led to increased economic distress, massive unemployment and insufficient provision of public and merit goods. To him public poverty existed not only in education but also in research and development, pollution control, foreign assistance for relieving hunger and starvation. Poverty could therefore be eliminated by more public spending (Tanzi 2000).

However, things moved in a different direction in the 1970s, when government policies proved ineffective in allocating resources efficiently, redistributing income in well targeted manner and stabilising the economy facing crisis. The 1973 crisis was ignited by huge hikes in oil prices by OPEC. Recession in early and late 1970s was singularly attributable to oil price hikes by members of OPEC. Exponential rise in oil import bills of the nations sapped their purchasing power, resulting in demand recession which adversely affected not only growth but even maintenance of the economy at prevailing levels. Private initiatives were not adequate to mitigate it. So, public intervention was needed.

However, this also occasioned the revival of neo-classical economics which moved round market based economic operations. Interestingly, public policy intervention was supported because of the failures of market, while replacement of public policy intervention by the market is advocated to overcome failures of public policy especially active public interventions. The above reasoning is obviously circular. But this debate inspired a number of studies, which highlighted the disincentive effects of high taxes and growing underground (black) economies (Tanzi 2000). For instance, supply side economists came out with an argument to refute Keynesian philosophy in 1975. Yje's argument was that too much government regulations and controls heightened economic stagnation of various Western economies. This view was supported by Jude Wanniski, Robert Mundel and Arthur Laffer, who collectively argued that economic growth can be most effectively managed by lowering barriers to people to produce goods and services by such instruments as tax reduction on capital gains, corporate income, to allow higher individual incomes along with reduction or elimination of various excise taxes. These economists believed that in a high tax rate environment, lowering of the tax rates to the right level could raise revenue by stimulating more investment in economy and expand free trade and free movement of capital. Hence, it will result in faster economic growth. Furthermore, as fiscal deficits and public debts were rising in the 1970s, many economists and policy makers considered size of government and public expenditure to have grown beyond the justifiable levels, undermining incentives, property rights and accrual of income to the future generations (Buchanan 1975). All these views heralded the birth of so called Reaganomics and Thatchernomics in early 1980s; it started in the US and the UK and there-from it spread to various corners of the world.

It is noteworthy that no economist has ever attempted to delineate the optimum size of public expenditure relative to GDP so far. No attempt has also been made so far to determine the most appropriate allocation of economic activities between the market (private enterprises) and public policy (government). The pendulum has been swinging back and forth periodically as one or the other view becomes dominant among economists. Question is–should the right type of public policy and structure be left to academic fashion and fad?

At political level, change in political philosophy in favour of a smaller government role or free market economic policies has gained ground ever since seventies. Margaret Thatcher and Ronald Reagan, the Prime Minister of the United Kingdom and President of the United States of America respectively were among the opponents of big governments. With their powerful positions, they carried out a political attack on big role for the government. Through 1980s and early 1990s, many social groups also began attacking what they considered excessive public spending and expensive welfare states. Ascendancy of this orthodoxy has taken place despite the frustrating and even disastrous consequences of liberalisation, privatisation and globalisation in countries of Latin America under the guidance of Milton Friedman or his followers (for a detailed review, see Shri Prakash 2005, Mathur 1992). The movement initiated by Reagan and Thatcher led to the rise of what is called Reaganomics and Thatchernomics. With two policy thrusts, privatisation of public enterprises and liberalisation of the economy were aimed to prevent public sector to put controls over the multinational corporations. This also resulted in a withdrawal of government and consistent cut of public expenditure in all directions, including education, health, social security services, transport and communication, public investment in irrigation and other infrastructure including power, subsidies to agriculture and exports.

Despite the changes in political, philosophical and economic theories, still debates have continued over centuries till date among various economists, leaders, policy makers and activists all over the world, whether the large increase in public expenditure contributes to improvement in welfare of the majority of citizens or whether citizens would be better off with lower growth of public expenditure. Welfare of citizens is linked to certain socio-economic indicators such as life expectancy, educational achievements, investment, literacy, infant mortality, and growth of per capita income, employment opportunities, inflation rates, consumption expenditure and all that government tries to influence through public spending.

Washington Consensus

The word Washington Consensus (WC) means those policies which were imposed by International Financial Institutions like IMF and World Bank on the poor nations in 1980s and 1990s. The word was coined in 1989 by John Williamson. Many people consider Washington Consensus to comprise those policies or economic strategies which were imposed by Two Breton Woods Institutions; these focus on (i) piberalisation of trade, (ii) privatisation, (iii) macro stability, particularly price stability. The policies referred as WC policies relate to 'neoliberal' policies because of their great emphasis on such liberalisation as was in vogue in the 19th century. It greatly emphasised the importance of minimum role of the state/

government and its expenditures on economic affairs. The WC policies are different from the successful policies implemented in East Asian countries like Hong Kong, Korea, Taiwan and Singapore. While WC used so called 'One-size-fits-all' policies without looking into different economic structures of various world economies, the East Asian countries regarded state or government to have an active role in the promotion of growth of the economy. The government or policy framework was meant to promote maximum investment to accelerate growth. The WC policies led to failure in many Latin American economies, the former Soviet Union bloc and Sub-Saharan economies in 1990s (Stiglitz 2008). The global financial crisis is also considered to be a result of WC policies.

WC policies were based on the theory of market fundamentalism as its proponents expected the state to be a mere overseer of rules of the game or regulator of the market to be only the passive (traditional) player by restricting functions of the state to those approved by Adam Smith. Emergence of the WC is also connected to the Reaganomics and Thatchernomics policies that had been prescribed for developing countries in the 1980s. These two ideologies were aimed at initiating free market mechanism and reducing state intervention and public expenditure.

Although many economists suggest that the WC strategies were initiated to promote economic development of the poor nations, they failed to provide answers to the problems facing these countries (Stiglitz 1998). It is thus believed that the countries, which implemented the WC strategies, experienced slower growth compared to those which did not. Besides the WC policies have increased inequality and corruption in many economies. Stiglitz further highlighted the following WC's 10 main reforms, which developing countries opting for LPG or those having taken loans from international agencies had to undertake:

(i) Fiscal discipline is advocated for those countries which had been having large budget deficits, especially fiscal deficit beyond a particular level. Such deficits have generally been manifested by balance of payments problems and inflation;

inflation affected the poor most. Incidentally internal imbalances also result in external imbalances;

(ii) Redirection of public expenditure towards health, education and infrastructure was advocated. Reduction and ultimately elimination of subsidies including those to agriculture have to be among the priority area;

(iii) Tax reforms, including broadening of tax base and cutting the high taxation rates were advocated as desirable policy goals;

(iv) Unified and market based competitive exchange rates in place of administered ones are suggested as advantageous. Besides, the following are also a part of the agenda of reforms:

(v) Conferment of Secure Property Rights;

(vi) Deregulations of market entry and enhancement of competition wherever it is stultified;

(vii) Liberalisation of International Trade;

(viii) Privatisation of State Owned Enterprises;

(ix) Elimination of Barriers to Direct Foreign Investment; and

(x) Financial Liberalisation including reduction in high interest rates.

All the above reforms are based on theory of market fundamentalism which had evoked great criticisms by Joseph Stiglitz (2003), one of the leading economists of the world. Following the financial crisis in Russia and South East Asia, Stiglitz scathingly criticised IMF-World Bank Agenda. Reasons are not far to seek. Structural Adjustment Programmes and Macroeconomic Stabilisation policies had caused negative impacts on growth and poverty in the poor countries. For instance, P.N. Mathur (1992) showed that Chili's per capita income in 1988 was reduced to the level of its per capita income 1962. Similarly, reduction/stagnation in public expenditure by the introduction of charges on health and education for the purpose of cost sharing led to a high level of unemployment, poverty and income inequality in some countries. Criticisms by various economists based on experiences of poor developing countries highlighted failures of the WC with reference to the goals stated to have been realised by its implementation. This led to the replacement of WC by Post Washington Consensus, or Washington Consensus Plus. This dealt a body blow to the proponents of WC. As stated earlier, previous WC policy objectives of development were too narrowly defined and these focused only on increasing GDP without taking into account issues related to improvement of living standard, promotion of democracy and equity all of which revolve round employment for all (Stiglitz 2008). The WC policies also failed to incorporate risks, associated with market failures, in the policy framework. But market failure often occurs in capitalist economies. The empirical evidence shows that the US economy had experienced demand recessions more than 17-18 times since 1980s. But even when American economy sneezes, the world economy gets cold and fever. Consequently, recessionary phases of US economy have been enveloping large number of developing economies. Market failures occur due to such reasons as asymmetric information, incomplete/imperfect markets, externalities and several others. But the proponents of these reforms forget basic empirical facts that modern economies are an intricate web of inter-dependencies; this facet results in spreading the impact of even marginal changes in any part or segment over the economy as a whole. As if this was not sufficient, envelopment of large number of economies under the canopy of LPG has created much greater degree of inter-national inter-dependence than ever before.

IMF-World bank Policies focused on Adam Smith's Invisible Hand but these policies overlooked operational conditions under which markets lead to efficient outcomes. Markets are efficient only if no cause/factor of market failure exists. But periodic recurrences of market failure necessitate an active important role for the government so as to contain adverse effects of market failure on the one hand, and eliminate factors that cause such failures on the other. This argument is supported by the historical experiences of East Asian Countries, China, the US, India and the governments of all EU member countries had to come out with financial rehabilitation packages in order to face the adverse consequences of worldwide economic slow-down in 2007-08 and recent debt crisis of Greece,

Spain, Portugal and Italy. Thus, dependence on market alone cannot lead to rapid development. It is also instructive that more rapid industrial development of all East Asian countries happened because of public policies. Public policies furnished incentives to people to save to provide capital to firms.

Post Washington Consensus recognised the need for an active role for the market as well as the government and these roles are beyond the traditional roles and functions of states, which had been emphasised by neo-liberalists, who focus on enforcing contracts and property rights alone. It also recognises that there are government failures as well as market failures. Under Post WC, government and markets are seen as complementary. Government plays an important role of correcting market failures and furnishes an environment for markets to work better. Therefore, a successful development regime requires not a limited or minimum government but the balance between market and government. However, exact role for the government may differ from country to country, depending on the state and level of economic development and public institutions. There cannot be a general policy package for all irrespective of socio-economic conditions and the nature of polity in place. This is like erstwhile German Historical Schools thought which challenged the universal character of British classical economic theory on the basis of differences of institutional structure and historical backdrop of attained level of development of each country of the world. This is also in consonance with Rostow's theory of stages of growth. Rostow averred that roles and functions of the state are varied and great in the early stages of economic development/ It is because increasingly high ratio of public investment to total investment is needed in such stages of growth. In the early stage of economic growth, government is responsible for accumulation of social capital through the provision of such infrastructure as roads, health, education, transport and communication, law and order. All these are necessary for pushing the economy towards middle stages of growth and development. Government will be required to provide social infrastructure in middle stages also, though public investment will just be complementary to private sector investment.

Government becomes important to correct inefficiencies associated with market and its resultant failures. Government intervention can enable the market to move towards higher stages of development. Role of the state decreases at mature stage. Rostow further argues that as the economy of a country reaches mature stage, expenditure of government tends to shift from infrastructure to health, education and welfare. But in the mass consumption stage, government focuses on development programmes to reduce income inequality. Musgrave also argued that as the economy grows and reaches higher stages, relative share of total investment in GDP rises, but the relative share of public investment in total investment tends to fall.

Post WC (WC Plus/Augmented WC) has the following agenda:

(i) Anti-corruption;
(ii) Corporate governance;
(iii) Independent Central Bank and Inflation Targeting;
(iv) Financial Codes and Standards;
(v) Flexible Labour Markets;
(vi) WTO Agreements;
(vii) Prudent Capital Account Opening;
(viii) Non-intermediate Exchange Rate Regimes;
(ix) Social Safety Nets; and
(x) Targeted Poverty Reduction.

The current phase is still in operation. Therefore, it shall be immature to judge its success or failure.

Conclusion

Above discussion has highlighted following important aspects of the theory of state and roles and functions of the government with special reference to public expenditure-the hub of public finance:

(i) Advancement in knowledge and accumulated experience of various shades and hues of states and their governments have resulted in the revision of opinions and dominant view among the thinkers and policy makers about the role of public expenditure in growth and welfare;
(ii) Emergence of new thoughts and theory have led to the revision in policy formulation and its implementation with

a view to overcome limitations and shortcomings in earlier policies and/or their implementation;

(iii) No individual or an international agency has the total wisdom to formulate policies which are universal in nature of 'fit all size' type which will benefit entire humanity uniformly;

(iv) Socio-economic and political conditions govern and guide the process of development and these conditions differ greatly among the countries at a given time and within a country between different time periods;

(v) Even though the ultimate objective is to attain convergence in world economy, results achieved have often been divergent and its accentuation from one to another stage of growth at international level.

It may safely be inferred that growth/development and welfare of all require great deal of balancing which is an eternal journey to Eldorado. Let all of us live the dream.

3

Budget and Budgeting

Introduction

Budget and budgeting is a ubiquitous feature of human society; these two are universal in nature since the need for budget and budgeting is felt by all entities ranging from micro to macro units. From households to schools/colleges and universities, private commercial and industrial establishments need some budget in order to avoid haphazard or wasteful manner of utilising resources and to keep expenditure within *a priori* determined limit. Upper limit of budgeted expenditure may be fixed according to income, nature and number of needs/wants, projects or programmes to be undertaken in coming financial year by concerned entity. But once income constraint is fixed internally or externally, it cannot be flouted in budgeting even by the government. The government, however, has the leverage to raise resources (income) according to needs of expenditure during the year. This is the universal norm followed by micro as well as macro units. Therefore, budgeting is done by individual micro units, including households, institutions, social and professional organisations, clubs, companies, labour unions, industry and professional associations as well as such macro units as national, state and local governments. Each layer and level of government and government organisations have to have a budget. In fact, both government and non-government entities have some or the other form of budget as the guiding principle for financial operations. The governments ranging from local/village *panchayat* or municipal committee to provincial/county government and from provincial to central government require budgeting and budget. Even micro level government organisations, departments within directorates, directorates within ministries and ministries within the central government require budget and knowledge of budgeting. But the concept, approach and theory of budget and budgeting are generally associated with the government and its agencies. The concept of budget is technical and process of budgeting is quite complex, intricate, elabourate and involved. Consequently, understanding of budget and budgeting cannot be acquired without proper explanation of technical concept, approaches and theories of the complex and extensive task of budgeting and intricate concept of budget. Complexities of conceptual framework of budget and budgeting arise from the multiplicity of its dimensions and universality of its practice, its need, formulation and implementation at different layers and levels of the government. Hence, the concept of the entity, called 'budget' cannot be rigid and steely-framed. It has to be extremely flexible and malleable so as to fit for use at all levels and layers of its requirement. This consideration warrants the concept of budget and the process of budgeting to be defined in an extremely flexible but comprehensive manner so as to make it suit every requirement. The concept of budget has to be like the job of tailoring done by the tailor who keeps every customer's size, physical structure, taste and preference in view according to the fashion of the times so as to satisfy want or requirement of each and every one. Besides, the concept of budget, especially the national budget, should be evolved so that it can always be molded, twisted and tuned according to the needs of the time and place, that is, the country or the entity of budgeting.

Technical Concept of Budget and Budgeting

Budget may refer to the budget of household, institution, company or public entity. The book is concerned with the analysis of public budget. First the concept of 'budget' is taken up for crisp discussion. It shall be followed by the discussion of the process of budgeting.

Concept of Budget

The term 'budget' is commonly used in day to day transactions among the people. The literal and commonsense meanings of 'budget' are well understood. It is because budget making prevails universally.

Budget relates to households, companies, institutions and all layers of government. Budget in common parlance refers to the total or maximum amount of money that an entity/individual unit is in a position to spend or plans to spend during the given period of time. But spending cannot occur without mobilising resources/income or having the same already in hand. Obviously, total expenditure intended to be incurred is constrained or limited by the expected amount of money earned or received or expected/planned to be received by the entity during the specified period of time. However, income/receipt does not constrain the governments to keep public expenditure under income constraint because governments can mobilise resources from several sources, including borrowing from domestic and/or international sources and fiscal deficit according to the needs. Individuals, households and institutions, including government organisations cannot resort to deficit financing. This lay in the power of central government of the country alone, though state governments, public enterprises and other public institutions may spend more than their actual or anticipated income. The difference between income and expenditure, defined as deficit, ultimately becomes the part of fiscal deficit of the central government. But technical meanings of budget and budgeting diverge from the common-sense meanings.

According to The Oxford Dictionary the term 'budget' refers to "Annual estimate of money needed or available". This definition is not self explanatory, and hence, it requires elabouration, explanation and critical evaluation. It is attempted hereunder.

'Money needed or available' implicitly carries two meanings: (i) Need means awareness of the want/desire or requirement of something. Desire/want is actual rather than hypothetical. Awareness of the existence of desire/want occurs in mind. The purpose of 'Need/want' may be fulfilment of physical or mental or intellectual or financial requirement; and (ii) Availability refers to the amount of money which can be used for financing public expenditure at the given time. First meaning refers to demand, while second stands for supply of money.

Oxford Dictionary's definition does not explain meaning, nature and type of need and entity whose need is referred. If the word 'need is considered in the context of budget, it may refer to financial requirement which is anticipated or expected rather than actually experienced desire or requirement of money'. As is evident from the meaning explained above, this is not the connotation of the word 'need in the context of the definition'. Now 'estimated annual amount of money' does not explain the purpose of need for money and its availability. The phrase should have read as follows: 'The need or requirement of total money for defraying expected expenditure to be incurred by the government during the incoming financial year.' Use of the word 'money needed or available' implicitly refers to both the requirement of public expenditure expected to be incurred and to the public revenue or the monetary income of the government expected to be received during the budget year. Therefore, the definition is absolutely ambiguous.

Use of the term 'or' between 'needed and available' implies the existence of an option between (i) available amount of revenue determining public expenditure, or (ii) public expenditure expected or determined to be incurred being the determinant of revenue to be raised. Use of such imprecise terminology in a definition is undesirable. Besides, money or income does not accrue to anyone, including the government, autonomously without making some effort for it. Efforts for earning the income or raising income yielding resources are involved in accrual of income.

Other question left hanging for an answer by this definition is the incompleteness of the phrase 'needed or available'. It does not explain 'available to whom' or 'available for whose need'. The proper terminology would have been 'money needed by or available to the government'.

As the term budget is used extensively by all types of organisations, institutions and households, missing elements in the definition leave it incomplete and vague. In the context of public budget, the definition may refer to 'central government or government at all layers and levels'. Thus, such implicit meanings have to be furnished by the learner or reader himself/herself.

Therefore, the definition propounded by Oxford Dictionary is imprecise and vague on these counts.

Let the definition from other dictionary, which offers better definition of budget than the Oxford Dictionary be taken up. Oxford Learner's Dictionary provides a better definition of budget than the one cited above. The definition of this dictionary runs as follows: The budget is a 'statement' of 'estimate or plan of how money will be spent over a period of time in relation to the amount of money available'. Alternatively, 'budget' may be defined as an 'annual statement of the government of a country's expenditure and how it will be financed.' This definition fills up the following gaps in the first definition:

It specifically mentions the government of the country to whom the budget relates and mentions the period of one financial year as the budget horizon. Budget is thus just a detailed statement relating to intended or planned public expenditure and public revenue. Interestingly, both these definitions rightly mention public expenditure as the guide post for government's revenue or income. Further elabouration of the above definition states that 'Budget is the amount of money needed or allocated for specific purposes.' But, budget is not only a statement of total public expenditure and public revenue but it also contains detailed description of items on which public expenditure is to be incurred and the sources from which requisite amount of revenue shall be raised. However, several times, the government presents supplementary budget in the middle of the year. In that case, duration of the budget is reduced by the time that lapses between first and supplementary budgets. The following aspects of this definition are also noteworthy:

Use of term 'shall' or 'will' is indicative of intention or plan rather than the figures reported in budgetary allocations being actually spent/collected ones. This is important. Anticipated/intended or planned figures are subject to error of estimation and/or plan or anticipated amounts may not be received or spent for some reason. But the error margins may differ from one to another case. Besides, error margins are likely to be involved in the estimates of both public expenditure and public revenue. It has many times been observed at the end of financial year that the expected/budgeted revenue is less/

more than revenue actually realised. Similarly, actual expenditure may be more or less than the anticipated figures. These differences are errors of estimation or figures being distorted by inflation or decline in specific or general prices. Divergences between estimated and actual figures of revenue and expenditure may also be defined as over shooting or falling short of planned targets of revenue and expenditure of the government.

The limitations of above definition of budget are attempted to be overcome in the following definition:

Budget is the statement of item-wise public expenditure planned or intended to be incurred by the government and the source wise resources to be raised to finance the targeted/planned public expenditure during the budget horizon. Statement of item-wise public expenditure embodies planned pattern of allocation of budgetary resources. Budgeted expenditure targets are assumed to be uniquely related to the expected achievement of physical targets of different lines of public expenditure. The validity of this assumption depends on correct prices being used in translating physical targets into targets of public expenditure. More often than not this does not hold true. For example, World Bank granted loan of $800 million to India for brick lining irrigation channels in the state of Punjab during late 1970s. Irrigation department worked out estimated expenditure in first year at a price of ₹13 lakh per sq km. Actual price turned out to be ₹17 lakh per sq km at the end of the year. But the next year's allocation was determined at a cost of ₹15 lakh per sq km, while the actual price turned out to be ₹19 lakh per sq km. Consequently, physical target was under achieved in both the years. Over-shooting of monetary or shortfall in physical terms may be accounted by change in observed prices or underestimate of future prices. This type of overshoot or shortfall in achievement of monetary or physical targets may be used as the measuring rod of evaluation of budgetary performance during the fiscal year. Incidentally, financial performance may also be an indicator of performance in physical terms.

Structural features and pattern of shortfalls in achievements become visible when each item of expenditure is examined with reference to expected or planned targets. Comparison of physical targets with actual achievement also removes the monetary cover or money illusion. Monetary shortfall or overshooting of monetary targets may be easily explained by the differentials between actual and estimated prices in which monetary expenditure is expressed. But the differences between targeted and actually achieved physical targets require investigation of causal factors underlying such differentials. These causal factors may be constraints and bottlenecks, shortage of materials or delay in their supply, breakdowns in machinery and equipment, labour problem or capital shortage. Non-availability of intermediaries may also be among these causal factors. All above factors are important for evaluation of performance. Qualification and competency of the evaluating team is an important factor in the whole process. Up and downward movements in prices during the financial year often leads to over or under achievement of physical targets. The reason is that item-wise allocation of total budgeted expenditure is based on the prices prevailing at the time of budgeting.

The example of irrigation department of Government of Punjab, one of the Indian states, may be cited again. The Government of Punjab used US $800 million for brick lining of irrigation channels to take canal water to farms. The initial year's estimate of total expenditure was based on a cost of ₹13,00,000 per sq km. Physical target was planned according to this cost estimate. But actual cost after the end of the year turned out to be ₹17,00,000 per sq km. Therefore, physical target achieved by the allocated amount of money fell far short of planned target. But the department again and again allocated money in a similar manner for targeted goals of achievement for next two years. Physical targets were over estimated relative to even the observed price of the first year of the project. Monitoring and Evaluation committee of Planning Department of the Government of Punjab cautioned the officials for such mistakes which actually *prima facie* appeared deliberate. This type of errors may be avoided at the time of formulation of budgetary proposals. Budget proposals sometimes themselves result in escalation or decline in prices of particular items of expenditure. The contractors entrusted with specified jobs of the government may indulge in reckless profiteering with the connivance of government employees because of which budget proposals affect prevailing prices in the market. For example, proposed cut in excise duties on specific items will result in decrease in prices of these goods/services. Similarly, increase in commodity taxation rates will induce prices to rise. A 10 per cent cut in total expenditure by Margret Thacher on assuming office of Prime Minister of UK in 1979 drastically reduced the government spending. This automatically affected the physical targets.

But, prices move up and down during the different phases of business cycles. Business cycles occur periodically in capitalist countries. Such price movements should be taken into consideration at the time of formulation of budget proposals. But it requires proper coordination between the departments of taxation and expenditure. At the end of the spectrum, budget department of the ministry of finance has to iron out inconsistencies contained in budget proposals of different ministries and different departments of the ministry of finance itself. Failing this, observed prices during the fiscal year will belie budgetary expectations. It is, therefore, incumbent on budget makers to anticipate such price changes consequent upon the presentation of budget before the legislative bodies. This will also reduce the error margins of budget estimates.

General Principles of Budgeting

Above discussion does not mean that there are no general principles of budgeting which are different from specific principles. General principles furnish guidelines for making national budget or budgets of other levels of government. Following may be considered as general considerations or basic criteria for budgeting.

Budget and budgeting are regular annual affairs of governments of all levels and layers. Budget furnishes a blue print of expected income from all sources and expenditure planned to be incurred on all lines of spending, all items and areas of public concern during the coming financial year. Therefore, people entrusted with the task of budgeting are experts or those who acquire learning and skill by doing the job over the years. Therefore, a careful evaluation of potential revenue yield of each source and desired extent of its exploitation are required to be done before hand. It implies that social, political and economic considerations are weighed before making the plan of action for raising revenue or income for the government.

As the national annual budget is the instrument of implementation of public economic policy in general and fiscal policy in particular, budget is required to be dovetailed into the objectives and targets of policy. Policy and budget part of it govern and guide the financial operations of the government in the coming/given financial year. Thus, budget of a national government facilitates governance of financial affairs of the nation in accordance with the pre-determined programmes and plans. Budget enables the government to express its intents and purpose of financial management of the country during the coming financial year.

Annual budgets take the economy, and hence, the country forward from its current to intended or planned and aspired status during the specified period of time, generally one financial year. Budget has, therefore, to be used as the tool to make appropriate financial decisions to implement fiscal policy already in place and in operation in the economy.

Finalisation of the budget should be preceded by an in-depth review of the performance of the economy during the preceding year in which budget for next year is discussed and prepared. The budget making is referred as budgeting. Budgeting involves following steps for the preparation of an annual budget.

Evaluation of Past Performance

Evaluation of performance during the preceding year is done with a view to determine shortfalls and achievements relative to targets fixed for the budget year under review.

Evaluation of performance of the budget of the preceding year facilitates the identification of enabling and debilitating factors in the realisation of pre-determined targets of the preceding year.

Review of performance is undertaken with a definite purpose. It focuses on revenue collected relative to amount of revenue planned or targeted to be raised from all sources in the preceding period.

Public expenditure incurred on each line of expenditure relative to planned or budgeted amount is determined for the purpose of evaluation of shortfall in achievement or realisation of the target(s). If actual expenditure on any item is less or more than the budgeted amount, then its causes have to be determined so as to avoid its recurrence in the coming financial year.

If the physical target has been achieved with less or more than planned expenditure, it implies that the estimation which was used for budgeting was erroneous and such errors are needed to be avoided in future. The explanations of such differentials have to be incorporated in proposed budget.

Actual fiscal deficit relative to its intended level has to be determined. Similarly status of outstanding borrowings, interest liability thereon and newly taken loans from domestic and foreign sources are to be assessed. The review of borrowings involves assessment of the success of (i) realisation of targeted borrowing from each instrument and source; (ii) provisions made in the past for the timely debt redemption and their implementation are to be examined.

At no point of time focus is to be taken away from the medium and long run objectives of policy. A mid-year course correction necessitated by emergence of exigencies or mal-functioning of the policy implementation, if any, has to be done.

Divergence between actual and desired or planned outcomes of implementation of budgetary proposals arises from imperfections in implementation of policy and errors of formulation and faulty design of policy. Defective formulation of policy causes percolation errors in its implementation. But the distance between policy makers and its implementers more often than not makes implementation go awry. It largely accounts for failure of policy more often than not. However, over-ambitious targets may also cause failure of policy. Resource constraints may also impinge upon the successful implementation of policy. The purpose of the exercise is to avoid recurrence of such errors.

Evaluation of successes and failures, strengths and weaknesses in all areas of fiscal policy is an important part of review of performance. This exercise prepares the ground for the making of budget for coming financial year. This is the common approach and steps for evaluation of the success of policy are generally taken by the government of all countries. Governments of India and Tanzania are no exception to this.

Concurrent monitoring and evaluation is undertaken for the minimisation of chances of failure or imperfect implementation of policy in several countries including India. But the budget and budgeting are guided and governed mainly by the objectives of fiscal and monetary policies.

Policy objectives are classified into short and long run goals and these goals are decomposed into annual targets of plan or budget horizon.

General Objectives of Budgeting

Budgeting is a long drawn process and hence, it involves time and several sequential steps, different ministries and departments, though it is primarily the responsibility of the Ministry of Finance. Statement of the primary objectives of Budget and Budgeting is the first and preliminary step. Annual budgets of Governments of India and Tanzania are the instruments of implementation of plans of development. The plans of development are translated into planned targets for the realisation of which policy and programme of action for its implementation are prepared in advance. An illustration may help in the elabouration and explanation of general concept of budget and general process of budgeting. Linking of each budget with the fiscal policy or planning horizon is essential. The need for this arises from the fact that fiscal policy and budgets are related to the strategy of planned development during each plan horizon. Each plan and project, and programmes of development under it has some general and many specific objectives of development and all these are required to be interwoven in policy and budgeting. The following may be stated as the general objectives of budgeting.

Each budget is linked to the fiscal policy for the coming year, say, 2016-17. It is important to make the fiscal policy and budget under it serve the same short and long run objectives so that each budget is the part of the chain of steps required to fulfill national priorities of growth, welfare and maintenance of political, social and economic stability. The national priorities are generally envisaged in strategy of planned/envisaged economic and social development of the country. The development strategy strives to achieve the aspirations of long run perspective or envisioned plan of economic growth. But long run objectives are broken into smaller parts of short run targets and objective. For example, Pitamber Pant, the then Director of Perspective Planning Division of the then Planning Commission, developed in 25 years the long run perspective plan of economic development of India from 1950-51 to 1974-75. Abdul J. Kalam, then President of India, formulated a long run perspective for India up to 2020.

However, the capitalist economies may have no long term planning per se. But countries having capitalist economies do have a definite vision for future growth of the economy and social development of the country. Since the signals released by the market may be oscillating through time and different groups of people may impute different meanings to the same, short and long run perspective of the economy, as revealed by the market, falls within the purview of ministry of finance and/or economic affairs and the Central Bank. The political leaders and administrators have close links with the political establishment of the country and economy of the nation. Such perspective or vision may be treated as the guiding direction for the budget and budgeting. For example, Government of France periodically releases market signals to the people, especially to the corporate houses, which are expected to use the same for formulating their own vision or expected state of the market for employment and growth of output.

General Properties of Budget and Budgeting

Each budget is generally formulated for one financial year. Thus, national budgets normally have one year cycle. But calendar dates of financial year differ between countries. For example, financial year of India runs from 1st April of the current year to 31st March of the succeeding calendar year. As against this, financial year of

Tanzania commences on 1st July of the current year and ends on 30th June of succeeding year. But an annual national budget is neither independent of preceding year's budget nor is it delinked from the budget of succeeding year. Thus, each budget is a link in short or long run chain of budgets. Each budget is one short run organic component of the link in five/seven year plan of economic development.

For example, if an economy is in the grip of deep recession, 2-3 consecutive budgets may have recovery packages and each package shall be the follow up of preceding one. Therefore, each annual budget is one in the chain of the continuum of budgets of different years. In a five year plan of development, there shall be 5 annual budgets. In non-planned capitalist economies, there may be only 2-3 annual budgets, depending upon the phase of business cycle in operation in the economy.

Main Objectives of Budget and Budgeting

Priorities in the national plan of development are translated into targets for achievement during the planning horizon. Each target fixed for the period as a whole is decomposed into annual targets. Annual targets are then translated into programme or project or scheme. Appropriate financial allocation is made in the budget so as to facilitate the realisation of the annual target of the scheme/programme. The budget target for each fiscal year has to be followed and implemented mandatorily. There is no scope for manipulation of budgeted allocation for a specific programme/project once the priorities are translated into programmes and projects which are translated into targets for realisation.

Budgetary targets are generally related to expansion of current level of achievement in a given field, structural transformation of the economy and changes in institutional and social set up. Therefore, budget embodies the implementation of priorities, directives or thrusts of fiscal policy.

Budget may also focus on structural transformation of the economy step by step. Structural transformation of the economy involves investment in such programmes and projects which change the input-output relations of production processes and pattern of commodity/sector composition of GDP. But social development focuses on uplift of specified segments of population and promotion of setting up of specified social and economic institutions. It also involves promotion of non-economic activities. For example, topmost priority to the development of women and promotion of their education means that the largest proportion of budgetary resources allocated to education may be used for the realisation of this objective. Therefore, greatest proportion of budgeted expenditure is allocated to the programmes of uplifting of social, educational and occupational status of women. This will raise the competence and competency of female human resources. This has been assigned an extremely high urgency and importance in plans of national economic development, especially in the twelfth five year plan of India. Structural transformation focuses on reducing the relative share of conventionally dominant primary economic sector(s), including agriculture, fishery, forestry etc. and mining. The move for 'Make in India' focuses mainly on manufacturing in the current Indian thinking. The reason is that the erstwhile primary dominated Indian economy is now tertiary dominated without having traversed the path from primary to secondary and from secondary to tertiary sectors domination in the economy. The shift in emphasis is not only an effort to correct the errors of the past but it also represents an attempt to make India compete successfully with countries like China, South Korea, Japan, Singapore and Malayasia.

An important objective of budget and budgeting in the context of recent global experience suggests the insulation of national economy, especially a developing economy, from sudden external shocks. 'Economic Slow-Down' and 'Euro Debt' crisis of recent years have taken a heavy toll of the developing economies in general and Indian and Tanzanian economies in particular. Such external shocks cause immense damage to the economies which depend largely on export earnings of few goods and exports of commodities prices of which are susceptible to high degree of volatility in international market. This suggests the choice between export-led or import-substitution strategy of growth. A mix of these two strategies may probably offer a better option to the national governments.

The stage of budgeting is appropriate for the course correction as well as switching from one to another policy regime.

Determination of basic contours of fiscal policy for each budget horizon serves an important objective of budgeting. Each fiscal policy of budget horizon is an organic component of long run fiscal policy.

The budget setting process, which starts 6-7 months before the presentation of budget before the legislative wing of the government, determines the mechanism for formulating annual budget. This preparatory period is used for widespread consultation with wide spectrum of industry groups, lobbies/leaders of different interest groups, experts, different ministries, departments and lower layers of government.

Annual estimated/budgeted expenditure furnishes requirement of revenue which the government has to raise from different sources by use of different instruments. But budgeted expenditure has to follow the direction and guidelines of fiscal policy. Fiscal policy determines upper limit for public spending within the year. Besides, fiscal policy has itself to be dovetailed into broad spectrum of economic policy and planning. Fiscal policy has to be in sync with monetary policy. This implies mutual concordance and consistency between the maximum public expenditure to be incurred during the specified budget year and expected revenue to be garnered from all sources. Sum of total budgeted expenditure of all annual budgets of the plan period thus constitutes the total size of plan. The plan covers five years. Mechanism of setting state budget with reference to the priorities of National Plan of Economic Development is operated at the level of individual ministries and other public entities. The mechanism is based on the principle of pursuing pre-determined priorities, programmes and projects of planned development.

An important facet of budgeting is the spelling out details of budget precisely for each ministry and government entities within each ministry. This reflects devolution of funding from top to bottom. Detailed schemes of public expenditure of the ministries and government entities are out in advance for successful accomplishment of the tasks assigned to different ministries, departments, public enterprises and other levels of government.

This is accompanied by the evaluation of performance of preceding year's budget. Evidently, performance evaluation follows the completion of the process of spending of the public funds on designated items and programmes on the one hand, and the realisation of targeted revenue source wise on the other.

Appropriate planning, funding according to planning accompanied by right resource use warrant the possession and development of competence and competency of human resources involved in budget making. This requires relevant and adequate level of education and acquiring of appropriate skills for the performance of assigned jobs. This involves intricate planning of education and relating it to the manpower planning (Shri Prakash 1976, 1977).

There are two alternative approaches to planning of education and accumulation and development of manpower. According to the needs of the time and place, planning of development of education precedes manpower planning. Manpower planning then focuses on utilisation of human resources, prepared by educational system, in productive activities. This approach suits those countries which have low base of educated manpower, especially the manpower with higher and professional education (Shri Prakash 1977).

The second approach focuses on manpower requirements of future economic growth and social development. Then, educational processes are adapted and adjusted to prepare manpower of requisite level and type of education in adequate numbers. The education-occupation profile of jobs expected to be available in the economy should match the education acquired for fulfilling occupational requirement by those produced by the educational system. This approach aims to eliminate the probability of unemployment among the educated persons. This approach revolves round the matching of requisite number of jobs with the required education-occupation profile of would be job seekers per unit of time.

First approach is useful for countries where illiteracy rates are high and education base of population is low. But population size is not very high. Second approach is useful for more populous countries with high literacy rates, high availability of educated manpower in the job market, but there exists rampant unemployment. But ideal situation is one in which number of qualified persons emanating from education system at different points in time is matched by the availability of jobs requiring the qualifications broadly approximating qualifications of job seekers. But exact matching of these two may not be possible. The supply and demand should broadly synchronize both in time and place.

General Criteria of Budgeting

Preceding discussion has paved the way for the enumeration of some general criteria for budgeting; these criteria may be followed in the preparation of national budget. Basic objective of the pursuit of these criteria in budgeting is to make the national budget reflect the following:

(i) Size, structure and composition of national income at the time of budgeting;

(ii) Stage of economic growth already attained by the economy;

(iii) Peoples' aspirations for future growth;

(iv) Natural resources and capital endowment of the nation at the time of budgeting and the utilisation of the same for realising the current budgetary goals with the focus on sustainability and inclusiveness;

(v) Current as well as future population size, its gender and age structure;

(vi) Education profile and occupation composition of those employed and the changes envisaged in the same;

(vii) Desired/targeted level of GDP and its structure; and above all each budget is the building block of self reliant and sustained growth of the economy over long period of time. This requires that each budget should be an essential link in the chain of budgets of budgeting/planning horizon

Concept and Approaches to Budgeting

Concept of budget has already been discussed quite elabourately. But the meaning and concept of budgeting, which has been used at several places in above discussion, needs explanation and elabouration. Making of budget, known as budgeting, is a complex and intricate process; it involves a definite but finite set of inter-related and sequential as well as non-sequential steps. The undertaking of these steps requires a great deal of care and caution to be exercised by the functionaries, who are entrusted with the task of preparing the budgets of different ministries and the departments within the ministries. Functionaries of the ministry of finance have to have full understanding and the grip over the nitty-gritty of budgeting since budgeting is mainly their task. The officials and lower order employees of the ministry of finance have to be adequately qualified with proper educational background, skills and experience required for budgeting. Detailed knowledge of economics and accounting is the basic knowledge needed to be possessed by these functionaries. The reason for this is that finance in general and public finance in particular has emerged as a highly super-specialised area of knowledge and expertise. Besides, the intricacies and nuances at several stages of budgeting may require specialised knowledge of financial econometrics.

Budget and budget making may be approached in different ways. The process of budgeting differs from approach to approach. It is, therefore necessary to understand the differences of underlying process of budget making under each approach. Approaches to budgeting which may be used by the ministry of finance are discussed hereunder.

Budget and budgeting are universally prevalent. Budgets are made by households, corporate houses, institutions and governments. But government exists at different layers and levels. There are local self governments, regional/state and central governments. Besides, there exist government owned and operated institutions and enterprises. All such entities run on public funding and/or control and regulation have to do budgeting.

It is obvious that each decision making public unit prepares an annual budget. Budget making involves the process of budgeting, which is a lengthy and complex exercise. The budget making requires several months for preparation. It also involves decision-makers at various levels. However, final authority of approving the draft budget proposals of each ministry and departments under it lies in the hands of one single authority. The minister of the concerned ministry exercises final authority to approve and forward the draft proposals to ministry of finance. In a democratic polity, parliament/legislative assembly is the last arbiter of the national budget.

Composition of Public Budgets

Government budgets are the pivot of public finances. Public/ Government budgets comprise four heads/accounts: (i) Public Revenue (PR); (ii) public expenditure (PE); (iii) public debt (PD), and (iv) fiscal deficit (FD). It is assumed that public debt is designed, and hence, public Debt Policy is formulated and activated to cover the gap between public revenue from all sources and public expenditure.

The importance of sequence of determination of targets of PR and PE arises from both theoretical and practical aspects of public budgets. Each component of public finance such as revenue, expenditure and debt has its own policy thrust which has direct implications for economic policy in general and fiscal policy in particular. For example, public debt policy has direct implications for public policy dealing with all components of public finances. The question to be addressed is the sequence of determination of the need for and requirement of the four heads of accounts as stated above. But the sequence of determination of these components of budgets depends on the approach used in budgeting. Two alternative sequences may be used for the determination of the magnitudes of PR, PE, PD and FD. These may symbolically be shown as follows:

(i) PR→PE→PD→FD, and

(ii) PE→PR→PD→FD.

PE, PR, PD and FD stand for public expenditure, public revenue, public debt and fiscal deficit respectively.

Public Expenditure as Determinant of Other Budget Components

Under this approach, total PE is fixed according to the *a priori* defined criterion. Important criterion used in budgeting is to examine all the ongoing programmes and projects and stage of their completion and the work to be completed during the coming financial year. Then, new projects and programmes according to planned or stipulated targets of growth and development are taken into account and the expenditure required to be incurred on these is estimated. Sum of the above two furnishes an estimate of total public expenditure targeted to be incurred during the incoming financial year. This expenditure guides and governs the targeting of PR and public borrowings (PB) during the coming financial year. Given these estimates, FD is determined as the difference between PE and the sum of PR and PD. This may be shown symbolically as:

PE=(PR+PD+ FD)

So, PE→PR→PD→FD

The above indicates the direction of flow of sequence.

Given the estimate of total PE, gap between PE and sum of revenue and public borrowings if any, is determined. The difference between PE and the sum of PR and PD is covered by FD.

Alternative Process of Determination: Public Revenue/ Income as Determinant of Budget

This approach assigns pivotal role to the magnitude of PR which is expected to be raised from all sources and it leads to the determination of PE. The classical principle of balanced budgeting treated the magnitude of PR as the determinant of PE. There was no scope for PD and FD. The magnitude of PR, that government considered feasible to mobilise, set the upper limit of public expenditure. No space was granted to public borrowings and FD in this principle. Later developments in the theory of public finance accorded due role to the public borrowings and fiscal deficit in public budgeting.

First approach reverses the roles of PE and PR in the process of budgeting. Shortfall in PR relative to requirement of PE, that is, (PR-PE). It determines the difference between PE and PR which is to be filled up by PB. FD entered the equation a bit later. Therefore, the second relation means that the difference between the PE and the sum of PR and PD is filled up by fiscal deficit. Thus, fiscal deficit may be defined as the residual used as the gap filler.

Components of Public Expenditure and Balancing Revenue and Expenditure

Expenditure refers to the sum of amounts spent or to be spent on (i) administration of public services and expenditure on governance; (ii) performance of different activities of the government, including policy formulation and implementation and (iii) purchase of goods and services used by the government in the discharge of administrative and other responsibilities.

The distinction between the spending by the (i) public enterprises, government owned establishments and publicly funded institutions of health and education etc. and (ii) the government, should be kept in view. This is essential to avoid errors of omissions and commissions. Public refers to the government and its agencies.

Governments in most of the countries have different levels and layers for efficient governance: Central government, state governments, and local authorities. Public agencies are established by the acts of parliament and legislative assembly, local councils and their orders. Public enterprises stand on a different footing. But these are owned and operated on behalf of the government.

Any imbalance in the earnings/revenue and expenditure of these enterprises is generally covered by the government grants. One theory is that what holds true for households should also hold true for governments. Just as households should not and cannot live beyond their means forever, governments should not and cannot spend more than their revenue from taxes, fines, penalties, donations, etc.

Short-run spending by households in excess of their incomes and the short-run spending by the governments in excess of public revenue may be feasible and economically viable. But the critical question is how short should be the short-run? Long-run is only an envelope of the multitudes of short-runs. Besides, what is the magnitude of deficit or imbalance between revenue or earnings and expenditure that may be considered tolerable and/or desirable? Besides, can imbalance be taken forward year on year or it has to be halted at some point? These are critical questions. Indian Rural society, especially farming community suffered from perennial indebtedness in the past. It was carried through generations. In recent years also hundreds of farmers committed suicide due to their inability to repay their debts. Sub-prime crisis of the US also emanated from excessive private spending financed by bank credits. Then, suicide is not an option for the government. Euro-debt crisis has also affected the world economy.

These aberrations lend substance and empirical support to the public prudence embedded in balanced budgets rather than deficit public budgets.

Alternative streams of thought emphasise that all budgetary proposals are anticipatory. So it is inevitable that errors of estimation, unforeseen occurrences and random factor will make the expected and actual to diverge from each other. Consequently, even if the government has prepared a balanced budget and got it passed by the legislative body, imbalances are more likely to occur than balances *ex post facto*. The budget proposals are formulated for the fiscal year much before its commencement. So, estimation errors, errors arising due to faulty implementation, and un-anticipated price changes make actual figures diverge from the anticipated or planned targets. But in balanced budgeting approach public revenue is the first charge on planning and formulating budgetary proposals. Generally, preceding year's observations and experience are used in the formulation of current year's draft proposals of the budget. But the future is seldom the replica of the past. Therefore, estimation errors and errors arising from implementation process make the observed figures at the end of the fiscal year and the planned targets.

Alternative Forms of Budgets

Zero budgeting offers an alternative to the use of preceding year's observed values and experience of the past. Zero budgeting starts on clean slate. It means that no public debt, surplus/deficit of revenue over expenditure in the past is taken into account. Preceding year's fiscal deficit, revenue and expenditure are overlooked. Zero budgeting is based on the assessment of current needs of public expenditure and possible amount of revenue feasible to mobilise. Public borrowings and fiscal deficit are then entered into the draft budget proposals.

Zero budgeting may be useful in such economies that face extraordinary inflationary pressures and fiscal deficits at rates running into hundreds or five digits, such scenario was observed in some of the Latin American Countries in mid-1980s. However, zero budgeting is not known to have been used in any country. It not only seems difficult but improbable also to disregard the outstanding public debt, or half completed projects/programmes brought forward from the preceding years.

Level of Utilisation of Public Resources

It is also possible in some cases that the revenue mobilised by the government remains under-utilised at the end of the fiscal year. So, the differentials between: (i) budgeted public revenue, public debt, past public expenditure are carried forward from the preceding to the current year. But actual figures willy-nilly become the reference frame at the outset of the budgeting. Future perspective over a span of few years also comes into reckoning in budgeting. The future perspective furnishes the base for the formulation of policy. Growth target to be achieved within the financial year serves useful purpose in budgeting. These facets and aspects of budgeting act as the guide post. The growth targets are three-fold: (i) correctives needed to fill up the shortfalls of preceding years. These shortfalls are necessary to be made good; and (ii) completion of the ongoing development projects, and welfare programmes; and (iii) new projects and programmes of growth and welfare are an addition to the above.

Past levels and patterns of expenditure and anticipated inflation also become the base of current budgeting. Level and pattern of public revenue are determined in the given sequence. Public expenditure needs to govern and guide the determination of public revenue. Current level of public revenue, taxation rates, and sources of revenue are taken into account in the determination of public revenue. The shortfalls in achievement of preceding year's targets to meet public expenditure requirement are also an important consideration.

Alternative Paradigms

Some of the above aspects may need rethinking for the removal of weakness, if any:

(i) Pragmatism and commonsense suggest the use of different fiscal measures during recession or depression and inflationary phase of the business cycles. This implies different type of budgeting in different phases of business cycles.

(ii) The conventional theoretical postulate is made irrelevant by the development of new forms, strains, structure and levels of competition in the markets of different goods and services in modern economies. The modern economies are broadly characterised by the existence and operation of two types of markets: flex-price and fix-price markets.

(iii) Markets in which items of food, agriculture and goods are sold and purchased by auction are governed by future price expectations of independent intermediate traders. Their price expectations govern the accumulation or depletion of stocks they hold. Their stocking behaviour makes flex prices rise or fall. So, interest rate policy does not affect the price behaviour in such markets.

(iv) Flex price markets are characterised by atomistic competition among independent intermediate traders. These traders are the makers rather the takers of the prices (See, Shri Prakash, 1981, Shri Prakash, and Goel, 1987, Sharma, Shalini, 2004, Shri Prakash, and Arora Bhatia, 2012).

(v) Fiscal and other measures to affect the behaviour of these intermediate traders should be the part of budgeting during the inflationary phase of the cycle. But the fiscal measures, including increased interest rate may be targeted on these selected markets. Uniform fiscal policy will not deliver the desired goods.

(vi) The fixprice markets are dominated by intermediate traders who act as commission agents of producers. They own and operate sales outlets on behalf of manufacturers of industrial goods-basic and heavy goods, consumer durables etc. These markets have oligopolistic competition.

(vii) The traders of these goods are the takers rather the makers of prices. Prices in such markets are determined by the long run average cost of production.

(viii) Even in the midst of demand recession phase of the trade cycles prices of such goods are not reduced. This perpetuates rather than mitigates the demand recession in the market. Therefore, fiscal measures for such markets should differ from the measures formulated for flex-price markets.

(ix) Unlike the past when either inflation/boom or recession prevailed in the entire length and breadth of the national markets, today's modern economies are characterised by the prevalence of recession in fixprice markets in the midst of inflation in flex-price markets. Therefore, fiscal measures for flex price markets should be different from those devised and implemented for mitigating demand recession in fixprice markets. Recession in fix price markets require injection of doses of investment. Demand for investment may be increased by reducing cost of intermediate goods by scaling down commodity taxation and incentives to investors. For example, tax holiday may be given on returns on new investment.

Process of Budgeting

Process of budgeting requires the arrangement of the items of expenditure in accordance with the priorities and objectives of economic policy and planning and development targets. This facilitates allocation of amounts of money adequate to meet the needs of spending on different lines of expenditure.

Adequacy of proposed amount of allocated expenditure on a given item/line of expenditure relates to the physical quantity of goods to be purchased or the physical targets to be achieved at the price expected to prevail at the time of purchase. Total amount of money allocated for the particular item is seldom spent in one go. Therefore, quantities of purchases at different points of time during the year and the price expected to prevail at that time are the variables to be taken into account. This facilitates avoidance of the locking of public money in extra quantity of purchase. Total quantum of inventories required for the complete work to be done will also involve the additional cost of storage and maintenance of the stores. The concept of 'Just in Time' Inventory may be used in dovetailing the purchasing according to the schedule of use. Each line of public expenditure involves a set of goods and services. The payment of purchased goods and services require requisite amounts of money at the prices expected to prevail at the time of purchase. Such amounts have to be allocated in advance. This necessitates estimation of prices expected to prevail at the time of purchase.

Public expenditure includes, (i) interest payment on outstanding loans, (ii) repayment of matured loans, (iii) transfer payments and subsidies, (iv) wages and salaries of employees, (v) maintenance and repairs of assets of the government, (vi) acquisition of new furniture, furnishings and entire equipment, (vii) other consumable items, and (viii) payments due to contract work. In some cases, old machines and equipment have to be replaced with new machinery and equipment having new technology. Expenditure on public consumption and public investment constitutes substantial proportion of total public spending.

The balancing of income and expenditure can be done by having proper matching of total expected expenditure on all directions and total income/revenue expected to be available during the course of budget horizon. Not only over all total expenditure and revenue have to be matched, but the amount of money allocated to each direction of expenditure has to be matched with the expected amount of money from each direction/source of revenue. The Ministry of Finance should possess the information about the overall amounts allocated and overall amounts of money needed by items of expenditure at the budgeting stage. Discrepancies between the expenditure caps imposed by the ministry of finance as per directive of the leadership or the government have to be borne in mind. This is needed to ensure that the priorities of policy and planning are not transgressed.

This part of the exercise is very detailed and great deal of care and caution are required to be exercised at each step of every stage of budgeting. This is an essential element of establishment of consistency between budgeted revenue and budgeted expenditure in each line of action.

Participatory Nature of Budgeting Process

Budgeting is a participatory process. Minister of finance may start the process of budgeting by calling a meeting of leaders of industry, agriculture, mining, trade, transport, communication, education and health. Experts, public opinion makers, and leaders of different interest groups like farmers, trade union leaders and political leaders may also be involved in such brain storming meetings which may be used to ascertain problems and policy gaps also. The meeting is held to seek the information about the problems and challenges they had faced in the preceding year(s). The meeting will furnish the information about the problems of all above activities. This facilitates process of budget making. This will also furnish a broad view of the status of the economy and its business to the minister. It will greatly help him/her in performing the function of budget making. Such meetings may be followed by the convening of the meeting of group of ministers to acquaint the finance minister with the views of his colleagues. Separate meetings with the Prime Minister will apprise the minister with the thinking of the top leadership of the country. The meeting of the Cabinet may follow this. The meetings of the senior officers of different ministries and directorates may also be helpful. As this process is quite involved and time consuming, preparation for the next year's budget generally commences 4-5 months before the presentation of the budget before the parliament. This process ensures the participation of wide spectrum of ministries and their respective directorates or departments, leaders of public opinion, though the Ministry of Finance is the apex body in the making of national budgets

Cooperation of leaders of opinion plays the catalytic role in the containment of possible discontent with the policies of the government. It goes without saying that the fiscal policy and annual budgets directly and indirectly affect the lives of the people greatly.

The ministry of finance not only coordinates and synthesises the budgetary proposals of the ministries but it has also to dovetail the proposed expenditure in the synthesised and integrated whole, called national budget, in a manner that it does not transgress the overall expected revenue receipts (expenditure caps) on all sources and directions. The duplication or triplication of expenditure on the same items by different ministries of the central government and other layers of government, public institutions is required to be weeded out by coordination. Thus, achievement of consistency is a complex and intricate exercise involved in budget making. It is obvious from the above discussion that the complex but sophisticated process of budgeting is a multi-layered and multi-faceted exercise. The following constituents are included in an organically integrated whole/entity, which is called budget; these have to be taken into consideration in the process of budgeting.

The budget is prepared for the total amount of expenditure proposed to be spent by the government and its agencies during the specific period of time. This requires the determination of anticipated total amount of resources to be mobilised for defraying the spending by the government. Total planned public expenditure determines the target for the income/revenue to be raised from different sources.

The knowledge and information about the item/line and direction wise planned expenditure is required for incurring specified amount of expenditure on all lines and directions of expenditure. This is an essential input for fixing the total figure. This is the bottom-up approach to budgeting.

Alternatively, the Ministry of Finance may adopt the Top-Down approach to budgeting. In this case, the Ministry of Finance anticipates and determines the total expenditure of the government during the budget horizon.

Alternative Approaches of Determination of Total Expenditure

Proposed total spending of the government may be determined in two alternative ways.

Ministry of Finance on its own or in consultation with the apex planning authority and in accordance with the policy and planning for the year determines the overall target of growth of the economy during the budget horizon.

The target of overall rate of growth of GDP is used to anticipate total public expenditure in general and investment in particular. This includes both public and private investment needed for the attainment of target of growth. Overall target of growth of GDP is decomposed into growth of constituent sectors of GDP.

The easiest way to do it is to use the technique of projection. Projection is done on the basis of growth performance of different sectors in the past. Projection takes into account past changes in economic structure due to diversification. Diversification is an essential consequence of growth. Trend analysis is one of the important techniques of projection.

Trend analysis involves decomposition of the time series. This may be done by the method of moving averages or regression analysis. Regression function may be specified in alternative forms.

This part of the exercise helps in the allocation of total expenditure among different sectors and items of expenditure. The desired acceleration or deceleration of the pace of change in sector/commodity composition of GDP may be effected to provide direction to the economy for moving on its growth path in accordance with the priorities of national economic policy.

Second option is that the Ministry of Finance first arrives at the maximum amount of resources that it considers feasible and viable to be raised from different sources during the budget horizon. The expected revenue/resources are then used as the base to determine the expected total expenditure to attain the targeted objective of growth. This furnishes the base of allocation of total expenditure proposed to be budgeted into different components; allocation is guided by the targeted growth of specific sectors and regions and population living there.

Whichever of these approaches is used for budgeting, current level of expenditure and revenue of the government furnish the backdrop of budgeting. This helps in neither to look into the future with too pessimistic an outlook nor to be too ambitious and unduly optimistic in fixing the growth targets and expenditure and revenue required for attaining the future targets of growth.

Technical Feasibility and Economic Viability

Twin criteria of technical feasibility and economic viability have to be the guide posts in decisions relating to the determination of growth targets irrespective of whether the target relates to sectors or economy as a whole. In this exercise, technical feasibility of each project and programme has to be determined in advance. If some project or programme is not technically feasible it has to be pushed out of the window at the initial stage itself. There are specialised agencies which undertake the study of feasibility of sector specific projects and programmes; their services may be used in this part of the exercise. Such agencies may be private or public. For example, Government of India commissioned the services of Dastur and Dasstur technical consultancy company to study the technical feasibility of Bhilai Steel Plant. Government of U.P. has established a corporation for managing and operating Noida-Greater Noida Metro. The corporation has entrusted the task of execution to Delhi Metro Corporation.

A project or programme may be technically feasible but technical feasibility alone is not sufficient for the incorporation of any project and programme in budgeting, unless it is economically viable. Economic viability depends on two factors: affordability of cost of the project or programme from the stage of initiation to its completion; and the benefits expected to be gained from the operation of the project after completion. This involves operational costs and revenue or benefits. Benefits may be economic or social though these have to be weighed in monetary terms.

Alternative Approaches for Determination of Public Revenue

Like the options available for the determination of public expenditure, options are also available for the determination of targets of revenue to be raised during the fiscal year. This involves evaluation of source-wise feasible amounts of resources which can be raised. Amounts of resources to be raised from different sources should not only be feasible but these amounts should also be needed to meet stipulated public expenditure.

An important aspect of budgeting is pursuit of the objectives of optimisation and consistency. This has three facets: consistency between (a) expenditure needed for meeting growth targets of specific sectors/areas and the budgeted expenditure for the same, (b) total as well as item wise budgeted expenditure and allocated resources both at macro and micro levels have to be matched, and (c) planned amounts of resources to be raised from each source should be consistent with the constraints to the raising of resources from the targeted sources.

These objectives can be attained in budgeting provided that the techniques of data analysis of consistency planning and optimisation are used in the process of budget making. Consistency model is known as inter-industry/activity or input output model. Consistency model requires the availability of input output matrix. So far as India is concerned, CSO prepares input-output tables of the economy every five years. The currently available CSO's table relates to the year 2007-08 and the new table is likely to be released in near future. But Tanzania lags far behind India in this field. The last input output table of Tanzania relates to 1993.

The optimisation techniques are known as programming models. There are models of mathematical programming, linear programmeming, non-linear programming, fuzzy programming, quadratic programming and programming under risk and uncertainty.

Steps Involved in Budgeting

Allocation of total budgetary resources among different ministries is an essential step in the budget making. Ministries in turn allocate funds for budgeted expenditure to their directorates which, in turn, have to allocate their respective allocated budgetary resources among different activities of the respective directorates. Alternatively, this exercise may better be done by the Ministry of Finance itself.

Discrepancy between expenditure and revenue of the government has to be covered by fiscal deficit and/or public borrowings. Fiscal deficit and public borrowings are inversely related because of their additive nature. This is evident from the following: Discrepancy between revenue and expenditure given by PE-PR equals shortfall in available resources=SFAR, public revenue here stands for revenue expected to be raised by taxation at the proposed rates. SFAR, shortfall in avialable resources, is covered by fiscal deficit, FD and public debt, PD. Therefore, SFAR= FD+PD. Thus greater the public borrowings, smaller shall be the fiscal deficit at any time and vice-versa.

Objectives as Guiding Principle

The discharge of these roles and performance of the functions involves following objectives as over-riding consideration:

Determination of the bearing capacity of the burden of taxation by the economy and the people of the country depends on the stage of growth of the economy and the level of income. Higher the level of GDP, greater is the tax bearing capacity of the economy, and higher the level of per capita GDP and lower the degree of inequality in personal income distribution, greater is the tax burden bearing capacity of the people.

(i) Absorption capacity of the economy and ability of the public to derive requisite benefits from the planned public expenditure on different lines at the given point in time. At each higher stage of economic growth and social development of the economy, capacity of absorption of public expenditure of the country tends to grow while the ability of the people to derive benefits grows with increase in their personal disposable incomes.

(ii) Public/government has to avoid un-necessary and wasteful splurge while essential and growth promoting expenditure is not to be shunned.

(iii) Determination of an optimum pattern of allocation of total budgeted expenditure among different lines of expenditure in accordance with the policy and planning furnish the guiding principle of resources allocation. This involves the use of programmeming techniques in budget making.

(iv) Change in priorities and objectives leads to a change in the objective function of programming model, which is sought to be maximised while the constraint constants tend to be loosened at each higher stage of economic growth.

(v) Conversion of the primal into its dual facilitates the determination of shadow prices or real resource cost of each pattern of allocation of public expenditure. This enables the decision makers to avoid the pitfalls of wastefull or unproductive spending of the public money.

(vi) Similarly, the objective function associated with the determination of the pattern of resources to be raised from each direction/source also tends to change with the priorities and objectives of policy and planning and the changing level and pattern of income distribution among different strata of population and sectors of the economy. But in this case, one likes to minimise the real cost of revenue resources to be raised from different sources.

The current level of growth and the sector composition of GDP tend to change in the course of development. In fact, transformation of structure of the economy holds the key to accelerated growth. These changes have to be viewed and reviewed at every stage of budget making in order to determine the direction of future change. This is necessary to ensure efficient and effective utilisation of allocated budgetary resources by all units. The objective is to make the given resources go the farthest. This requires the determination of productivity of expenditure relative to its real resource cost of each use.

Monitoring and Evaluation

Monitoring and evaluation (M&E) of implementation of budget and its outcomes is an essential component of overseeing the process of implementation. Incidentally, M&E exercise offers two options. The exercise may be performed at the end of the programme or completion of the projects. But the shortfalls and divergences from the desired path would have had already happened; so no corrective measures are feasible and admissible in such cases. Alternatively, the Ministry of Finance or Ministry of Programme Implementation should undertake concurrent M&E exercise. M&E exercise should be both internal and external. External evaluation is required for overcoming the human tendency to cover up and hide one's own mistakes which may be judgmental or self-interest induced.

Budget Multiplier

Budget multiplier is an important parameter for analysing the impact and effect of budget proposals, if the purpose is to know the impact of budget proposal on the economy before the budget is finally adopted for implementation. The analysis may be performed on past data to have an idea of the likely consequences of the implementation of the proposed budget. As against this, impact of budget may be assessed after the implementation of the budget. The impact is captured by budget multiplier.

Concept of Budget Multiplier

The moot questions are: what is the budget multiplier; and what is the process of its application to the economic data? Answers are as follows.

Budget multiplier generally refers to the effect of the public budget on national economy in general and national income in particular. But in the narrow technical sense, budget multiplier relates to the effect of change in government expenditure and government revenue on national income. But the public expenditure is incurred on a multitude of items and projects/programmes. Therefore, overall impact can be derived from the analysis of impact or effect of public expenditure on each line or direction of expenditure. The sum total of all these shall furnish an idea about the overall effect of expenditure. Impact and effect relates to the outcome or the change in the value(s) of the variable(s) which bear the impact and carry the effect of given change in public expenditure in a specific direction. Similarly, public revenue is raised from different sources. Taxation is an important source of public revenue. So, the amount of change in revenue and demand for liqueur if the rate of tax/excise duty on, for example, liqueur, is raised by 10 per cent. Such estimates of changes in revenue have to be made for all sources of taxation. Thus, the budget multiplier captures the causal relation between the changes in public expenditure and changes in public revenue and national income during the budget horizon. Sensitivity analysis may be performed in order to acquire a comprehensive view of the impact of budget on the economy during the budget horizon. Budget horizon refers to the length of the period, generally one financial year, for which the budget is made. For example, public expenditure is raised by X per cent and tax rates are increased by X per cent for generating additional revenue needed to meet the increase in expenditure of X per cent. It reads 'If aggregate demand as a result of these changes remains constant, then it is contrary to general expectation. If, however, the proportion of decline in personal disposable income is due to increase in tax rate by X per cent and the corresponding increase in revenue is Z, then Z, is the budget multiplier. So, reduced savings will depress the aggregate demand. But the rise in public expenditure exactly by the same percentage by which tax has been increased raises aggregate demand. Besides, reduction in personal disposable income reduces savings rather than consumption. If the savings ratio of households was also X per cent of their personal disposable income, the percent by which tax rate is increased, then aggregate demand could have risen by X per cent as the value of budget multiplier (Cf. Bannock et al. 2012). The assumption behind this is that the elasticity of aggregate demand with respect to public expenditure is equal to one. However, the underlying assumption is the neutrality of rise in income to savings. This may not be supported by empirical evidence. The above definition of budget multiplier does not take into account the impact of increased tax rates on consumption expenditure. It takes consumption expenditure to be inelastic with respect to increased taxation. Hence, reduced disposal income of the households does not affect consumption according to this assumption. Alternatively, budget multiplier may be interpreted differently. The concept of budget multiplier implicitly assumes negative effect of enhanced tax rate to be balanced by positive impact of increased public expenditure on consumption. But it overlooks the investment induced accelerator which relates to savings.

This important point is missed by the definition of budget multiplier cited above. Correct assumption shall be that public expenditure is partially productive and partly unproductive. Thus, only additional public expenditure used for investment is productive. But production involves time lags. Hence, the rise in income caused by increased public expenditure does not occur instantly with the increase in tax rate. But the disposable income is decreased immediately by the taxation at increased rate.

Increased expenditure incurred on promotion of consumption of public and merit goods, and subsidies on necessities also increases purchasing power of the households and consumption. It activates consumption multiplier of growth. Increased expenditure on public investment financed by enhanced revenue raised by increased tax rate activates growth accelerator. Besides, increased public expenditure on people's welfare contributes to long run growth.

Pragmatism dictates that public savings/investment do not necessarily increase by the same percentage as public expenditure. The national income is expected all the same to rise by the same percentage rate by which the public expenditure is increased. This would have been the case if the elasticity of aggregate demand with respect to public expenditure is one irrespective of percentage rise in taxation rate resulting in reduction of disposable income.

Other Approaches to Budgeting and Steps in Budgeting

Budgeting refers to the process of formulation of the national budget. The budgeting is a multistage exercise. Each stage in budgeting involves multiplicity of steps. Budgeting involves various stages in the finalisation of the budget of the national government. Budgeting may be approached in several alternative ways. Two approaches to the making of public budgets need further explanation.

These approaches are: (i) zero budgeting which totally disregards what has happened in the past and what is likely to happen in future. It is as if the present stand alone by itself and totally disconnected with the preceding past and succeeding future. (ii) Treatment of current year's budget as the continuation and supplementation of budgets of the preceding years, especially the last year which also clears the path for the future or the preparation for the future budgets in the given budget cycle, say of 5 years duration. It means that the current budget is one of the five budgets that have to be made in the given cycle. Second approach is based on the assumption that the system operates in social and economic arena in a vacuum.

Zero Budgeting

Zero budgeting exercise starts on a totally clean slate since zero budgeting does not take the past into account. It also does not consider the future. First step in zero budgeting is to list the objectives and priorities of the coming year for the realisation of which the budget is being made. This implies that resources for financing the item-wise capital and revenue account expenditure at the prices expected to prevail in the coming year are to be estimated first. Expected expenditure is obviously already fixed. This, however, needs consideration of trend of movements of prices of goods required for achieving the targets fixed for the year. But estimated total expenditure is the sum of expenditure on all public activities, including public administration, social and economic activities expected to be performed for the realisation of the budget targets in the financial year. Negligence of likely changes in prices at the stage of budgeting sows the seeds of achieving less than targeted goals. Materialisation or realising budgeted expenditure will raise demand in the market. If the extent of rise in demand is not matched by supply, prices will rise. For example, if 1,000 households are provided one room tenement of 16x16 sq feet, then number of bricks, cement, steel, electricity, water and wage payments to construction workers on the basis of man-hours/days required for completion of the project have to be determined in advance. Besides, the prices of all the above goods to prevail in the market at the time of actual purchase have to be estimated. Physical quantities can then be translated into monetary terms in order to make adequate provision for this budgeted programme. The budgetary provision for this housing project should be matched by the programme of increasing the output of construction material so that rise in demand and supply synchronise both in time and space.

Second step of zero budgeting is the determination of sources of revenue required to finance the budgeted expenditure on all items/lines of expenditure. Quantum of revenue from taxation is determined first. All items of taxation have to be looked at from the point of view of their revenue yielding capacity. Increased tax rates should not cross the limits of people's capacity of bearing the tax burden. At each stage of economic growth, tax burden bearing capacity of the economy and households' tax burden bearing ability increases; and it sets the upper limit for taxation. Actual taxation should not cross this limit. So, the tax burden has to spread judicially on all segments of the population and sectors of the economy. But the revenue elasticity of each tax has to be kept in view so that revenue yielded by taxes does not fall short of the target.

Budgeting in Continuum of Past Budgets

This is the commonly used approach to budgeting across the globe. In this case, current budget is one of the many in the long chain over the medium or long run. Following steps are involved in this approach to budgeting.

First step is the review of performance of the preceding year's budget. The entire budget is carefully and thoroughly scrutinised for the evaluation of its performance in each arena of budgeting; it facilitates determination of current status of the economy and its finances. The current status is used as the building block for current budgeting. Second step in this process of budgeting relates to the identification of strengths and weakness of performance in each area. Fulfilment of budgeted targets and/or area wise shortfalls in the achievement of targets is considered which reveals the strengths and weaknesses in performance. Realisation/fulfilment or more than targeted achievements in specific directions highlight strengths of the preceding year's budgeting. These strengths have to be further improved in the current budgeting exercise. Third step is detailed analysis of causes of failures. Failure may partly or wholly be accounted by over-ambitious targets which makes the realisation of targets difficult. Another factor of failure may relate to inappropriateness of strategy for achieving the stipulated targets.

Other factor of failure may be faulty implementation of the budgeted activities. Such activities may relate to revenue generation by taxation, or public borrowings, or mode and items of public expenditure in the past.

One reason often encountered in the area of implementation of budgetary programmes and projects is under or over estimation of prices expected to prevail at the time of budget implementation. If the prices are lower than expected, part of budgeted public expenditure will be surplus. As against this, under-estimation of expected prices will result in budgeted expenditure falling short of requirement. Past experiences over the years furnish guidelines to avoid the possible pitfalls in budgeting. However, inclusion of new projects, programmes or activities relating either to public expenditure or the raising of additional resources from hitherto totally unexplored sources and untapped areas will have no advantage of past experience. But one may become wiser on hindsight due to the lapse of sometime after the approval of budget. Such insights as are acquired on hindsight may be useful in future. But it is of no help in the present.

Conclusions

It may be concluded from above discussion that:

(i) Budget and budgeting are inter-twined and complex concepts.

(ii) Process of budgeting is prolonged and consists of several steps.

(iii) Widespread participation in budgeting is an important ingredient of budgeting in order to evoke popular support.

(iv) There are alternative approaches and principles of budget making including general principles and objectives of budget and budgeting.

(v) Each budget furnishes a link in the long chain of budgets in the budget cycle.

(vi) Zero budgeting, however, does not follow the above postulation.

(vii) Size and composition of budget may be determined either on the basis of requirement of public expenditure or alternatively public revenue may be taken as the guidepost for the formulation of budget.

(viii) Evaluation of performance of budget of the preceding year is an important aspect of budgeting.

(ix) Monitoring and evaluation of budgetary performance may either be concurrent or it may be done at the end of the fiscal year.

(x) If the budgetary performance is evaluated at the end of the financial year, then there is no scope of initiating corrective measures for correcting errors in implementation.

(xi) Shortfalls in achievement of budgetary target may either be due to over-ambitious nature of target setting or faulty implementation.

(xii) Part of the failure may also be accounted by imperfections and errors in the policy formulation.

(xiii) Budget is an important instrument of fiscal policy.

4

Concept and Theory of Economic Growth and Public Expenditure

Introduction

Theme of the book in general and this chapter in particular raises a host of questions which need answers. Following are some of the important questions that need explanation in order to provide conceptual clarity and to delineate the theoretical framework of the study.

(i) What is economic growth?

(ii) Does economic growth differ from economic progress and development?

(iii) How is growth measured, or what represents growth?

(iv) Is economic growth related to public finances, especially public expenditure?

(v) Is there a relation between theory of economic growth and economic policy, especially fiscal policy, including policy of public expenditure?

(vi) What does public expenditure connote?

(vii) What are the determinants of growth?

(viii) Why and how does public expenditure affect economic growth and what is the degree of its influence on growth relative to other determinants of economic growth?

Answers to some of the above questions are explored in this chapter. Answers to other questions shall be attempted in other chapters. The chapter mainly explores the conceptual and theoretical underpinnings of answers to some of the above questions. This chapter however does not furnish empirical evidence to support the answers to the questions as it concentrates on concepts and theory.

The book attempts to portray Indian and Tanzanian economies in econometric framework with special reference to public finance. It uses econometric modeling to highlight what underlies the inter-relations of economic growth with core macro financial variables. The determination of degree and direction of inter-relations between growth and public finances will facilitate explanation of inter-temporal behaviour of these two economies in different phases and stages of growth. This may be helpful in forecasting future scenarios also over the horizon of short period.

The main objective of this book is to determine economic growth and its relation with public expenditure of India and Tanzania in a comparative framework. One single model or model of a particular hue and dimension may not serve the purpose of analysis of data of two countries of the world with lot of differences but with certain level of similarities. The study will, therefore, explore the routes for evolution of econometric models for empirical evaluation of special features and structures of the economies under study. This may pave the way for forecasting.

The forecasting necessitates such models as are adequate to explain the past and current behaviour of the economies under study on the one hand, and furnish the base for future scenario building for sensitivity analysis on the other. Therefore, the models outlined in this book have been designed to be consistent with the fully blown and developed macro econometric model(s) of the economies under consideration and these models have to be a part of building blocks of final macro-econometric(s) model for economies of both countries in future. Another aspect of the models evolved in the book is their characteristic of appropriateness for time-series modeling.

Answers to the following questions are also needed at this stage: (a) What is a model? (b) What is a macroeconomic model? (c) What does distinguish one from other type of model(s) under consideration? How does model differ from method and viceversa. Answers to these questions will highlight the contents of this book while answer to the last question of earlier set of questions will put the models developed and used in the study in proper perspective.

Core Concepts of Study

Model, economic growth, policy, public finances, economic and fiscal policy, public expenditure are some of the core terms that have been and will be used extensively in the text. Some of these concepts have already been explained in an earlier chapter. For clarity, the concepts of these terms are explained in the ensuing pages.

Model and Method

The model and method are two terms which are often used synonymously. Thus, the distinction between the concepts of these two is lost sight of at times. Almost all sciences, including science of economics, use models for the explaining and testing of the empirical validity of one or more theories; models and methods are also used as an instrument of research investigation and forecasting. But what is a model? Does model differ from method?

'Model' in day today parlance is the representation of reality in a miniscule form or minimum size. Reality is hugely vast, complex and comprises intertwined relationships. This makes understanding of reality in its totality difficult. Reality is compartmentalised into different disciplines to make it understandable; each discipline comprises numerous theories consisting of concepts/constructs, assumptions and causal relations. Models are formulated as shorthand statements of theories. A model may represent one or more theories. But theories are very concise and precise which exclude myriad of inessential details of the phenomena under study. So, details of information are drastically reduced and irrelevant aspects/factors are kept out of a model. Model is, therefore, like the mapping of a building planned to be built. The structure of the building depicted in the map may be converted into miniaturised model of clay or wood. For example, many vendors around Taj Mahal and Red Fort in Agra sell white/red coloured models which look like Taj Mahal or Red Fort. The model maps out only the basic features and essential details of the object of modeling.

A model is thus, an abstract representation of reality, which brings out what is relevant to a particular question/aspect of study and neglects all other aspects. Therefore, a model is a Miniaturised replica of reality. Miniaturisation involves abstraction from details and focus on core features and facets in order to be the mini mirror image of vast phenomenon under consideration. This objective is attained by exclusion of non-essential details from the model so as to make it focus more on structure than size, more on operational facets than environmental matrix, core variables of the system and the causal relations than non-core and peripheral elements of phenomenon under consideration. Model may alternatively be defined as architecture of operational design. It is reality in action/operation. The model is an instrument of expression of abstract theory, its constructs, assumptions and statement of causal relation(s) in concrete terms; it makes theory applicable to the complex reality. The model may however be expressed or shown in symbolic or literary language; it may also be depicted graphically.

A model reflects a definite idea or a set of ideas about reality. In most of the social and behavioural sciences, a model does convey the idea but nothing more than that (Cramer 1972). One may or may not agree with Cramer, since a model involves concepts, assumptions and relations among the variables involved in the model even though each of these facets of the model revolves round one or more ideas. Cramer is probably referring to such social sciences as focus merely on facts and their description. Practioners of such social sciences take pride in calling their discipline pragmatic and realistic.

Methods

Models differ from methods. Method may be defined as 'know-how to do how'. In other words, methods are designed or developed for application to the observed or conceived and perceived facts of some part of reality. So, methods comprise knowledge of procedure of application of the given method to data or information, derivation of concrete results from application and performing the analysis of results derived from the application of method with a view to draw inferences or offer relevant and meaningful interpretations. There are two distinct methods of data or information analysis: deductive method and inductive method.

Method of deduction may use perceived facts; perceived facts may be based on observations or on *a priori* reasoning. Such facts facilitate proceeding from general to specific proposition. Deduction may also use facts as these are conceived by researcher(s) to reach a particular conclusion from some general proposition.

Method of induction as against deduction uses observed facts which facilitate step by step proceeding from particular to general proposition. Thus, methods consist of a well defined procedure to be pursued in the process of application to observed or even hypothetical facts. The procedure of application comprises sequential steps required to be taken for the application of the method for the analysis of facts. But each method has its own theoretical base from which it is evolved in a finished form or format; methodology furnishes the theory of methods. But every method has its own theory, its assumptions, strengths, weaknesses, sample spread and power. All above aspects distinguish one method from another. Alfred Marshall (1890/1963) has given an analogy to explain the need for and concept of 'method'. The analogy is that of a saw machine. Trees may be cut manually into pieces of wood of different size, shape and structure. But the manual performance of this job is both tedious, monotonous and involves hard physical labour. It is obvious that the saw of a definite size which depends on the size and thickness of wood has to be moved to- and-fro time and again. The job can be done much quicker and easily by a saw mill. The machinery of the saw mill embodies the method of cutting of wood. Similarly, 'Method' of Investigation and/or analysis may be defined as the machinery of research (Shri Prakash 2005).

Features of Economic Models

Economic models are a special class of models in social sciences. Specialised facets of economic models arise from the following features of economic models:

(i) Economic models stand out favourably in comparison to models of other social sciences. For example, one may have a glance at the comparison and contrasting of economic and managerial approaches to the modelling of consumer behaviour (Shri Prakash 2010).

(ii) Economic models are fairly exact and precise; these models are usually elabourated in terms of well conceived and properly defined variables and concepts associated with these variables;

(iii) Economic models basically encompass functional relations which make these models theoretical;

(iv) Economic models are methodological and/empirical in orientation since the objective of economic theory and its models is to furnish as accurate analysis of economic reality as is possible;

(v) Economic models of modern economics are often detailed out in mathematical terms which are apt for application to data;

(vi) Mathematically formulated or translated economic models are amenable to conversion into econometric modelling. This makes economic models precise and accurate;

(vii) Mathematically stated models are also of two types: (a) models which are exact translation of economic theory in mathematical terms, and (b) mathematically expressed models which have been developed by mathematical methods to become a part of mathematical economics, encompassing economic theory;

(viii) Economic models are generally evolved as devices of application of economic theory to observed facts.

Types of Economic Models

Economic models may be classified according to: (i) theory or facts as base; (ii) size or unit of analysis as base, and (iii) method or methodology as base.

Theory or Facts as Base of Economic Modelling

Economic models may be purely theoretical or these models may be constructed on the basis of extensive empirical observation of facts. Purely theoretical models use deductive logic for formulating and testing of model's consistency and relevance to reality. Knowledge of the economy shapes and guides the model builder to formulate constructs, propose premises and assumptions with a view to reduce complexities so as to focus on variables of interest which proposed theory relates to. Adam Smith's theory of cost advantage as the base of international trade, or long run cost of production as the base of price determination, Ricardo's theories of rent, long run falling rates of profit, comparative cost as base of international trade, Marshall's distinction between theories of price determination in market, short and long periods are examples of purely theoretical models.

As against purely theoretical models based on deductive logic, facts based or empirical models use inductive logic. Malthus's model of population growth was based on extensive empirical evidence of population growth in several countries of Europe. Milton Friedman used his extensive observations of world economy during his travels across the globe about comparative advantage in growth, that is conferred by the nature of government in power and economic systems in place in different countries in the formulation of his theory of market based growth. This, in turn, led him to advocate the policies of liberalisation, privatisation and globalisation (for details, see, Shri Prakash 1995) which have practically engulfed most of the economies of the world. Dada Bhai Naoroji and M.L. Darling have probably been the first analysts in the recorded history of thought to have used empirical facts for the formulation of their respective economic theories. Dada Bhai Naoroji used his observations and knowledge about Indian and British economies of his times in the formulation of his Theory of Colonial Drain as the cause of under-development of Indian economy. In fact, he must be considered as the founder of Economics of under-development (See, Mathur 1986, 1992, Shri Prakash 1992). M.L. Darling, then Governor of British Punjab, used facts of the farming in Punjab to highlight the theory of backwardness of Indian agriculture due mainly to small size and scattered nature of holdings which did not permit adoption of improveds methods of cultivation known at that time. The economically unviable holding size did not leave the peasants with sufficient funds to invest in their farms.

Unit of Analysis as Base of Modelling

There are two approaches to model building: (i) top-Down approach, and (ii) bottom-up approach. Top-down approach is generally the hallmark of macro-modeling. Modeling of public finance pursues top-down approach and these models are macro in nature and orientation. Bottom-up approach to modeling relates to micro-modeling. It is generally followed in non-public finance. Modeling of stock market is an example (For example, See Shri Prakash and Bhatia Arora 2013).

Macro and Microeconomic Models

Macroeconomic models refer generally to economy wide models. Such models deal with macro-aggregates and averages like GDP and its growth, volume of international trade, employment, savings/investment, aggregate consumption expenditure, public revenue, public expenditure, public debt, inflation, etc. These models do not involve the analysis of individual human behaviour, or individual firms and industries which fall within the domain of microeconomic models.

General Equilibrium (GE) and Computable General Equilibrium (CGE) models furnish the bridge or link between the micro and macroeconomic models. Such models focus on micro units, that constitute the macro aggregates on the one hand, and seek to determine prices and output of all commodities in the state of equilibrium of all commodity and factor markets on the on the other. Thus, these models analyse the behaviour and decisions of consumers and determine outcomes of decisions of all firms of all industries. CGE models differ from GE models in so far as these models use theory and structures which yield empirical equilibrium solutions in the general frame-work of the economy as a whole. Such models may be econometric, or input output, or programming ones. However, general equilibrium models may not be implementable in certain cases due to some specific reasons.

Theoretical Model

The theoretical model may also be conceptualised on above lines. A theoretical model is defined as the miniaturised replica of theory; model replicates only essential characteristics such as causal relations, definitions/concepts and assumptions or premises of theory in concise and precise form. The model may be expressed either in literary language like the Maslow model of basic needs; or Adam Smith's labour theory of value/prices. Alternatively, model may express the theory in mathematical or econometric form. For example, Mahalanobis' two sector model of economic growth, or Harrod-Domar macro model of economic growth comprises a set of identities and equations. Like the theory, model also avoids incorporation of inessential details to focus on basics. Model like the theory comprises causal, definitional, concepts and assumptions based inter-relations among the variables of theory, which are expressed in mathematical and/or econometric terms as equations and identities. The model equations comprise variables and parameters. However, equations based on causal relations consist of dependent and independent variables and each independent variable has a parameter attached to it. As against the mathematical models, an econometric model also contains an error term which is assumed to be random in nature; it is in addition to the causal relation of the theory. Parameters attached to the pre-determined or independent variables of mathematical and econometric models quantify degree and direction of causal relation between variables of the model.

For example $Y=2.54+0.85X$ is a causal relation. Here, 2.54 is the minimum or autonomous value of Y which is independent of any influence of X while +0.85 tells us that X and Y are causally related positively and corresponding to unit change in the value of X, value of Y increases by 0.85 units.

This classification of models uses method as the main base of categorisation. Following are the major categories of models based on methods:

(i) Graphic models display and explain the features and behaviour and/or inter-relations of variables under consideration by means of charts, figures, diagrams and graphs;

(ii) Mathematical models are of two types: (a) models that use mathematical methods for developing economic theory.

Such models fall in the domain of mathematical economics; (b) models which use mathematical methods to explain and elabourate existing micro- or macro-economic theories;

(iii) Statistical Models are those models which use statistical techniques of data analysis. The choice of techniques may be from any branch of statistics. Such models like the mathematical models also use symbolic language. Statistical models have now come to be used to complement the mathematical models. Statistical methods/techniques are used to quantify the relations contained in mathematical models;

(iv) Econometric models constitute the specialised branch of Quantitative Economics. Such models are based on econometric tools of data analysis. Econometric models employ tools of both statistics and mathematics. But these models draw heavily on economic theory. Besides, theory of probability also plays some role in these models;

(v) Programming, input-output and game theoretic models also fall in the category of methods based models.

Modelling Approach to Study

Economic/econometric modeling, as has already been explained, may follow either Top-down or bottom up approach. Top-down approach moves from macro modeling to the modeling of micro units of the economy. But bottom-up approach to modeling begins with the building of models of each micro unit to end up with macro model to represent the economy as a whole or some parts of it. First approach, adopted in this study, focuses on economy as a whole in order to furnish the back-drop for understanding and forecasting the behaviour of micro constituents of macro entities. Incidentally, general equilibrium model, including input output model, furnishes a bridge between micro and macro modeling.

The study is a step towards the building of model which comprehensively and exhaustively captures inter-relations between public finances and economic growth. The model is evolved to envelop almost all important facets of the economy such as growth of GDP, temporal changes in public finances, investment, interest rate, consumption, employment, trade, and inflation. All these variables affect not only overall business environment but also the state of business of individual enterprises of industries. But model building is preceded by an explanation of concepts, which lie at the base of theory which the model embodies. Focus of this study is, however, confined largely to the analysis of inter-relations between public expenditure and economic growth. Following are other core terms involved in this particular part of the study: Growth and Public Expenditure.

The term 'growth' has often been used interchangeably with such terms as 'economic progress' and 'economic 'development'. Therefore, this study distinguishes growth from both progress and development. The concepts underlying all three terms are taken up for elabourate explanation. Incidentally, this study tries to break free from the shekels of obsolete terms and their meanings; it attempts to furnish new and more contemporary meanings and does not hesitate in proposing new terms with innovative interpretation of empirical results wherever it is warranted. The study thus moves away from mechanical interpretations of results by delving deep into the causes or consequences of observed facts. All such interpretations are then woven into the theoretical framework.

Progress, Growth and Development

Distinction between these three terms, economic progress, economic growth and economic development is needed because these terms have often been used synonymously in literature for quite some time. The concepts of progress, growth and development need to be distinguished as their features/characteristics are distinct, their relations with their respective determinants are varied, scope, nature and coverage of each term widely differ. But all three concepts have some common features also which are related to the process, causes and outcomes of change. Change is the hallmark of all three terms.

Trade Cycles, Growth and Economic Dynamics

Concepts and theories of growth and development emanated originally from the analysis of trade cycles. Magnitude, rate and direction of growth and/or development in different phases of business cycles and their consequences for the economy and its business generally differs sharply. Consumption/demand, and hence, output and supply differ between and during different phases of business cycles; these differentials affect investment, output, prices and employment. All such changes directly affect profits of the enterprises in different phases of the cycles. These differentials make business and economic environment starkly different during different phases of trade cycles. Changes in all above variables relate to growth as its propellants or as its consequences.

Profits are the propellants and drivers of investment in general and private investment in particular. Both investment and consumption affect growth directly as well as indirectly. In fact, consumption and investment are causes as well as consequences of growth. This bi-directionality of interrelations involves lead and lag structure. Concepts of growth and development, therefore, were initially related directly to the concepts and magnitudes of profits/losses during the different phases of business cycles. Profits/losses manifest specific state of the economy and its business in the distinct phases of business cycles in a capitalist economy. In the boom phase, profits, and hence, output, consumption, investment, and employment all are in a state of buoyancy. As against the boom phase, doom or down phase of cycles is associated with falling demand and prices, and hence, profits, at times even resulting in losses which result in reduced production, low or no investment, prevalence of high unemployment and negative growth. High profits, rising investment, expanding employment and output are both a cause and consequence of growth. Fluctuations in the state of business and health of the economy were and are reflected by fluctuations in profits, investment, output and employment.

Common Factor of Progress, Growth and Development

Changing magnitudes of profits and other core economic variable are essentially related to economic dynamics; its concept emerged from analytical differentiation between economic statics and economic dynamics. A third concept of 'comparative economic static' lies between these two ends of the conceptual spectrum.

An economic/business system in a stationary state is changeless, and hence, this state is without progress or growth or development. In nutshell, it may be called a change-less state as it is associated with stagnancy in the economy and its business. The stationary or static state of the economy refers to such a state as was and is a timeless economic system, since passage of time does not bring change in values of any core variable in a stationary state. This state is a conceptual benchmark for comparative analysis. Real life economies in modern times are seldom in a stationary state; as there is always change of one or other type. Change, in fact, is the salt of life; everything is destined to change through time. But change has varied hues and shades some of which are discussed in ensuing paragraphs.

Stationary and Dynamic State

Approach of this study is quasi logical and quasi empirical. Rationale of this approach is that the concept(s) of Growth and Development have been evolved on the basis of observed major facets of outcomes of the processes of change associated with growth and development of different nations over a period of time. Evolution of these concepts has thus been empirical and experiential in nature and orientation (Shri Prakash 1992a,b). Concepts and analytical thrust of such studies have been developed partly on the basis of Sraffa's model of self replacing, self reliant, sufficient and closed economy, which produces just enough to keep itself going without any surplus over the needs of production even for meeting increasing requirements of growing population from one to another period. However, it is implicitly assumed that like other core variables of the model, population is also changeless. Consumption in such economies is also assumed to just fulfill the needs of maintenance of workforce/manpower required for operating the production process. The stationary economy/business shows no expansion of output. It is also closed to outside world. It just reproduces itself year after year without any change taking place in quantum or structure of output of commodities produced within the economy. This is as if the economy is timeless, and hence, growth-less, since the passage of time does not leave any mark on an economy of this genre.

As against a self-replacing, self reliant and growth-less economy in a static or stationary state,[1] developed and developing or growing economies produce surpluses either for being retained as profits of enterprises, or for financing investment to raise capacity to produce greater output than before so as to meet temporally expanding demand for goods and services. In such economies and their buoyant phase all core variables such as consumption, investment, output and employment tend to grow in magnitude through time. Time itself enters the system as a variable in such dynamic states (Ragnar 1953, Hicks 1967). Variation in time is a feature of dynamic state. Growth and Development are thus major characteristics of the Dynamic State.

This study also distinguishes those growing economies, which generate profits only for retention by entrepreneurs from those which invest such profits in better technology, borrowed or indigenously developed, for imparting momentum to growth. It differentiates the factors that lead to: (i) growth of an advanced economy; and (ii) development of a developing economy. It also highlights the difference in growth and development based on technological changes involving replacement of production function with lower by higher productivity. It is implied that economic growth is the feature of developed economies, while development relates to developing economies of the world.

Historical Perspective

Growth is propelled by autonomously driven forces of the market In an open capitalist economy, entrepreneurs, traders, professionals and other agents are pivots as well as direct beneficiaries of growth. As against this, in a socialist and planned economy, benefits of growth may accrue largely to the people. But conceptual clarity is required in order to avoid confusing wood for the trees. Let us first explain the concepts of growth and its varied connotations. Similarly,

1. Solow imputed growth of productivity only to capital accumulation and technical progress both of which he postulated as the cause of shifts in production function. Technology is defined narrowly to overlook the contribution of human and intellectual capital to growth. Further, he disregards the role of twin factors of organisation and enterprise so greatly emphasised by Marshall (1890).

working out empirically relevant and logical definitions of economic progress and economic development are formulated in the study.

Growth

Growth has been defined differently by different thinkers, who emphasize one or the other aspect of the process and its causative factor(s). But growth is a process of deliberate and conscious, or autonomous change that involves time. Growth changes the current status of an economy and its business. It involves the evolving and use of new technology in the production of goods, number and nature of products, and process of production, or product designs. All these changes result in the rise of output/income both in absolute and relative terms. Therefore, growth embodies change in the production function rather than use of the same function for the production of higher output on a higher scale with the same production function but more amounts of inputs of the same quality may be used. Evolution/development of a new technology, process, new product or new design of current goods requires investment in R&D (Research and Development). R&D, in its turn, needs specialised infrastructure of research, institutional set up, highly specialised research–oriented manpower and other resources. Most of the developing countries do not have the quantity and quality of such resources, including manpower, required for inventions and innovations in general and development of advance technology in particular. So they depend upon imported technology, process, products and their designs. Induction of imported technology, however, involves substantial change in the currently prevalent production arrangements which directly and indirectly affects social, psychological, economic and other factors. The developing countries' capacity to absorb and use advance technology and changes required for its absorption in the business and economy is extremely limited. Absorption of these elements, associated with new technology, warrants radical transformation of institutional, organisational and social structures and managerial techniques (Shri Prakash and Balakrishnan 2005a, Mathur 1962). For example, if all self employed hand-loom weavers move to wage employment in organised mill sector where production is based on use of automatic looms in a given location, it will bring sea change in the life style, working conditions, income, transport, and financial infrastructure like banking, insurance etc. Such wide by ranging socio-economic changes and huge investment needed for fostering this process restricts induction and use of advance technology by the developing economies. Process of absorption and utilisation of imported technology to produce more quantities of goods and services in the economy is defined as economic development. But the indigenous development of advance technology and its commercial utilisation by developed economies is defined as economic growth. Economic growth occurs only in the developed countries of the world. The developed countries have the infrastructure, institutional and organisational base, greatly qualified R&D manpower and above all investment resources to initiate and develop the advance technology. It does not involve such wide-ranging economic, social and psychological changes as is the case with the developing economies. Inter-temporal rise in per capita income in developing countries is related to the process of Economic Development (Mathur 1962, also see Bhatia 1966 and Shri Prakash 1977). This distinction between economic development and economic growth is technology centric, which is narrow in its sweep and nature, though it takes into consideration the social and psychological changes involved in economic development. It is implicitly assumed that development and subsequent commercial utilisation of advance technology does not involve any social or psychological change in individual and institutional behaviour other than that pertaining to resources in developed countries. This is, however, belied by recent experience of high technology turnover occurring at much shorter intervals than ever before resulting in shorter life span of each technology. Such huge leaps in technology embody wide ranging effects on developed economies of the world also. For example, life-span of technologies of different vintages differs significantly. Replacement of old by new technology renders the technical know-how, skills and education profile, and hence, expertise and knowledge of currently available manpower redundant; many persons lose their jobs; re-training and redeployment involves huge resource cost both for individuals, institutions and society. Compulsory apprenticeship programme in Germany had been rendered obsolete by such rapid changes in technology. It may therefore be surmised that Mathur's hypothesis has been rendered empirically invalid by observed changes. Experiences are based on the nature of consequences of first, second and third industrial revolutions which stand testimony to the above inference.

This study overlooks this conceptual difference between growth and development. Development involves large scale changes in social, economic, institutional structures for absorbing and utilising imported technology. The manpower requirements of the operations of new technology are totally different from those of traditional technology. Even lifestyles of those, who move from self employment to wage employment in industrial units, change radically. This brings psychological, social, and economic transformation in the lives of the people involved in such process of change.

The general conception of growth recognises the fact that investment is its main propellant. Growth operates on two pillars: first is consumption multiplier and second is investment accelerator. Investment is of two types: autonomous and induced. Current consumption expenditure induces producers to raise output/supply during the next period which warrants investment in capacity creation (fixed capital) and its utilisation (working capital). Both capacity creation and its utilisation activates backward linkages to induce growth of output of inputs used in the production of consumption goods on the one hand, and generates additional employment, and hence, income on the other. Thus, current consumption expenditure results in increase in income which is a multiple of consumption expenditure. One part of incremental income induces more consumption which propels secondary multiplier process, while other part is invested, which activates investment accelerator. As marginal propensity to consume is less than one, additional income emanating from multiplier process tends to decline from one to another round of income generation from initial consumption expenditure. This is the reason why Finance Minister of India raised exemption limit from income tax of that part of income which is invested in designated savings instruments from ₹1 lakh to ₹2 lakh with a view to leave larger income in the hands of households for spending.

But economists of 18th century did not distinguish between growth and development. Connotations of both these terms referred to greater output than before. For example, the title of the book of Adam Smith, *Nature and Causes of Wealth of Nations* itself suggests that development/growth refers to creation of more wealth, which necessitated the identification and the utilisation of factors of production. Creation of more wealth was envisaged to be related to more and more investment in industries which have had greater potential of wealth creation. Factors have to be deployed to sectors where the productivity was higher. Wealth in Smith's conceptualisation emerged both as the cause and consequence of rising incomes. Subsequent economic analysis also focused on the means and ways of mobilising and utilising such factors of production as land, labour and capital for the maximisation of their output. Raw materials and intermediate inputs were probably treated as part of working capital. Thus, the mobilising and utilising more resources was considered to hold the key to development associated as it was with production of more output/income. Resource extension or factor multiplication was hypothesised to be the pivot of growth/development. Production was hypothesised to depend mainly upon the factors of production. Smith's analysis was greatly enriched and extended rigourously in a more comprehensive manner by Ricardo. Ricardo also incorporated agriculture and international trade into focus as possible contributors to growth though industry still remained the main driver of growth in his analytical framework. Limited supply of land and its marked fertility differentials made agricultural production to remain in the domain of diminishing output per unit of factor inputs unless methods of production improved. This limited the role and contribution of agriculture to growth. International trade, by implication, has had also very limited role to play in growth since the volume and composition of trade depended on comparative cost advantage in production. As against this, industry was envisaged to be subject to falling rate of profits in the long run; and investment revolves round the returns or profits it fetches. In the short-run, industrial investment yielded greater returns than the returns yielded by investment in agriculture. Comparative cost advantage was also associated largely with industrial rather than agriculture goods. The classical thought on growth revolved round the insights of these pioneers.

The move away from classical supply side economics occurred with the emergence of utility school of thought which emphasised demand as the propeller of all activities, including economic growth. Emergence of Marshall signaled the attempt at synthesis of classical and utilitarian thoughts. Marshall also incorporated organisation and enterprise as separate factors of production, and hence, growth. He explicitly recognised the importance of investment in man as distinct from investment in physical capital. In this process, he highlighted the roles of investment in (a) education and training, (b) health, (c) child bearing and rearing, and (d) migration in economic growth (Marshall 1890/1963 and Shri Prakash 1996).

The consensus that income, and/or per capita income may be treated as the index of growth emerged among the economists in the evolution of theory of economic growth. This came to be challenged for the first time by economists like Adleman (1967). Kenneth E. Boulding (1966) also opined that

> As technology did not change, and hence, remained constant for a prolonged period after the first industrial revolution, it was assumed as given exogenously. The production function, based on invariant technology, remained implicit in above conceptualization of development; improvement in methods of production had not been envisaged to raise output. But the assumption of invariance of technology was not valid when pre-industrial revolution economy shifted from its primitive production function to one based on post industrial revolution technology.

Movement from manual to mechanical processes, associated with the technology of first industrial revolution, involved a technological leap forward at that time. Subsequently, it had settled down at a stable level. In the then state of know-how, the technology and hence, methods of production were, therefore, assumed invariant. Conceptually, focus was on 'economic progress' rather than 'growth and/or development'. Term 'economic progress' in the sense of growth/development was used probably for the first time by Colin Clark (1954) in his book titled *Conditions of Economic Progress*. He postulated economic progress to revolve around investment in industries which results in industrial capital.

Second industrial revolution, which involved a movement away from mechanical to autonomous processes of production, again had a technological leap forward; it resulted in gigantic transformation of operational scales. Besides, replacement of erstwhile technology by more advance modern technology of production resulted in new designs and structure of previously produced goods, several of which were also replaced by new products and several totally new products were also produced. This raised the range of products available to consumers exponentially and new intermediate goods were also produced for the production of such new goods for the first time in the world economy (for changing number and designs of products etc, See, Shri Prakash 2010). Above discussion exemplifies the fact of non-shifting production function before the change in technology and shifting production function between the periods of change in technology resulting from two industrial revolutions. The shift of production function involved a quantum jump from the technology embodied in the mechanical processes. This technological leap forward took slightly more than two and a quarter centuries, a much shorter period than that involved in the occurrence of first industrial revolution. The third industrial revolution, based on micro-chips, occurred even in a shorter period than the period involved in first and second revolutions. The third industrial revolution embodied a movement away from automated to digital processes of production. In today's knowledge economy, there is a high degree of convergence in so far as one single product can embody services of two or more than two IT based production technology and multiple uses of its outcomes. In the modern knowledge economy, production based on modern technology involves processing of information and knowledge rather than materials. These changes again represent a technological quantum jump. Conceptually, changes involved in the development of technologies are associated both with growth and development rather than progress (Shri Prakash 1977). Economic progress stands for more of the same things which are produced in the same way as before. It involves invariant technology, number and quality of inputs, number of units of the same quality as produced before. Economic progress falls in the domain of factor multiplication process of production of greater output from the use of more quantities of same inputs processed by the same processes of production as before. This involves no change in production function.

Growth and Concealment of Micro Effects of Trade Cycles

Growth has been materialising in the midst of trade cycles and as a part and consequence of trade cycles. Growth had largely been a subject of macroeconomic analysis. Consequently, progress, growth and development have traditionally been treated to be in the domain of macroeconomics. This has pushed micro facets of business and economy and consequences of business cycles on micro units into oblivion. However, expansion of economies/business may be conceived as an outcome of growth and development of the individual sectors, industries, enterprises and companies within them. Growth and development of macro entities pertain to aggregates or averages and their indices, manifesting performance of all the constituents units of the macro aggregates but not the performance of individual units. Macro analysis focuses on aggregates and averages, overlooking the constituents and their structural features altogether.

Progress, growth and development are invariably associated with change in general and change in national output or per capita income in particular (see for example, Viner 1958, Denniso 1962). As against macro analysis, micro analysis focuses on individual entities, their decisions/behaviour and their consequences. Consequences emanate from performance, productivity and operational efficiency of individual entities. Therefore, production depends on: (a) quantity and quality of factor inputs, including human and physical capital, intellectual/knowledge capital, and (b) technology. Capital in this study is distinguished into physical, human and intellectual/knowledge capital. Institutional set up, organisational behaviour and managerial techniques/practices/expertise may be treated as institutionalised part of knowledge capital. However, the analytical apparatus generally used in analysis and the focus that emerges thereof treat these as if these were irrelevant or disjoint. This is not really the case. This leads the conceptual and operational distinctions to be blurred.

This study is an attempt to rectify the above analytical focus by proposing an integrated and synthesised conceptual framework of analysis based on managerial approach. This is in contrast to the fact that both growth and development have been an exclusive analytical concern of economists, though the management of resources, organisation of business enterprises in the economy plays an equally crucial role both in growth and development. This approach combines the paradigms of economic theory, authors' own analytical perspective and managerial orientation.

Shift of Focus

Development and growth have been among the important concerns of economists and policy makers since the times of Smith and Ricardo, irrespective of social and political structure or development status of the world economy or its national constituents. There has been a resurgence of interest in these subjects in the post Second World War period. Almost all the colonial countries got political independence and set themselves on the development path during this period. Cold War rivalry between the Eastern and Western blocs prompted developed countries to provide Liberal Aid for Development to the third world. Reconstruction of the war ravaged and damaged economies of the West and East European countries on the one hand, and Japan on the other also emerged as the top priority. Comecon, under the leadership of erstwhile USSR, helped Eastern Europe, while US, under Marshall Plan, facilitated the reconstruction of Western Europe and Japan. Development and growth naturally emerged as the pivotal theme of both analysis and policy during this period (Shri Prakash 1995).

Progress, Growth and Development- Formal Concepts

These terms have generally been used synonymously though the nature, dimension and structure of change may differ from progress to growth and growth to development. Classical economists used the term "economic progress" for growth. Colin Clark (1954) seems to have formalised the concept of economic progress.

Progress

Progress connotes 'more of the same by the same process'. Economic progress of an economy involves production of more quantities of the same commodities by the use of increased quantities of the same factor inputs of given quality with the same technology. Increased output is the result of Factor Multiplication, when the economy operates with invariant production function over time; only scales of operation change. In most of such cases, output increases in proportion to the increase in factor inputs, if economies of scale are not realised and production takes place under constant returns to scale. Such facets as quality of factors, organisational structure and behaviour, institutional set up and managerial techniques remain unchanged; finite quantity of inputs can be transformed only into finite quantity of output. It is assumed that something cannot be produced with nothing used in production as input(s). Nothing can be produced with zero inputs. So, more factor inputs are required to produce more output. Change in operational scales is, however, compatible with production taking place under constant, increasing or decreasing returns to scale despite the technological invariance of production function. The constancy of production function need not necessarily be associated with the constancy of structure, that is, the technical coefficients or factor inputs required per unit of output. This is usually assumed in economic analysis. Increased output under this process results from an expansion of productive capacity, associated with higher operational scales, using increased quantities of the same factor inputs with the constant: a) technology, b) organisational behaviour, c) managerial techniques, d) quality of inputs, and e) technical features of the goods produced. Both the developed and developing countries can move along the path of progress during the expansionary phases of unchanging technology and other factors associated with it.

Development and Growth

Development is, however, defined as a process of technological transformation of an economy (Mathur 1962). It involves a choice of technology from the technologies available from the developed countries, relative to resource base of the under-developed economy under consideration at a given point in time. The objective may be to determine the most efficient path of transformation for moving the economy from less to more efficient technology. The choice of endogenously developed or imported technology for use in production basically distinguishes the developing from developed countries on the one hand, and growth from development on the other. Developing countries can draw upon the stock of superior technologies, already developed and used by the developed countries. A developed country spends huge amount of resources on R&D to develop technology for itself for subsequent use in production. As it already uses the next best/advanced technology comparable to those already available and used for production by itself or other developed economies, it does not have any ready stock of more advanced technology to choose from. It has to create it. But the developing countries generally import technology from the developed world and then adapt the same to suit indigenous conditions. For example, adaptation may involve the tropicalisation of imported machinery and equipment to suit the Indian/Tanzanian conditions. Such technology may not be in tune with the resource endowment of the importing country, organisational structures, managerial techniques and socio-economic infrastructural base, though the technology may be on the verge of obsolescence in the parent country (Mathur, 2000). Imported technology from the developed world is generally capital intensive and labour displacing, which may not suit the factor endowment of importing (developing) country.

The process of consistent and continuous rise in income/per capita income of developing economies has been defined as economic development by Hicks (1967) as distinguished from economic growth. She points out that the problem that developing countries faced is the problem of development and utilisation of the unused resources they have, though the uses of such resources are well known as these resources have already been utilised by developed countries. As against this, growth relates to developed countries. Hicks somehow fails to recognise the differences between: (a) optimum and sub-optimum utilisation of known resources; and (b) efficient and non-efficient utilisation of resources; and (c) unknown resources which remain to be explored and discovered. Besides, economic use and the way of the utilisation of some of the known resources may be unknown to the developing economies. Hicks differs from Mathur on these counts.

Arthur Lewis and Report of UN Expert Group considered increase in per capita income/output as *sine qua non* of economic development. According to Lewis (1958), 'growth of output per head of population' is the essence of economic development. Jacob Viner also postulated that 'an economy which can maintain its current population on a rising standard of living, or the rising population can be maintained on the current standard of living' may be defined as the developing economy. Thus, Viner considers current capacity and/or potential capacity of an economy as the indicator of under-development. However, there is a logical fallacy supported by empirical evidence in so far as all the developed economies can maintain their current populations on rising standard as well as maintain rising populations on current standard of living. Thus, the distinction between developed and developing economies is blurred. But two important points emerge from Viner's proposition: (a) standard of living is the criterion of development or under-development; and (b) current or future population eliminates the need for consideration of per capita output. But output/income still remains the indicator of development.

The view that per capita output/income is the indicator of development has been challenged by several economists. For example, Frankel (1952) called the view of UN Experts as fallacious, though the view of Frankel has also been contested vehemently by those who support the views of Lewis and UN Experts. Sustainable growth revolves round increase in factor productivity over time; it also takes care of population size and its age and gender composition.

Capital and Economic Change

Technology is the key to modern growth and development. The process by which more output is raised with the same/lesser factor inputs of better quality and an advanced technology involves Factor Transformation (Barewald 1969, Mathur 1962). The process makes the production function shift to the right. Evolving a technology requires research and develop ment. Research may be original or repetitive, imitative and adaptive, including reverse engineering. Non-original, repetitive or imitative or adaptive research is generally undertaken by third world. Technology creation requires original research, which precedes development. The twin processes of technology creation and technology adoption for commercial exploitation (development) may be defined as the process of economic growth (Bhatia 1966). Generally, in the advanced countries, technology creation does not require the creation of R&D human resources, infrastructure, institutional base, organisational setup and managerial expertise, since these have already been in place. These are required as essential and enabling factors both for (a) R&D; and (b) use of new technology, emanating from R&D, in actual production of commodities. Growth may, therefore, involve only marginal changes in economic and other infrastructure. Social and organisational structure and institutional setup may also not warrant large-scale changes. Development would, however, involve the wholesale changes in R&D base, infrastructure, institutional setup, managerial skills and organisational structures. All these changes will warrant the knowledge and know-how of new managerial techniques required for implementation of programme of technology development and its subsequent utilisation. Growth and development, therefore, need management approach and a broader orientation for analysis (Shri Prakash and Balakrishnan 2005a).

Progress does not require research. But both growth and development need R&D. Growth and development are techno-centric. Progress is technology neutral. Physical, human and knowledge capital and outcomes of their use play the pivotal role in growth and development. But understanding of the connotations and nature of different types of capital and different technologies that each type of capital carries requires clarity.

Concept of Capital

The term capital is usually used both in 'real' and financial sense. Capital in real sense refers to machinery and equipment, infrastructure and inventories of factors of production and materials. Real or physical capital produces goods and services or creates value by the use of factor inputs. However, physical (or hard) capital is distinguished from non-physical (or white/soft) technology as well as the human capital, which is embodied in manpower, who develops and uses physical capital and technology embodied within it. Physical (hard) technology is embodied in the physical capital, that is, machinery, equipment/plants, tools and buildings. The non-physical or white technology is embodied in human capital in the form of skills, knowledge, and information, know-how and other human capabilities, that are reflected in organisational behaviour and managerial techniques. Knowledge capital is partially a part of human capital and partially a part of institutional and organisational structure and behaviour. Human capital is needed to develop and to use physical technology, whereas knowledge capital is required both to develop and operate the physical and human capital. Human and intellectual capital are the carriers of white/soft technology which, in combination with physical technology, leads to the production operations, and hence, factor productivity. In fact, hard technology can deliver nothing without soft technology. Knowledge or intellectual capital produces new 'intellectual property/capital' (Shri Prakash and Sharma 2005).

Growth Accounting and Human Capital

The neo classical approach to growth accounting is based on the concept of 'residual'. Residual is net of sum of increase in quantities of labour and capital used in production. The residual has empirically been found to be quite substantial. Change in output due to a change in quantity of labour and physical capital without change in technology, however, manifests progress of output of the same goods of the same quality. Estimated residual by the above approach to evaluate sources of growth is accounted mainly by human and knowledge capital. The residual manifests the consequences of operation of the process of growth or development which embodies the contribution of human and knowledge capital. This is over and above the contribution of technology.

However, Abramovitz (1962), Solow (1957) and Kendrick (1961) focused on hard technology as an instrument of raising productivity. Hence, they attributed residual to improvements in hard technology used in production. But Vakil and Brahamananda (1953), Dennison (1962) and Schultz (1959) focused on human capital as the major contributor to growth and development. The centrality of technology in growth and development thus yielded place to human capital and its skills and knowledge. This has shifted the emphasis from physical to human capital, institutional set up, organisational behaviour and managerial practices as instruments of transformation of factor inputs to yield higher output per unit than before. Therefore, productivity impacts growth directly. Transformation of input-output relations is no more conceptualised to revolve around development of physical technology alone. Intellectual and human capital play the pivotal role in transforming input-output relations. Technology creation and its adaptation/adoption for growth or development have the knowledge and skills as its main drivers. Findings of Shri Prakash and Balakrishnan (2008) lend empirical support to the above thesis, they found that the growth of most of the sectors of Indian economy has largely been the outcome of the growth of productivity. But growth of productivity is accounted more by intellectual and human capital than technology. Adoption of advance technology needs to be supported by human capital endowment with knowledge, skills and expertise on the one hand, and institutional set up, organisational structure, improved managerial techniques and the mindset of people on the other. Thus, technological transformation warrants a comprehensive chain of changes for development. In case of growth, changes in these facets/variables are, however, marginal or add-ons to the existing stock.

Interestingly, population has been viewed as a drag on development of developing economies all through the 1950s to 1970s. But going by Adam Smith's dictum that "growth is limited by the size of the market" and market size is essentially derived from population size and its purchasing power. Population size has now emerged as a positive factor of development. Population size and purchasing power endowment of India and China have now made them major destinations of FDI (foreign direct investment). But age, gender and knowledge endowment of population are also important.

Consumption and Investment as Base of Growth

Consumption multiplier process of growth is activated through the 'residentiary linkage' (Shri Prakash 1992). Larger the size of the market, greater shall be the growth effect of consumption multiplier. Induced investment based acceleration imparts further impetus to growth initiated by consumption multiplier. Multiplier effect on growth has been found to last as long as 17 rounds even if the accelerator effect on growth emanating from multiplier growth of income is overlooked (Shri Prakash and Sharma 2013a, b).

Accelerator operates through dynamic backward and forward linkages (Hirschman 1957, Shri Prakash 1992). Population constitutes the base of human resources; population constitutes the supply pool of human resources and human capital (Shri Prakash 2000). Effective exploitation of human resources (needing transformation into human capital) depends on the opportunities for its productive deployment, structure of organisation, institutional set up and managerial techniques in use. Information, knowledge and skills and their management have, therefore, emerged among the core factors of modern development and growth.

Diagramtic Representation

The typology of resources and capital along with their core concepts, discussed above, may be converted into a flow chart/figure. Figure 4.1 portrays the classification of resources into different typology.

It has been highlighted that progress, growth and development have change as a common core feature. Economic change may result either from factor multiplication or factor transformation process (Barewald 1969). Factor multiplication process is essentially associated with 'progress' and it operates if the technology of production, quality of output and quality of factor inputs remain constant. It means that production function is invariant. But returns to scale in production depend essentially upon technology in use, its operational level and above all factors-mix. Organisational behaviour, institutional set up and management practices also affect the returns to scale in production greatly. The last three factors have been consistently overlooked in the discussion of production possibilities and growth of output in economics. Ricardo is an exception to this.

Figure 4.1

Types of Change in Output and Returns to Scale

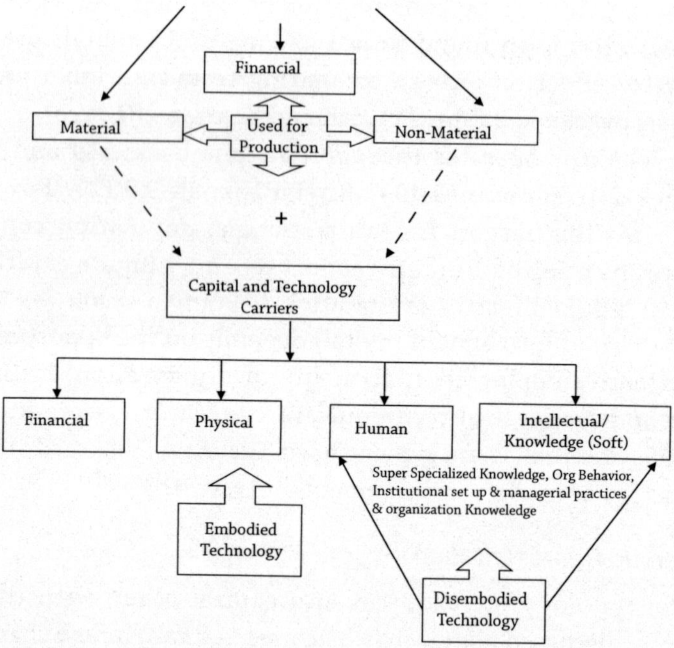

Source: Authors' own construction.

Constant/Diminishing Returns to Scale

Constant or diminishing returns to scale may obtain if technology, institutional set up, organisational structure and management techniques remain constant. Factor inputs are combined optimally under constant returns to scale; but inputs are combined sub-optimally under diminishing returns to scale. Thus, optimal or sub-optimal utilisation of factor inputs results in increase in output at constant or diminishing rate, though production function remains the same in such cases. Under factor multiplication process, factor productivity will, therefore, either be constant or decline, depending upon whether production takes place under constant or diminishing returns.

Increasing Returns to Scale

Increasing returns to scale may obtain under alternative scenarios even while technology remains constant; these scenarios are listed below:

(i) Managerial techniques, institutional set up and technology remain constant, while improvement in organisational/behavioural parameters like structure or culture or work environment facilitate the realisation of increasing returns;

(ii) Institutional set up and organisational behaviour remains the same, but improvement in managerial techniques facilitates the realisation of increasing returns to scale.

(iii) Managerial techniques and organisational behaviour remain the same, while improvement in institutional setup and support for workforce facilitates the realisation of increasing returns to scale.

(iv) If institutional support, organisational behaviour and managerial practices improve together, increasing returns would be much more pronounced even under constant technology.

Scarcity of resources and limits to improvement in all these cases will constrain the factor multiplication process of growth. Scarcity of resources has always existed and would always exist in future also. Progress through factor multiplication process will, therefore, always be limited and it may not be sustained forever due to these constraints. Therefore, the alternate route to growth and development is through factor transformation process for overcoming resource constraints and limits to improvement. Factor transformation process is techno-centric; it uses less quantity of better quality factor inputs, including human/intellectual capital to produce more output from same quantities of factor inputs. Factor transformation hinges both upon hard and soft technology. Therefore, techno-centrity has a wider connotation to include both soft and hard technology and know-how to do how. Naturally, output per unit of factor inputs tends to increase under factor transformation process more rapidly than under factor multiplication process. This results is a rise in total factor (aggregate) productivity.

Development of new technology requires high quality manpower for research and development, expensive and extensive infrastructure and other research facilities. Availability of high quality R&D manpower with requisite research facilities makes the development of technology and its market exploration feasible. Besides the above, advanced technology needs high quality manpower for its operation also. Advancement of physical technology augments the production capability of human and other resources on the one hand, while utilisation of higher level and quality of knowledge and skills endowment of manpower and better production facilities needed for such technology enhances the system's efficiency and resource productivity on the other. Consequently, quality of factor inputs cannot remain constant. Factor Transformation occurs essentially through Technological Change and Quality up-gradation of factor inputs (Mathur 1962, also see, Sharma 2012).[2] These two factors together augment the capability of factors to produce greater output with lesser amounts of inputs.

Alternative Operational Modes of Advance Technology

The preceding paragraphs highlight the role of factors other than hard technology in growth/development. However, advance technology may be combined with improvement in organisational behaviour, institutional set up and more efficient managerial techniques, all of which are embodied in human/intellectual capital. These alternative ways are listed hereunder:

2. Mathur considered movement from less to more efficient technology as the means to development. We, however, consider improvement in quality of other factor inputs, specially human capital, including intellectual capital, managerial and organisational inputs to be as much, if not more, important than technology carried forward by physical capital and embodied in machinery/plant and equipment.

(i) Institutional set up, managerial techniques and behavioural parameters of the organisations remain constant, but technology and quality of other factor inputs are improved to change the values of input-output coefficients or relations.

(ii) Managerial techniques change along with technology and the quality of factor inputs, while organisational and institutional set up remain unchanged.

(iii) Managerial techniques remain the same, while technology, quality of factor inputs, institutional set up and organisational behaviour change.

(iv) Changes in technology and quality of factor inputs are combined with improvement in organisational behaviour, especially processes of decision making, institutional set up and managerial practices.

Like the quality of factor inputs, organisation, institutional setup and managerial techniques also change with technology. All these four cases lead to the realisation of increasing returns to scale. However, the degree of proportionate increase in increasing returns to scale becomes more pronounced from first and last cases. Factor Transformation can *ipso facto* be associated either with growth or development.

Types of above changes are neither in a time continuum nor in a temporal vacuum; these changes are also not free from spatial dimension; such changes are neither nominal nor marginal. These changes are discrete and quite substantive. In fact, more often than not these changes may be catastrophic or even chaotic in mathematical sense. The chaotic or catastrophic nature of change is revealed by the response to or outcome of change. The substantially high value of cumulative outcomes, induced by change, is an indicator of catastrophic nature of change. Chaotic and/or catastrophic changes are not amenable to marginal analysis. Once changes have started occurring, these continue to occur for some time and become cumulative till the plateau is reached. It is, therefore, possible to combine above cases either with optimal or sub optimal factor utilisation which may result in constant and/or differential degrees of diminishing or increasing returns to scale. Varying nature of change, explained above, is shown in Figure 4.2.

Figure 4.2

Change and Variables Associated with Factor Inputs

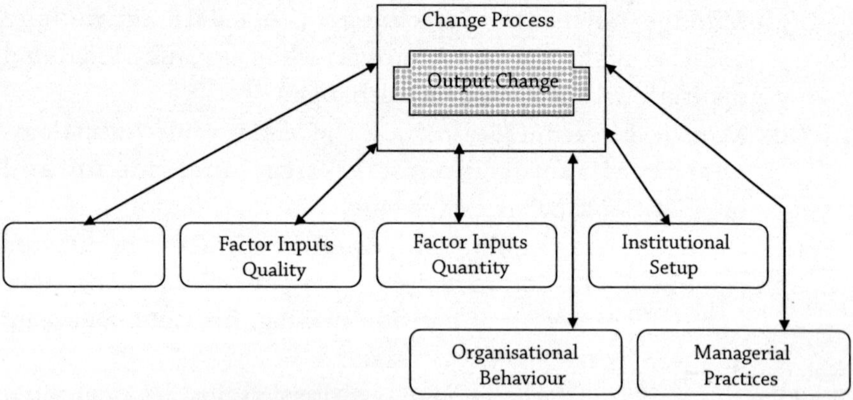

Source: Authors' own construction.

Figure 4.2 displays all possible causes/factors of change in output. Possible combinations of these factors in different ways may lead either to the occurrence of (i) progress; or (ii) growth; or (iii) Development.

The pattern and inter-relations of different factors under the process of (i) progress; (ii) growth; and (iii) development have been depicted in Figure 4.3.

Last box under the heading 'progress' implies that output may rise purely in response to (i) an increase in factor inputs, or (ii) change in one, two or all three elements of intellectual capital. Such changes have to be internalised within the company/industry or the economy as a whole. Economy comprises industries and industries comprise companies or firms. So, the process of change may move from down below to above, or from top to down below.

Various factors, their interrelations and combinations and the resultant consequences, involved in economic progress have been shown in Figure 4.4.

Various factors, their interrelations and combinations and the resultant consequences of economic growth have been shown in Figure 4.5.

Figure 4.3

Typology of Change in Progress, Growth and Development

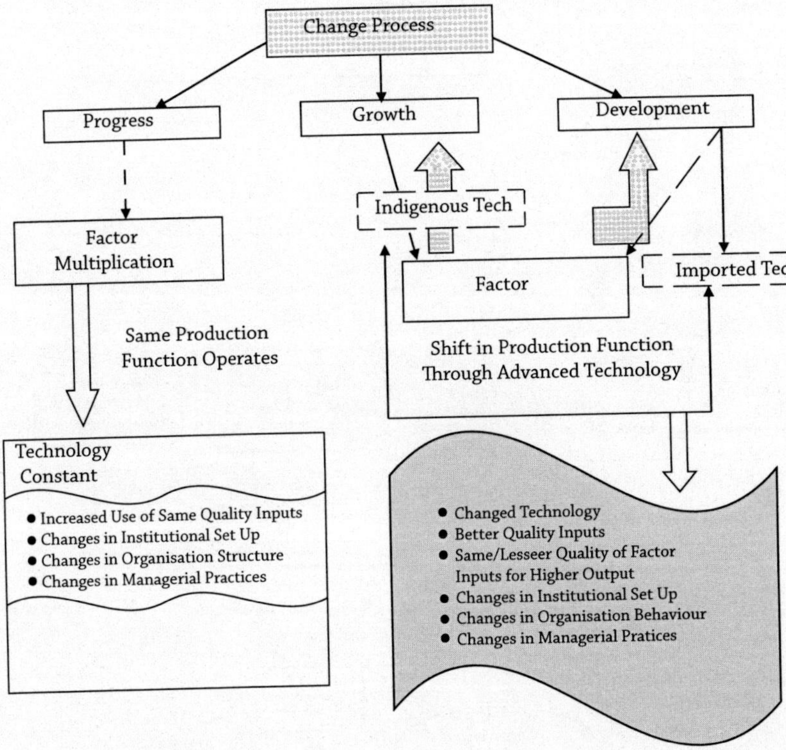

Source: Authors' own construction.

Various factors, their interrelations and combinations and their resultant consequences of economic development have been shown in Figure 4.6.

It is obvious that the nature of production function and its shifts play a pivotal role in all the three processes of progress, growth and development. The overall but comprehensive view of the production function, nature and causes of its shift and the consequences that flow from its shift are displayed by Figure 4.7.

Figure 4.4

Change Process and Economic Progress

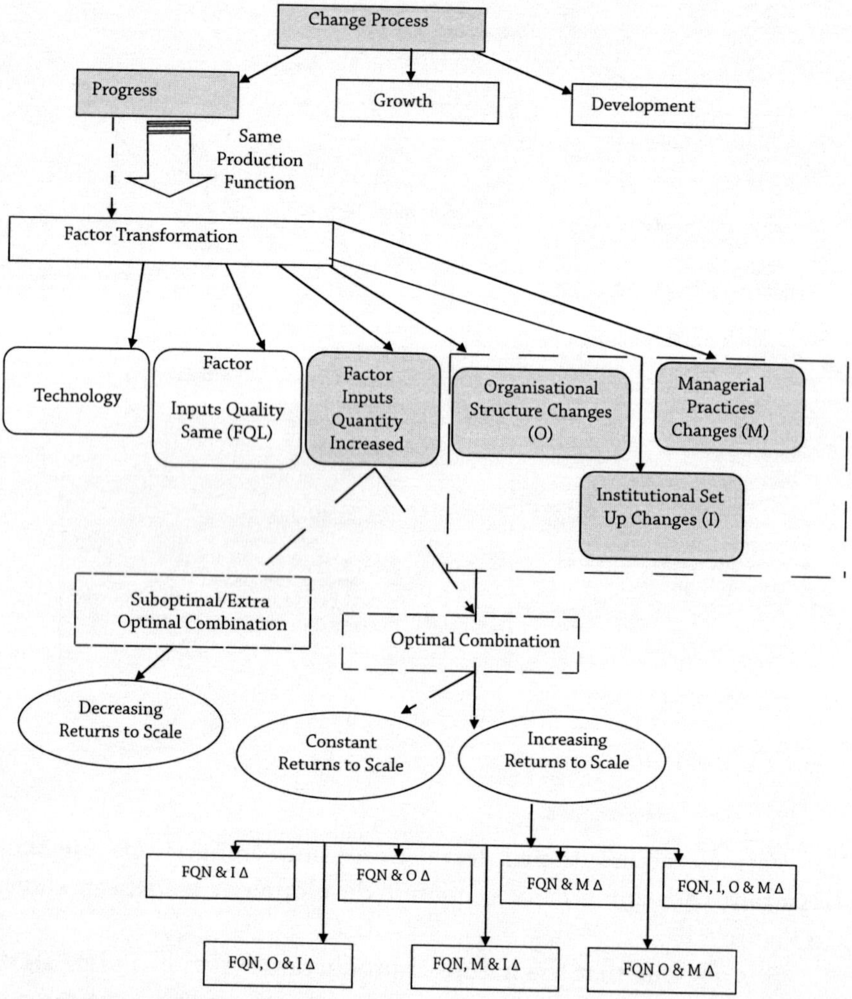

*Note:*FQN: Factor Quantity.

Source: Authors' own construction.

Figure 4.5

Change Process and Economic Growth

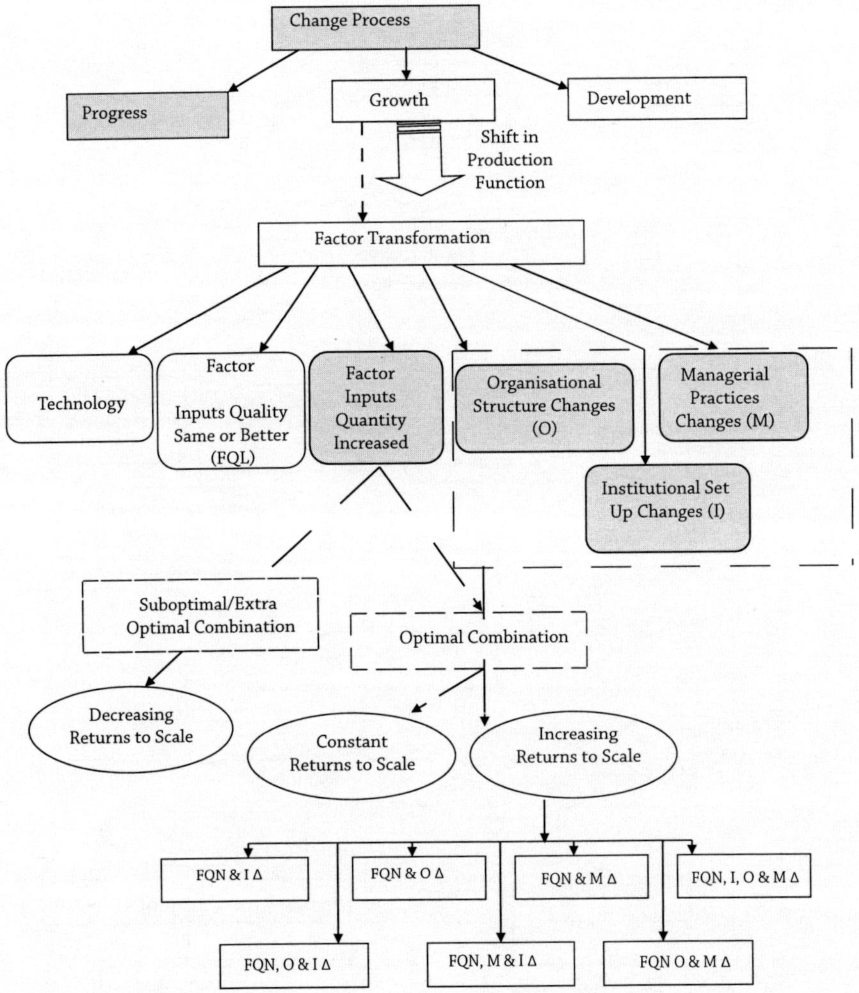

Source: Authors' own construction.

Figure 4.6

Change Process and Development

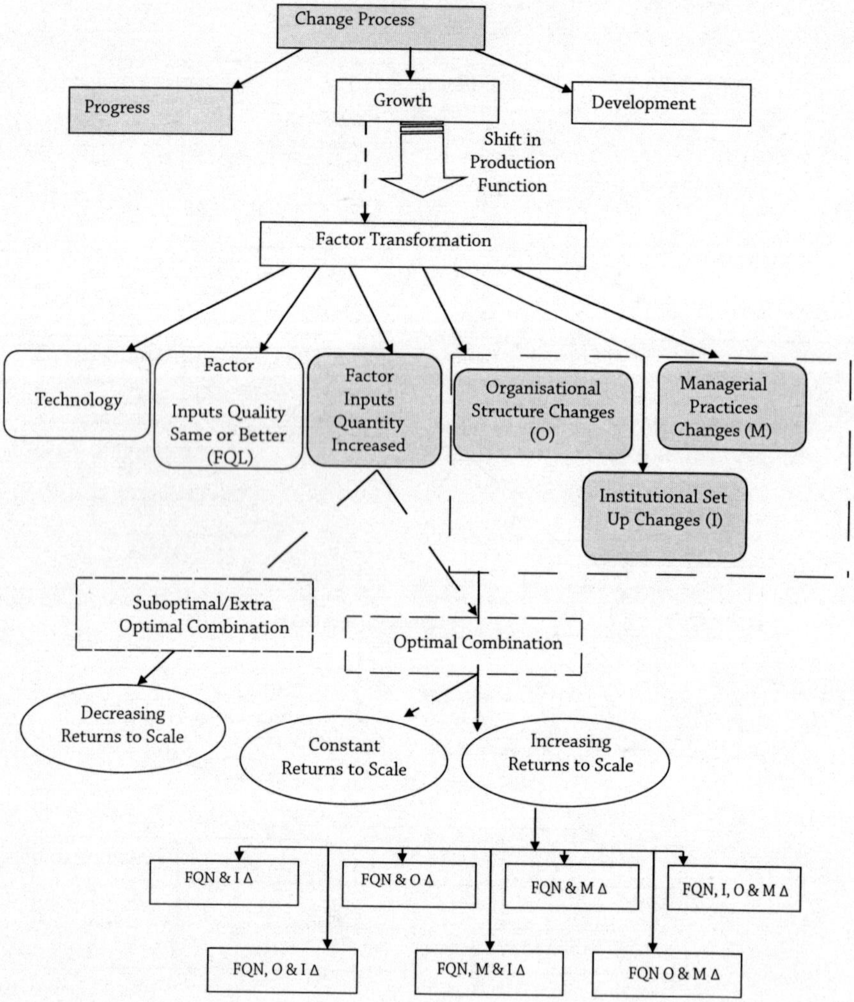

Source: Authors' own construction.

Figure 4.7

Economic Change and Production Function

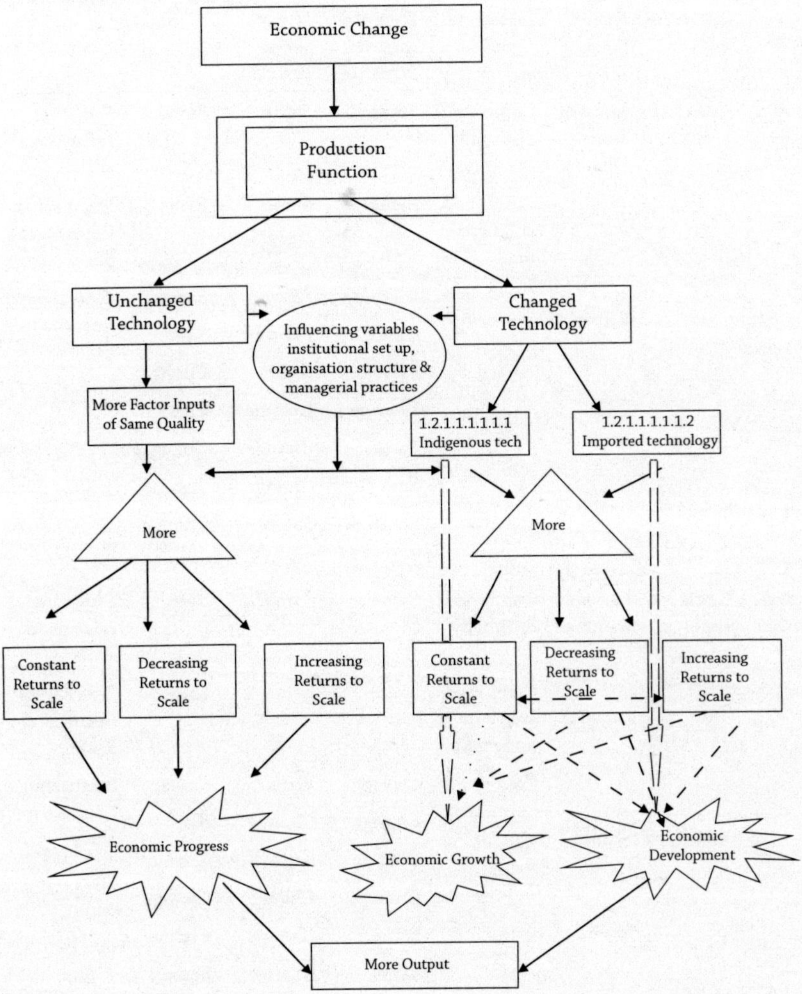

Source: Authors' own construction.

Table 4.1

Types of Change Processes, their Organic Structure, Causes and Consequences

	Technology	*Factor inputs*	*Institutional Set up*	*Organisational Structure*	*Managerial Practices*	*Returns to Scale*	
Economic Progress	Constant	More of Same Quality	Combined optimally	Same	Same	Same	Constant returns to scale
			Combined sub Optimally	Same	Same	Same	Decreasing Returns to Scale
			Combined optimally	Change	Same	Same	Increasing Returns to Scale
				Change	Change	Same	
				Change	Same	Change	
				Change	Change	Change	
				Same	Change	Change	
				Same	Change	Same	
				Same	Same	Change	
Changing							
Economic Growth	Using Indigenous Technology	Less of Same Quality	Combined optimally	Same	Same	Same	Constant returns to scale
			Combined sub-optimally	Same	Same	Same	Decreasing Returns to Scale
			Combined optimally	Change	Same	Same	Increasing Returns to Scale
				Change	Change	Same	
				Change	Same	Change	
				Change	Change	Change	
				Same	Change	Change	
				Same	Change	Same	
				Same	Same	Change	

contd...

contd.

Economic Devlop-ment	Im-ported	Less of Same Quality	Combined optimally	Same	Same	Same	Constant returns to scale
			Combined sub Opti-mally	Same	Same	Same	Decreasing Returns to Scale
			Combined optimally	Change	Same	Same	Increasing Returns to Scale
				Change	Change	Same	
				Change	Same	Change	
				Change	Change	Change	
				Same	Change	Change	
				Same	Change	Same	
				Same	Same	Change	

Source: Authors' own construction.

Convergence of Macro to Micro Entities

Conventionally, production function has been defined as a technical relation between quantities of various factor inputs and the quantity of output yielded by the use of these factor inputs. Production function signals the engineering process whereby all conceivable combinations of factor inputs are converted into the maximum achievable output of the same (quality) good (Shri Prakash 1996). Aggregating various inputs and heterogeneous outputs into volume related variable(s) facilitates the extension of production function "beyond a single production line to cover a plant, a firm, or even an industry" (Intriligator 1980). Then, aggregation over products, firms and industries furnishes the macroeconomic production function on the basis of the same logic. Aggregation may be based on the assumption that: (i) the coefficients of labour and capital inputs do not vary between micro units of production though the values of labour and capital do vary between production units. It implies the neutrality of coefficients to greater or smaller values of inputs; (ii) inputs of labour and capital do not differ between production units but the coefficients do vary. The factor inputs are then treated as weights. At the macro level, national product is taken as output, while total work force and total stock of capital in the economy are treated as factor inputs of production. In such cases, production function relates factor inputs to value added or output net of intermediate inputs used up in production. But the change in quality of either inputs or output or both has generally been overlooked. Thus, conventional analysis has focused generally on labour and capital as factor inputs. But the growth economists like Solow (technical change), Samuelson (surrogate production function), Kendrik (productivity) and others have brought technology directly or indirectly into focus in order to analyse and explain the process of growth. This puts production function, and hence, factor inputs in the centre stage of analysis of growth. In the growth accounting, after exhausting the growth of output attributable to expansion of inputs of two factors—labour and capital, a big chunk of output remains unexplained. Economists like Kendrik, Abramovitz and Solow attributed it to technology. But others just called it Residual Factor of Growth. Subsequently, attempts to identify the crucial determinant of growth led Schultz to hypothesise human capital, depending primarily upon investment in education, to be the leading factor of growth. Dennison followed Schultz's conceptual/theoretical framework to identify the contribution of investment in education to growth of GDP (42%) and per capita income (28%) in the US from 1901 to 1957. Shri Prakash and Buragohain's estimates showed that education accounted for 2 per cent in 1961 and it rose to about 4 per cent of total GDP of India in 1981. This share of education in (total) GDP is in contrast to the share of education in the growth of GDP/ per capita income of the US. In one of these approaches, investment in education and returns to it are postulated to be the contribution of education to total investment in economy and returns on it as the contribution to growth. Such analysis left entrepreneurial initiatives, innovations in managerial techniques and organisational behaviour beyond the scope of growth calculus in spite of Marshall's explicit recognition of organisation and enterprise as independent factors and management of resources as a pivotal factor of production. Subsequent generations of economists, supporting Marshall's viewpoint, incorporated these in production analysis though this was left out of the domain of production function. This study has attempted to fill up this gap. This study attempts to carry these theoretical paradigms and empirics of growth/development a step further by emphasising the role of managerial techniques, organisation, and human capital, including intellectual capital as core factors of growth.

Macroeconomic performance entails the analysis of policy issues, resource mobilisation, allocation and utilisation of goods for public activities. These facets of analysis have to integrate public finances, fiscal and monetary policies and their outcomes in analytical framework. Therefore, all above elements constitute the framework within which micro-units operate. In the market economies, production units at micro level make the basic operational decisions. In all these roles/functions, relative role of three types of capital, namely, Physical, Human and Intellectual/Knowledge capital is among the major determinants of output and its growth.

Reconstruction of war ravaged and damaged economies of Western Europe and Japan and their re-emergence as leaders of economic growth furnishes empirical evidence to support the above thesis. Despite the widespread physical destruction of the economies of Germany and Japan during the Second World War, their human and intellectual/knowledge capital remained, by and large, intact. They recorded spectacular growth in the Post Second War period, especially during the 1960s and 1970s. Besides, soft technology differentials explain why any two countries using same or similar technology and quantity of factors show variations in output, and differentials of cost and prices for the same quantity of output of given good/service of specified quality. Internal and external economic efficiencies, technology, transformation process through human/knowledge capital, quantity and composition of investment, all affect the industries' performance. Thus, macro performance is dependent on the performance of enterprises or micro units that constitute the macro entities. Role and importance of micro performance in macro growth may indirectly be inferred also from the fact that though the Indian five year development plans may be considered among the finest blueprints of development, yet actual performance consistently fell far short of expectations and targets due to the negligence of operational details at micro levels. The micro operational details depend upon: (a) organisational structure, (b) decision processes, (c) enterprise, and (d) management, especially the management of change.

Managerial Approach Distinct from Macroeconomic Approach

The proposition stated in the foregoing paragraphs that Factor Multiplication process is limited by the scarcity of resources and constraints to improvement in quality of factor inputs is empirically valid, especially in the developing economies. In India, supply of food grains (till the occurrence of Green Revolution), foreign exchange, professional manpower of requisite quality and capital had been among the major constraints all of which limited development. The way to overcome such constraints is through Factor Transformation, which is techno-human and intellectual capital-centric. Technological development in association with requisite quantity and quality of human and knowledge capital leads the process of factor transformation. The efficacy of this transformation depends both on 'hard' and 'soft' technology, embodied in physical, human and knowledge capital, organisational and institutional arrangements for effective and efficient use of all resources, and managerial practices for sustaining the process of growth and development. Benefits in terms of increasing returns to scale can be generated with the optimal utilisation of factor inputs, or with technological advancement and its quality associated with improvement in factor inputs.

Degree of increase in returns to scale would be dependent on the support for improvement in organisational structure and managerial techniques. In fact, each advancement in technology tends to displace labour and bring human and knowledge capital in its place partially or even fully, depending upon the nature and expanse of change embodied in new technology. As the quality of labour force and human capital improves, operational techniques of decision making and management need to be upgraded. This involves upgrading of skills and knowledge base of manpower (See, Shri Prakash 1977, Sharma 2012). When operational techniques change, networks of work-flows require modification and organisational restructuring for the performance of management functions is required. Job specifications, job descriptions and job analysis of changed work-design and its connectivity reflects change in the organisation design and its structure. Economic growth and development, therefore, have to be supported by improvement in the organisational and managerial capabilities. Thus, growth/development does depend upon labour and capital as much as on human, knowledge and intellectual capital.

Macroeconomic/econometric approach, which focused on growth and development on the basis of technological transformation and investment in factor inputs needs to be integrated into micro perspectives of sectors/industries and production units within sectors that account for economic growth and development of an economy at the grassroots. The importance of institutional support by way of corporate governance, infrastructure and stability of markets at macro level is as important as unit/industry/sector's own institutional support systems, organisational and managerial efficiency. Therefore, macro planning has to initiate support systems for micro efficiencies, while micro operations have to converge towards the realisation of macro goals.

Let us take the example of labour as factor input, a macro determinant of growth and development. The growth rate in size of labour is not matched by the growth of workers' participation, especially in the organised sector on the one hand, and skills and knowledge of manpower are not matched by those required on the job on the other (Prakash 1995). Employment scenario in India today indicates that 93 per cent of India's total employment is provided by informal sectors, while only a negligible 7 per cent of the total employment is provided by organised sectors. Employment in the informal sector has been growing far more rapidly than that in the organized sector due largely to growth of labour force and mismatch between education received and training for skill development received and the knowledge and skills required for the performance of the jobs. Emergence of tertiary sector as the leading sector of the economy has imparted its momentum to the growth of service providers, large, medium or small. But human and intellectual capital play a more dominant role than labour and capital in employment in tertiary activities, since the tertiary sectors are more knowledge intensive than others. An emerging feature is the sprouting of service activities in un-organised segment of the market. The non formal sector is not adequately supported either by the organisational or managerial capabilities, resulting in low productivity and decreasing economies of scales. Most of the employment in the informal sector can be attributed to the lack of employment opportunities in the organised sector[3]. Disappointed migrants from rural to urban areas initiate self-employment ventures, adding to the pool of informal employment. Given this scenario, the government has to set itself upon the task of organising the informal sector through cooperatives. The success of Prof Kurien in setting up Anand Cooperative, the Mumbai *Dabbawalas*, the setting up of '*Dastkar*' through the Crafts Council for marketing traditional handicrafts of India are examples for inspiring other such ventures.

There is a vibrant small sector also that needs the organisational and managerial support. Post globalisation, slightly more than 4 lakh small-scale industrial units were closed down. There is an urgent need to reorganise the millions of workers rendered idle on this account. Social entrepreneurship and their management models need to be introduced and supported with the training in managerial and organisational techniques. Initiation of unemployed/unused human resources into the growth process is the prime managerial challenge for the country today.

The organised sector in this globalised era has to rejuvenate the factor transformation process of growth with a view to acquire edge in competition both in terms of cost and quality. A new process of growth needs to be evolved and defined in order to bring about an indigenous development of technology. A comprehensive growth and development process, encompassing institutional, managerial and indigenous technology development, is necessary to activate factor transformation process in a comprehensive manner. Unfortunately, both the descriptive theories of growth (Clark 1954, Lewis 1958) and

3. For a detailed analysis of employment and growth in India, See Shri Prakash and Balakrishnan (2005, 2014) and Shri Prakash (2006).

other strands of growth theories and growth models have overlooked these factors of growth.

Conclusion

This conceptual framework will provide the clarity of thought and approach to Indian Corporate in formulating the strategic responses to global competition, growth, diversification, quality improvement and cost control. This view is in contrast to that of the classical economists, who discussed Economic Progress under non-shifting production functions. Neo-classical economists focused on technology as the production function shifter to be the pivot of growth or development. Analysts of both these streams of thought overlooked the role of organisation, management and enterprise as important factors of production and its growth, neglecting Marshall's emphasis on organisation and enterprise on the one hand, and modern emphasis on human and knowledge capital on the other. The study has attempted to partly fill up this gap by putting soft technology, embodied in human and intellectual capital in contradistinction to hard technology, embodied in machinery and plants, as the shifter of production function, and hence, as the prime mover of growth and development.

5

Economic Growth and Theory and Policy of Public Finance

Introduction

The chapter seeks answers to the following searching questions:

(i) What is public expenditure?

(ii) Is there a theory of public expenditure different from theory of public finance? What are the relations between public expenditure and public revenue and public debt?

(iii) What are the factors that account for the growth of public expenditure through time?

The following questions may also need explaining in the context of the above questions:

(i) Is there a relation between theory of economic growth and economic policy, including fiscal policy? Answer to this revolves round the basic ingredients of growth and policy.

(ii) Corollary of the above question is, 'what is the empirical relation between economic growth and public finances, including public expenditure? In other words, why and how does public expenditure affect economic growth?

The chapter seeks theoretical answers to the above questions. It also focuses on policy implications of expansion, direction and composition of public expenditure as a factor of economic growth and promotion of social welfare. The chapter, however, concentrates mainly on conceptual rather than empirical framework of the study.

Answers to first two questions are important in view of the fact that most of the countries of the third world, which got political independence after the end of Second World War, aspired to move out of the web of poverty, under-development and backwardness of their socio-economic systems at the time they got freedom from colonial rule. These countries attempted to develop their economies as rapidly as possible in order to catch up with their erstwhile colonial West European masters. The revolution of rising expectations of the masses even during the colonial rule had put leaders of independent third world countries under pressure to realise the goal of maximum rise in per capita income and standard of living of the masses in the shortest possible time. Naturally, the political leadership aspired to attain that level of economic development or growth of their economies in a few decades that had been attained by the developed countries in centuries that too by the extensive exploitation of resources of the colonies. The option of exploitation of the resources of other countries though colonisation was no more available to any country under the changed geo-political environment. It is noteworthy that the colonial rulers had successfully manipulated the international market for deriving the maximum economic benefits for economies of their respective countries. But this facet of manipulability of international market for the growth of developed countries through the exploitation of resources of the third world had been kept away from public gaze; this facilitated propagation of the ideology of capitalism (Mathur 1991). Meanwhile, USSR had furnished a model of rapid growth, which offered an attractive alternative to capitalist growth based on market mechanism. Consequently, many developing economies opted for planning as an instrument of not only rapid growth but also as the means to transform their social and institutional structure to suit their social, economic and political needs. Imperfections and consequent failure of free market have already been exposed during the Second World War; it has been recognised that the time involved in the response of the market to the emerging scenarios is extremely long and distorted, due to low and slow response rate. It has also been highlighted theoretically as well as empirically that industrialisation is the key to development of countries of the third world. Consequently, growth of these economies was sought through rapid industrialisation in general and development of heavy and basic goods industries in particular. This was an empirically observable fact then as it is now that the industrialised countries of the world were developed and levels of living of their people were much higher than those of the people of countries which depended largely on primary production (for example, see Myrdal 1955, 1968). Descriptive theory of economic growth, propounded by Lewis (1963), Clarke (1954), Ranis and Fei (1963) and supported by Singer (1989), Prebisch (1950), and validated empirically by Kuznets (1973) made this proposition highly attractive to newly independent countries of the third world. Spectacular success of USSR to match the economic might of great economic powers of the West in a period of few decades made Soviet model quite attractive to the leaders of the third world. Planning was chosen as the strategy of economic growth by several developing economies. But the developing economies faced severe shortages of capital and enterprise on the one hand, and educated and skilled manpower on the other. State has to shoulder the responsibility of not only initiating but also nurturing and sustaining economic development over a period of time (Shri Prakash 1995). Gigantic tasks of social development and economic growth could not have been left to the care of autonomously working forces of the market. In the first instance, market mechanism was not adequately and widely evolved in developing economies; failures of the market have been exposed quite prominently first by Great Depression, then by contemporary state of the world economy, demonstration of efficacy and effectiveness of development model of USSR, and prevalent political and economic paradigms taken together made planning as an attractive proposition of growth. Economic Structure of the third world countries was lopsided as these economies were dominated by primary production. Besides, low per capita income had restricted household savings and private investment to measly levels. Consequently, State had to shoulder the responsibility of mobilising public resources for investment in desired lines of production, offer the initiatives of state enterprise for growth and development. This has led to the emergence of public expenditure in general and public investment in particular in the centre stage of economic growth not only in the centrally planned economies of the Soviet Block but also in the developing countries.

Besides, the countries involved in the Second World War had also to use the machinery of State to mobilise men and materials for meeting urgent needs of War within the short span of time at hand. This has provided experience of enforcement of controls and regulation of economic activities to the administrative and political leaders of the West who had also recognised the limitations and infirmities of the market mechanism. Consequently, public expenditure has grown astronomically both during and post Second World War period. All these changes have also brought economic policy to the forefront of debate and discussion for formulation and subsequent implementation. It is not that concept and practical use of policy has not been known earlier. However, policy has emerged in an entirely new context.

Policy: Concept and Dichotomy

For explaining the meaning and nature of fiscal policy, concept of policy itself needs explanation. The context of discussion relates to public policy. Common sense meaning of policy refers to the broad framework containing specific rules of procedure to guide and regulate the decision making at macro level with a view to realise specific goals of public good. But public policy is a broad envelope which contains numerous policies relating to various fields of public and private activities both within and outside the country. But economic policy is a distinct envelope which contains policies relating to each economic activity. For example, there is an industrial policy, agriculture policy, trade policy and fiscal policy. But fiscal policy also comprises several policies such as taxation, public expenditure, public debt and fiscal deficit. It also has distinct relationship with monetary policy, which deals with all money matters. Policy of interest rate, open market operations, foreign exchange rate, money supply and its regulation, inflation and the like are the policies which fall within the monetary and fiscal domain.

Fiscal Policy: Concept

But what are the technical meanings of fiscal policy? Fiscal policy has two words: 'policy' and 'fiscal'. The adjective 'fiscal' delineates broad contours of scope and restricts it to the domain of 'public finances'. Hence, fiscal policy literally stands for the policy that deals with the finances. General connotations of policy relates to the public or government policy. Therefore, fiscal policy may be taken to refer to public policy that deals with finances of the government. But 'what is policy' still remains unexplained?

Schaffer (1995: 621) opines that the term 'policy' has been used in the following three different senses: (i) policy stands for the objectives for which the people associate in 'polis'; (ii) it also stands for review of information and determination of appropriate action; and (iii) policy focuses on securing and committing of the resources for the specified objective(s). The core ideas in the above three senses of policy relate to (i) objectives, (ii) consideration of information for determining proposed action, and (iii) collecting and committing resources. None of these definitions mentions either the time or space as frame of reference for implementation and evaluation of results emanating from implementation of policy. Policy implementation more often than is found to be misdirected and miss-delivered in implementation; or design of policy may be inappropriate for the conditions that obtain at the grass roots. So rather than waiting for the time frame of implementation to be over for taking up evaluation of results, it is desirable to institute concurrent monitoring and evaluation of results flowing from the implementation of policy. In view of the above limitations of the Schaffer's concept of policy, a satisfactory definition of policy is required to be wider in scope and inclusive in nature than any one of the above definitions. This is attempted in what follows hereafter.

Discussion of the connotations of policy necessitates differentiation between the concept of policy and theory of policy and formulation of policy and its implementation. Implementation involves an advance detailed programme of action. The concept has also to include evaluation of outcomes of implementation of policy and time of evaluation.

Concept of 'policy' refers to the idea or ideas, which its operational or implementation part relates to and which is designed for attaining chosen objective(s) in the given time-space horizon at the estimated resource cost not larger than the committed resources. This definition of policy not only includes all elements of definition of policy prevalent in literature but it also fills up the gaps in above cited definitions. Policy may alternatively be defined as the choice of one from available alternative actions in the set of choice in public domain which may best serve the pre-determined objective(s) in given time and space horizon with committed amount of resources. This definition of policy is more comprehensive than any one of the above three senses in which the term 'policy' has been used. But 'political economy', the earlier incarnation of economics comprised what is called economic policy. It dealt with the measures of regulation and guidance of trade, business, exchange, money, taxes and expenditure (Sutcliffe 1995). Policy may broadly be defined as a proposed set of measures to be taken or promised to be taken by the government, which will furnish the operational framework and guidelines for operations of institutions and decisions of individuals; it is generally designed to bring about changes in the prevalent material, social, economic and political conditions with a view to achieve pre-determined target(s)/objective(s) with the use of minimum resources. This definition combines Lasswell's (1971) 'maximisation postulate' and Simon's principle of 'bounded rationality' which characterise implementation of decisions. Now the theory of policy may be taken up for discussion.

Theory of policy constitutes a part of policy science; policy science itself may be treated as the constituent part of decision science. Theory of policy may refer to the set of assumptions, constructs/concepts and method of choice making from technically feasible and economically, socially, and politically viable options under the given conditions. The conditions and problems for solution of which policy is formulated are likely to be altered by the implementation of policy.

Conditions prevailing at the given time and spatial unit are sought to be altered by intervention/implementation of proposed policy in pre-determined direction. However, the concept of policy and theory of policy coincide with the policy making. The policy making refers to steps involved in the process of the formulation of policy proposals and steps needed to finalise broad contours and contents of policy. Policy in this sense may be treated as an outcome of policy making. The theory of policy treats the given conditions as its assumptions, goals and objectives set to be realised and expected to emanate as outcomes of implementation of policy. Thus, implementation of projects/programmes or actions stipulated to be taken under policy regime are the cause and its results are effects of policy. Policy making differs from policy implementation; policy implementation comprises determination of steps and their sequence for translation of policy into concrete actions. This is the function of POA (programme of action).

Policy and policy making signify the conceptual dualism, where policy is viewed as a 'unique stand-alone entity' in its 'own right'. But it distinguishes 'policy making' from 'policy' itself. Policy is outcome of policy making. It transforms policy into the dual whose primal is policy. Like policy, policy making may also be unique since each policy embodies its own process of formulation due to unique features that distinguish one from another policy. Bacon's approach considers policy and its making as the sole reason for the existence and acceptance of the state by the people. The twin meanings attached to policy and policy making signify the different facets of policy and policy making. Policy is something 'just to be uttered', or 'to be out there' in the open for all to see, or 'just chosen as definite promise' which is expected to be fulfilled in due course of time. It is this multiplicity of meanings of policy that accounts for there being 'galaxies of policies' (David Steel, Leader Liberal Party, Speech, UK General Election, 1983, Quoted from Schaffer 1995: 621).

Factors of Policy Duality

The dualism between policy and policy making emerged gradually from the Middle of Victorian Age to the decade of radical philosophical thoughts about state. Following two factors account for duality of the concept of policy and policy making: (i) Emergence of modern state which differed radically from the concept of ruling and monolithic state under the autocratic Kings/Emperors, who could be law unto themselves. This is amply signified by the statement of Julius Caesar, "Caesar and His wife are above Law." The modern states are caring and growth and welfare promoting states for the good of their people. That is why Durkheim observes that the "State is not an enormous coercive power but a vast and conscious organisation" (Quoted from Schaffer). Several other institutions have also emerged along with the evolution of modern state. The state is responsible towards the people and is accountable to its institutional set up. It is these institutions which prompted J.S. Mill to postulate Politics and Policy arguments to stand in contrast to each other. This probably is also the reason for Baghot to conceive the Political Minister to be above dirty policy making process. The policy making process becomes dirty for person holding political power because he has to bear the agony of patiently listening to conflicting views and logical and even illogical arguments in the process of finalisation of the policy. More often than not the process of policy finalisation may tend to be an arduous and long-drawn exercise in comparison to finalisation of thoughts that constitute policy proposal. The time that has lapsed between the formulation of Proposal by UPA-2 for replacing current laws and policy of indirect taxation by GST and efforts by the new government of NDA to make it a law by the Upper House of Indian Parliament is the testimony to this. Thus, the long drawn process precedes the state's actions, which are guided and governed by well deliberated and carefully drafted and adopted policy for the benefit of the state and its people; (ii) Most of the modern states have been democratically elected governments. Therefore, the policy making is not the prerogative of one or some privileged persons' thoughts; policy has to be approved and adopted by the elected representatives of people. This makes 'policy making' sneak into the scenario as a distinct entity in its own right (Cf. Schaffer 1995). In fact, policy making has now emerged as a fine art and a scientific discipline in its own right, which has brought professionalism into the system of policy making. The policy formulation is supposed to fall in the domain of experts, while its approval and mandate for implementation is in the zone of political class. Thereafter comes in the bureaucracy at implementation stage of policy. Thus, administration of the implementation process is the function of management experts, who may also undertake the task of concurrent monitoring and evaluation of outcomes of implementation of policy. They furnish feedback to the policy makers on the basis of monitoring and evaluation exercise. There is a voluminous treatise on policy making in US Congress. Besides, dichotomy between policy and policy making has created a cleavage between policy making and policy implementation which may pose problems of coordination and misinterpretation of the thrust of policy and accountability. Most serious problem emerging form this divide is the problem of accountability, since policy makers blame implementers for any shortfall in achievements, while implementers of policy blame faulty design and/or improper identification of targets and targeted beneficiaries.

The above discussion clears the way for defining the fiscal policy.

Fiscal Policy Elaboration

Fiscal policy refers to the framework and the rules of procedure for operations and management of public finances with a view to achieve chosen objectives and goals of economic policy of the state in the best possible manner that is politically and socially feasible and financially viable. The term 'best' may be interpreted in the sense of 'minimising the resource cost of realising the outcomes expected to flow from implementation of fiscal policy'. Fiscal policy, therefore, deals with management of public finances which comprise public revenue, public expenditure, public debt and fiscal deficit. Fiscal policy covers all these facets of public finance. Therefore, fiscal policy focuses on raising and allocating public revenue, effective and efficacious utilisation of public expenditure, and fixing targets, raising and liquidating public debt. Policies relating to all these facets are the constituent parts of Fiscal Policy. Fiscal and monetary policy are, in fact, inseparable components of economic policy. But fiscal policy has a greater role than the monetary policy. Monetary policy is generally expected to supplement the functions of fiscal policy in an economy, since these policies are highly inter-related. Monetary policy generally falls within the purview of the Central Bank of the country, while the formulation and implementation of fiscal policy is the responsibility of the Ministry of Finance of the Government.

The roles and functions of fiscal policy are derived from social, political and economic objectives of the government in general and from economic policy in particular. Economic policy of the country is directly related to the stage of economic growth of the country and its future directions and dimensions. The objectives of fiscal policy are most of the times also derived from the economic policy, especially when the government moves away from existing to new policy regime for the economy. This generally happens with the change in government of the country. For example, attainment of political independence by India and Tanzania offered an opportunity to both these countries to move away from the policies of the colonial regime. Then both these countries opted for the policy of liberalisation, privatisation and globalisation in 1986 and 1990-91. Both these changes were quite radical and transformational. But radical change in economic, and hence, fiscal policy do not occur very frequently, since the governments are concerned with the continuity in policy. The reason is that an unwarranted change for the sake of change may result in the loss of the gains of the past. However, if the outcomes of the policy diverge a lot from the objectives and targets set for the policy, then necessary corrective changes are made. Besides, if a set of policies are found to have outlived their utility and/or the success of past policy has changed the conditions so radically that previous policy becomes redundant and obsolete, then new policy package becomes essential. For example, Second and Third Five Year Plans of India laid great deal of emphasis on the establishment and expansion of basic and heavy goods industries. The fairly successful implementation of these plans made it necessary to change gears and direction. Thereafter, the emphasis of policy changed to economic reforms which focused on making public enterprises, especially power generation and distribution entities/electricity boards and public road transportation corporations of the states efficient so that these enterprises became economically viable; under utilisation of capacity and below cost pricing made several of these enterprises incur huge losses. So, the public enterprises were made to fix prices for earning profits (for details, see Shri Prakash and Ghosh 1977). Subsequently, now-on-then-off policy of economic reforms in second half of 1980s also brought some new policy paradigms into operation.

Role and Functions of Fiscal Policy

Above discussion has not explained the role and functions of fiscal policy. So, the question is what are the main roles and functions of fiscal policy? Following may be considered to be the main role and functions of fiscal policy:

(i) Fiscal policy strives to maintain the current financial system and its constituent elements; it involves continuation of on-going projects, maintenance of the operations of completed projects, and initiation of such new projects and programmes as are the part of current programme of economic growth and welfare;

(ii) Focusing on newly chosen objective(s) and projects and programmes for their realisation;

(iii) Fiscal operations are not confined to the ministry of finance alone and/or its departments; it covers all the ministries of the government and their departments. Therefore, fiscal policy has to coordinate and agglomerate the basic operations of all ministries and their departments at the formulation as well as implementation stage;

(iv) Fiscal policy is an instrument of mobilisation that quantum of resources which is adequate for the realisation of the chosen objectives and utilisation of resources in accordance with the pre-determined priorities;

(v) Public revenue, public debt and fiscal deficit are three distinct sources of resources of the Ministry of Finance. The ministry has to formulate an integrated policy framework so as to keep these three distinct sources in sync with each other;

(vi) Fiscal policy has to determine the allocation of mobilised resources from various sources among different lines of expenditure. Allocation has to conform to *a priori* determined priorities and objectives underlying the same in an optimum pattern. Allocation pattern has to conform to the specified public resources constraints and chosen targets for each line of expenditure. Therefore, fiscal policy has to have an expenditure policy as its important component;

(vii) Fiscal policy is an instrument of promoting growth of the economy. Economic growth is greatly influenced by investment and its structure. Investment comprises both public and private investment. Besides, resources for investment are raised from within and outside the country. A balance is needed to be maintained between the resources mobilised for public/government and private investment so that both these components/sectors play their respective roles effectively. Thus, fiscal policy has to keep public and private investment required for desired rate of growth of the economy in view;

(viii) Resources for public sector should not be raised in a manner and in magnitudes which lead to the total crowding out of private investment. This is a delicate act of balancing and it includes determination of the line between actual and desired levels of resources available and accessible both to private and public sectors respectively;

(ix) Just as public investment requires appropriate focusing of fiscal policy, private investment also needs incentives and inducements based on public policy and overall conducive environment. In other words, private investment requires (a) an appropriate business environment and incentives/ inducements and minimum policy disincentives, if any;

(x) Fiscal policy embodies an in-built mechanism of incentives and inducements for private investors, these are furnished in two ways: (a) provision of basic infrastructure- physical, institutional, policy framework, and environmental protection. Meeting this requirement needs public investment in transport, communication, power, banking, insurance, etc. These measures lie in the domain of public expenditure both on revenue and capital accounts; (b) Provision of direct subsidies to products of certain lines of production and/items of exports. Besides, supply of such facilities as power, transport, etc., at prices lower than cost of production, land at concessional rates to those engaged in priority sectors, etc., are needed wherever promotion of growth or welfare requires. These policy measures require public expenditure; (c) Rates and structure of taxation have to be aligned to targets of resource mobilisation and needs and priorities of growth, welfare, equity and inclusiveness, and economic stabilisation, including price stabilisation. These policy measures relate to resource mobilisation;

(xi) Fiscal policy is an important instrument of promotion of growth. This task is performed in two complementary ways: (i) government directly invests in selected lines of production. Choice for this capital account expenditure is generally guided by (a) magnitude of investment which may be beyond the means of private investors, (b) Long lead time involved in the attainment of break-even point which dissuades private investors from entering such lines of business; and (c) Low returns on investment. These factors dissuade private investors from entering such lines of production. Filling up of certain other gaps in economic structure may also require public investment on priority basis. Then, public and merit goods also qualify for public rather than private investment at least in the initial stages of growth of the developing economies. Strategic lines such as defence production and environmental protection, social and economic stability in the country may also qualify for public investment;

(xii) Requirement of equity, justice, and growth, including inclusive growth, and welfare programmes fall in the purview of fiscal policy as essential components. If high incidence of unemployment prevails, government may come forward to promote programmes of employment generation. Government of India has been financing various employment generation schemes such as MNREGA/NREGA. Government of India promoted opening of one crore bank accounts of the people with zero deposits and provision of insurance of ₹ one lakh for the poor families recently. This has been prompted by the need for financial inclusion of the poor. Food Security Act and other arenas of social security also constitute a part of focus of fiscal policy. Provision of two main types of subsidies: (a) subsidies for promotion of production of intermediate or capital goods like fertilisers, power, exports of selected goods, and (b) provision of subsidies on mass consumer goods of necessities like food, LPG, petrol/diesel, etc., are an important element of public expenditure;

(xiii) Rapid capital formation is required to be promoted as a matter of priority for the industrialisation of developing countries. Therefore, taxation and other instruments of fiscal policy are used for this purpose. For example, income tax payers are allowed to deduct 20 per cent of total payable tax, if they have invested their savings up to ₹1.5 lakh in approved instruments during the fiscal year. In tune with the factor endowment of the developing countries, prices of capital goods or interest on loan capital may be deliberately kept low relative to the wages of labour which is the abundant factor. Such factor pricing may greatly diverge from the prices dictated by the relative demand and supply of capital and labour in the economy. As against this, alternative line of argumentation is that capital may be taxed and labour may be subsidised to generate more employment and for the promotion of relatively labour intensive technology. However, the trend witnessed in developing countries has been contrary to this theoretical paradigm;

(xiv) So far as developing economies are concerned, it is not only inadequacy of physical capital but they have inadequate human and intellectual capital base also. Therefore, public expenditure has to focus on investment in education, training, nutrition, and health care services also. These priorities have to be reflected in fiscal policy;

(xv) Certain activities and/or their products may be heavily taxed if these are deemed to go against national/individual interest. Heavy taxes on tobacco and its products is an example of this;

(xvi) It has been witnessed in several cases that direct public investment in productive activities and incentives/ inducements and even direct grants are provided for the promotion of private investment in priority sectors of the economy. However, constraints of structural rigidities, institutional framework, market imperfections and resultant distorted inter-sector relations, absence of market mechanism in certain areas and inadequate experience and expertise in development administration impose limitations on efficacy and effectiveness of fiscal policy in developing economies.

(xvii) Deliberate individual actions for private profit such as corruption, black money deposited in banks outside the country, tax evasion and smuggling etc., constitute bottlenecks to fiscal policy's effective operation. These are needed to be tackled by effective fiscal policy instruments;

An important aspect of the developing economies is that their per capita incomes are low, which limits their capacity to save and accumulate adequate amount of capital. Therefore, fiscal policy has to be used as an important instrument of mobilisation of resources for investment. Besides, private enterprise is also scarce. So, the government has to fill up both these gaps. This raises the problem of proper balancing of public and private investment in a mixed economy or a capitalist economic structure in a developing country. Fiscal policy has to be actively pro-growth in the initial stages of development of developing economies. Government has not only to act as an entrepreneur but also as the financier of growth to break the centuries old stagnation; government has not only to initiate but also nurture the growth process till the mature or Rostow's take-off stage is reached. It requires massive mobilisation of resources for investment and also to establish appropriate public enterprises. Revenue shortfalls relative to revenue and capital account public expenditure may have to be made good by public debt and even fiscal deficit. This runs contrary to the paradigms of classical theory of fiscal policy of raising minimal public revenue but also the principle of balanced budgeting. In fact, autonomous market based rapid growth even in advance countries of West was not realised with the pursuit of neutral fiscal policy. Hansen (1949: 115) observed that "as the 'high' capitalistic period receded before the advance of state interventionism, taxation was seized upon as a convenient and highly effective instrument for regulation and control of economic life." During the post Second World War period, fiscal policy has been used and is being used as an instrument of economic stabilisation and growth in the developed capitalist countries. When Indian academics were heatedly debating the proper balancing of public and private sectors, John Galbraith, then US ambassador to India, in one of his public speeches in 1962 remarked that public sector approximately accounted for 20-22 per cent of all economic activities in US at that time. In contemporary world economy's or national economy's balance rather than budgetary balance is assigned the key role in policy.

An important problem of balancing is posed by backwardness of agriculture which constitutes the main stay of developing economies in terms of its contribution to GDP, exports and employment. This also poses the problem of maintenance of structural equilibrium in the economy, which may cause some intractable problems to growth as industrialisation gathers momentum. As Myrdal (1955, 1966) pointed out if the autonomous forces of the market were left free, their operations would result in cumulative causation of imbalances both between and within the economies and the international divide between the rich and poor countries and rich and the poor regions and their people within the countries are likely to be perpetuated. The vicious circle of poverty and backwardness cannot be broken without the intervention of state. Fiscal policy offers the potent weapon of such public intervention. Inadequately developed money and financial markets in developing economies are also formidable problems. Without an adequately developed financial infrastructure, a necessary condition of financial development, monetary policy and money market may not function effectively. This discussion has cleared the way for considering other aspects of fiscal policy.

Public Expenditure: Concept and Types

Full understanding of the concept, scope, types and nature of public expenditure is needed for explaining the roles and functions of public finance, sources of financing of public expenditure and the theory of fiscal policy and theory of public expenditure.

The term 'Public expenditure' comprises two words: 'public; and 'expenditure'. The word 'public' is an adjective, which stands for some entity or authority of or under the government of the country. Therefore, word 'public' refers to those items of expenditure which fall in the domain of the state or its government and the payment for which is made from the treasury. Expenditure refers to the outcomes of the process of spending, or the utilisation of resources, including money at the disposal of the spending entity. Thus, public expenditure denotes acts of spending or utilising of resources by the government and its authorised representatives on chosen items/objects/lines of expenditure during the period of one financial/accounting year to realise social, economic and political objectives of economic and/or fiscal policy. Public expenditure is the sum of amounts spent on (i) the performance of all activities by the government, (ii) expenses incurred on the purchase of goods and services used in the discharge of these activities, and (iii) defraying or paying for the liabilities incurred by the government. Public refers to the government and its agencies. Besides, government in most of the countries have different levels and layers of their composition: Central government, state governments, and such local authorities as municipal corporations, municipal committees, *gram panchayats* etc. Public agencies are established by acts of parliament and legislative assemblies, local councils and their orders. Public enterprises stand on a different footing, though these are owned and operated on behalf of the government. Any imbalance in the earnings of these enterprises between revenue and expenditure is generally covered by government grants. Public authority refers to the government of the day. The public expenditure is, however, governed and guided by the budget sanctioned by parliament/assembly/members of municipal/committees/corporations/*panchayats*, and authorities of public sector enterprises, etc. Amounts of public expenditure are drawn from the government treasury. Thus, public expenditure has the following characteristics:

(i) Public expenditure is designed to be incurred on pre-defined and *a priori* chosen lines or items;
(ii) The chosen lines of expenditure relate to the objectives of fiscal policy adopted by the government;
(iii) Public expenditure has prior sanction of an appropriate legislative or administrative body. If some expenditure has been incurred in some emergent situation without proper sanction, it will require *ex post facto* sanction;
(iv) Magnitude and composition of public expenditure is a part of annual budget of the government or an authorised public agency;
(v) Money for public expenditure is drawn from the common source of treasury.

Types of Public Expenditure

Public expenditure is incurred on myriad lines or items of expenditure by a large number of spending entities located in different areas and public entities.

Larger the geographical area, greater the population size and higher the development stage, greater is public expenditure in magnitude and more diversified is its structure. However, magnitude and degree of diversification of public expenditure depend on the number of items of expenditure and the degree of priority and importance attached to the different lines of expenditure. Relative importance assigned to each of the following determines the relative magnitudes of expenditure on (i) investment for growth, (ii) productive or non-productive expenditure on items of peoples' welfare, (iii) structure of development expenditure which depends on the importance assigned to inclusiveness, equity and justice as objectives of fiscal policy. One school of thought postulates that in the initial stages of growth, regional inequalities of development and inter-personal inequalities of income distribution tend to rise but these inequalities generally decline at mature stages of growth and (iv) Level of internal and external security that prevails in the country also affects the level and nature of expenditure. Disturbed internal conditions and external threats are generally given higher priority than development expenditure, since such conditions not only compromise welfare of the people these also retard the development of the economy.

The government and its agencies have to perform a variety of roles and functions, including those listed above. Nature of these roles and functions constitute the base of classification of public expenditure in distinct categories. The following are the main categories of public expenditure:

(i) Maintenance and expansion of administrative machinery of the government and its agencies account for substantial proportion of total public expenditure. The size of administrative machinery varies with geographical and population size of the country, number and nature of welfare programmes and projects of growth on which public expenditure is to be incurred;

(ii) Administration of justice and maintenance of internal law and order generally accounts for very high proportion of total public expenditure. Social, political and economic conditions govern the quantum of expenditure on these lines of expenditure. But frequent internal political or other disturbances such as communal strife, demonstrations and strikes by political opponents of the government and social activists, internal revolts such as Naxalite or Maoist movements related turbulence in certain parts of the country, such political agitations as in J&K, Manipur, Nagalnd, or demonstrations against social evils or tragedies necessitate unusually high magnitude of public expenditure;

(iii) Management of natural or political, social or economic disasters evoke responses from the government with a view to either prevent recurrence of such disasters or containing the adverse effects of disasters after their occurrence or both. More frequent the occurrence of such natural or man-made disasters or turbulence and disturbance, greater tends to be the public expenditure on such items. Floods and famines, earthquakes and tsunamis, and landslides are natural disasters while wars, agitations and communal or political unrest are examples of mad-made disasters. Some of the natural disasters occur periodically almost at regular intervals. Expenses incurred on second and third categories adversely affect other lines of public expenditure. However, Musgrave (1953) in his study of British data treated such expenditure as an important cause of substantial hikes in public expenditure despite the fact that such expenditure is not the part of general and regular budgeted expenditure. He assumed that once such expenditure has been incurred, it does not remain once for all affair, it tends to become the part of general rather than specific public expenditure. It may, however, be surmised that public expenditure, like consumption expenditure, is downward sticky but upward flexible. Ten per cent reduction in public expenditure across the board in 1979 is an exception. This may not hold true for other countries or other times. For example, Europe used to witness frequent battles among the countries during Pre-Second World War Era. But the disastrous consequences of Second World War and emergence of European Union has resulted in the reduction of expenditure on such battles.

(iv) Expenditure on external security of the country against periodic foreign incursions or conduct of wars with a view to seek and establish peace and secure borders of the country happens to be among the biggest items of public expenditure. Larger the length and breadth of international borders, greater the number of countries on the borders and higher the degree of disagreements among the neighbours/countries, larger tends to be the absolute and relative size of defence expenditure. This expenditure also depends on the status of the country in the comity of nations. For example, US is the greatest economic and political power of the world, consequently it has to incur extremely high volume of expenditure on defence. International disturbance in any corner of the world induces it to intervene. Iraq and Afganistan are the latest examples of such intervention by the US or other countries in internal affairs of a country by other countries on one or the other counts leads to the victim country to incur relatively large expenditure on this. Islamic Jehadi or IS disturbances or terrorists disturbances in many countries of the world may also be bracketed in this category (compare with Shri Prakash and Chowdhury 1995: 18-21).

(v) Public expenditure related to economic activities is an equally important category of public expenditure. Economic activities and expenditure on the same may be distinguished in three categories: (a) Maintenance of ongoing economic activities and the enterprises/undertaking of the state; (b) expansion of the ongoing projects and programmes, and (c) initiation of new activities in the existing or new areas of activity. This largely depends on the nature and objectives of the government in power. For example, if the government follows the dictum of minimal government action and/or intervention in economy and its business, then it tends to reduce the absolute and relative size and lines of public expenditure. As against this, the government with socialistic leanings will be undertaking the responsibility of not only regulation but also control and ownership of economic activities under the aegis of its policy package and great responsibility will be entrusted to the public sector enterprises operating in the economy. This will result in increasing the size of expenditure and its diversity. Greater the number and size of public enterprises in the country and larger the number of economic functions in the domain of the government, greater tends to be the magnitude and more diversified structure of public expenditure.

Most of these activities will fall in one of the following areas: (i) growth initiating, promoting and sustaining activities; (ii) activities relating to the people's welfare; (iii) regulation and control of activities which are treated as socially, politically or environmentally undesirable in nature or consequences in general and private activities of this genre in particular. For example, regulation and control of monopolies, and promotion of activities, which enhance the degree of competitiveness in the economy result in raising the public expenditure. Preventive and punitive, and/or promotional or incentives and inducement furnishing activities fall in this category of public expenditure; and (iv) economic activities; designed to promote inclusiveness and equity and justice in the process of development of the economy and transformation of social structure constitute a distinct category. Reservations of number of seats in educational institutions and job opportunities/posts and scholarships for weaker sections of society, subsidies on essential commodities, and or adoption and enforcement of dual pricing policy of specified goods are the activities which fall in this domain. Pricing of sugar and cereals is an example of dual pricing policy in India.

Modern governments are members of a number of inter-national agencies like UN and its constituent institutions which are supported by periodic financial contribution. Besides, during political strife like prolonged armed insurrection in a country, which inflicts heavy loss of human life and property and national government of the day is unable to cope with it, UN intervenes in such cases and the member countries contribute their armed forces as a part of international peace keeping force as well as aid is provided in money and materials. In many instances, if any country of the world faces serious natural disaster, friendly countries help it in terms of men, money and materials. All these are also a part and parcel of public expenditure. Most of the countries of the world partake in financial aid both as a recipient and donor which is a charge on public expenditure.

Interest on public debt, both domestic and foreign, is paid regularly till the debt is liquidated. Besides, government enterprises may have to remit profits to foreign investors, if the enterprise has absorbed such investment. This becomes a part of regular expenditure. Expenditure on the provision of public and merit goods such as health, education, transport, communication, water and power, conservation and sanitation, environmental protection, etc. constitute an important part of public expenditure.

Such public enterprises as incur losses over a period of time are provided the financial grant to compensate them for the losses so as to bail these entities out of trouble. In some cases, government takes over the management or ownership or both of sick private enterprises if these are on the brink of closure. During the 1960s and early 1970s several cotton textile mills were taken over by the Government of India (GoI). This is necessitated by the need for protecting the employees of such units and also to keep the units running for the maintainance of their contribution to GDP.

All above categories of public expenditure, incurred in accordance with the roles and functions of fiscal policy, are conceptually quite distinct and different in nature and scope. The complex, intricate and inter-woven nature and consequences of each category of expenditure are difficult to demarcate and distinguish from each other empirically since their causes and consequences overlap. For example, the government of a country at war with some other country(ies) will concentrate all its efforts and resources for fulfilling the needs of war. Consequently, public expenditure on growth and welfare will slide into the background during the war period. Theory and practice of war finance is, however, a distinct branch of public finance. The theory and practice of war finance are consequently different from theory and practice of Public Finance of Economic Growth. Besides, the practice of developmental finance of developing countries differs from the public finance of growth of developed countries (See, Tripathy 1970, 1985). If, however, the country is entrapped in internal strife, large amount of energy of its government and large proportion of resources of the country shall be subsumed in the control or elimination of strife and turmoil; besides, lot of resources will be required for salvaging and extricating the economy out of the morass into which wide spread political or social strife may push it. Absorption of large chunk of total national resources in control of strife and turmoil in the country will adversely affect expenditure on growth and welfare. It is noteworthy that public 'expenditure on law and order machinery or judiciary and general administration may, at the first sight, appear to be routine expenditure of the government on maintenance and governance. But the disorderly and disturbed conditions will directly hamper not only welfare and development activities but will raise the routine expenditure on maintenance and governance also' (Shri Prakash and Chowdhury 1997: 18). The discovery of new source of national resources also affects public expenditure. A historical precedent illustrates this facet of public expenditure a great deal; it relates to the discovery of one silver mine in Laurium in the city State of Athens. Several members of the assembly suggested equal distribution of silver available in the mine for the promotion of welfare of the people for meeting the ends of justice and equity. The reasoning was that the mine belonged to the State, and hence, all citizens were entitled to have an equal share in its reserves. But Themistocles pleaded that the mined silver be used for strengthening the naval forces of the State. His argument was that the satisfaction derived from the feeling of security for all times to come and future benefits from this expenditure on increasing military might of the nation will far outweigh the immediate gains of equal distribution of mined silver among all the people and these gains will not last for long (Quoted from Shri Prakash and Chowdhury 1997: 18).

In the first instance, expenditure on law and order and secure external borders furnish not only a great deal of psychological returns to the masses but it also promotes growth and welfare. Growth and welfare, as has been explained earlier, are adversely affected by internal disturbances and external wars. But increased expenditure on the strengthening of defence and internal law and order machinery results in the generation of additional employment and furnishes purchasing power in the hands of the people who get employment; they spend the income on consumption and also save a part of it. Besides, requirements of maintenance of police and armed forces lead to increased production of articles used by these two forces; this directly enhances productive capacity to generate output/income. Hence, it is difficult to classify public expenditure in water tight compartments.

However, enhanced expenditure on containing or mitigating internal disturbances, or the managing of the consequences of outbreak of war may also confer some benefits in the form of increased public expenditure; the increased expenditure will lead to the reduction of deficiency of effective demand, if it exists, otherwise it will raise effective demand in the economy. This will initiate the process of recovery from recessionary phase of the economy. This is what happened after the outbreak of Second World War, which extricated the economy from Great Depression and its adverse growth effects. Similarly, big financial bail-out packages, given by the US, European, Indian and Chinese governments and those of several other countries in order to mitigate the adverse growth effect of World-wide economic slow down in 2008, did initiate the process of recovery in the world economy. It is noteworthy that the bungling by business houses or ill effects of their failure may be contained and the economy could be extricated from the deep morass by government action. This reflects the imperfections of market mechanism and the invisible hand which it works with.

An important question is 'who will bail-out the bankrupt national governments like the governments of Greece, Portugal, Spain and Italy, who faced the economic crisis triggered by such heavy public debt as could not be liquidated by the governments?' Similarly, the government of India faced economic crisis of unprecedented proportion in the beginning of 1990s, which erupted partly due to unproductive splurge in public expenditure during the late 1980s (see, among others, Shri Prakash 2005 and Nayyar 1993). The answer to the question is that the governments have to act rationally and manage their economic affairs prudently. Otherwise such government as perennially indulge in unproductive splurge of public expenditure will be forced to go to the international agencies or the governments of other countries for bail-out. But there are no free lunches.

Inter-relations of Economic Theory, Fiscal Policy and Source of Public Expenditure

Public expenditure is the core part of public finance, which depends on monetary and economic policies in general and fiscal policy of the government of the day in particular. Fiscal policy is, however, an integral part of economic policy. The nature and scope of economic policy and consequently fiscal policy and public finance have changed from time to time. Magnitude and structure of government finances also tend to change with the change in government and its fiscal policy. However, the stage of economic development and programmes of future development have a direct bearing on the finances of national governments. Public finances of modern governments are naturally the offspring of fiscal policy of the government of the day. This makes fiscal policy and its theory largely empirical rather than theoretical in orientation, influence of theory on policy notwithstanding. Political theory and philosophy of the ruling party in democracy and the rules of international political climate influence economic and fiscal policies. Another important aspect of fiscal policy is its relation with economic theory in general and theory and models of welfare and economic growth in particular. Fiscal policy as has already been discussed is determined largely by roles and functions of the government, which change from time to time. The theory and philosophy of the state and its government have been the guide-posts of the government's functions in society and its economy. Thus, public finance and fiscal policy are to be viewed in quasi theoretical and quasi empirical framework.

But what is fiscal policy? Black et al. (2013: 158) defines fiscal policy as follows: Fiscal policy is "The use of taxation and government spending to influence the economy. This may work *via* changing tax rates or the rules about liability to tax, or *via* changing government spending on real goods and services or transfer payment. Fiscal policy can be used both to influence the level of aggregative demand in the economy and to change the incentives to firms and individuals so as to encourage or discourage particular forms of activity." It is thus obvious that fiscal policy has wide ranging scope of influence from individuals to firms to industry to the nation as a whole. It has been described that the national budget is the main instrument of designing and implementing the fiscal policy of a country. This is known as fiscal stance of the budget: "The tendency of tax and spending policies embodied in a government budget to expand or contract the economy. The fiscal stance can be found by comparing the full employment budget surplus or deficit with some normal level" (Black et al. 2013: 158). It is implicitly assumed above that deficit or surplus budgets are indicator of fiscal stance. It may be added that growth and inflation effects of a national budget may reflect the fiscal instance better than the fiscal deficit or surplus associated with full employment in the economy. Oxford Dictionary's yardstick may be more theoretical than practical since hardly any economy of the world attains full employment in normal conditions. Level of employment changes with the alterations in the boom and doom phases of the business cycles. As against this, growth and inflation effects are usually present in the economy during all three phases of the business cycles. Incidentally, fiscal drag may then also be easily related to fiscal stance. It is because "the tendency under progressive tax system for the proportions of incomes collected in taxes to rise under inflation. This results from the fact that threshold at which income tax becomes payable and the threshold for the application of higher tax rates are fixed in money terms. Inflation thus tends to increase the proportion of incomes collected in direct taxes. The existence of some 'specific taxes tends, however, to reduce the proportion of incomes collected in indirect taxes when prices rise, and the fact that many taxes are collected in arrears also tends to reduce the fiscal drag" (Black et al. 2013: 157). The above quote needs consideration in the light of two contradictory facts: First, purchasing power in the hands of the people is reduced both by increased prices and increased tax liability; and proportions in which total expenditure on essential goods rises and proportion in which the expenditure on other goods falls may not be balanced by each other (For a contrary view, see, Shri Prakash and Sharma 2016, Sharma 2016). Therefore, reduction in fiscal drag in inflationary conditions is debatable. Besides, the Dictionary seems to assume that there are no subsidies on certain goods to counteract either inflation or taxes and that tax rates are never adjusted for inflation. Both these assumptions are not empirically valid. For example, Government of India (GoI) arranged to distribute onion at controlled prices when its prices rose too high. Besides, exemption limits of income and wealth tax are adjusted downward though belatedly order to increase purchasing power in the hands of people.

Analysis of fiscal policy with reference to paradigms of economics of welfare and growth greatly hinges on the envisaged roles and functions of the government. As policy of public expenditure is a part of fiscal policy, it is essential to discuss the theory of fiscal policy in detail. But the theory and practice of fiscal policy have been evolving through time to time.

Classical Theory of Fiscal Policy and Public Finance

The classical theory of fiscal policy stands on the following two important pillars:

(i) Principle of minimal government intervention in economy for maximal efficiency in the allocation and utilisation of resources among different activities is the first important paradigm of classical theory of fiscal policy. Idea underlying the principle is that the government is *ipso facto* inefficient in economic management and the government should not undertake any social or economic activity which can be done better by individuals (Shri Prakash 2006);

(ii) Principle of balanced budgeting is the second pillar of classical theory of fiscal policy. Balanced budget stipulates equality between public revenue and public expenditure. Just as households cannot and should not live beyond their means, governments should also not spend more than the public revenue expected to be raised in coming financial year. This may also be stated that the government's planned spending during the financial year should match the revenue planned to be raised during the same period so that spending and income are balanced.

Principle of Minimal Government for Maximal Efficiency

First ever fully blown and grown up account of theory of fiscal policy may be traced to the classical economic theory, rudiments of which have already been discussed earlier. The explicit elaboration of the classical concept and theory of fiscal policy is found in the formulations of (i) Jefferson's account of public finances of US, and (ii) Gladston's precept of the ideal fiscal management of England.

The concept of the ideal state of public finances revolves round (i) the freeing of the market mechanism to the maximum possible extent from the clutches of public policy; and (ii) removal/reduction of the constraints and bottlenecks of institutional structure, which limit the free operations of the market. Both these are complementary to each other and require the reduction in government' roles and functions in economic and social affairs *a la* Adam Smith's *laissez faire*.

Efficient market is envisaged to attain optimum pattern of allocation of resources between different lines of production, which leads to full employment on the one hand, and maximum output on the other (among others, see, Tripathy 1970, 1985: 34-56). The attainment of optimum pattern of allocation of resources between different lines of production or public uses hinges upon transfer of resources from less productive or efficient use to more efficient and effective use of the resources so that marginal benefit and/or marginal productivity in each use is equal. Obviously, such allocation pattern is not hit upon in one go. Then how can this objective be realised in one financial year? This is not taken into account by the adherent of this principle. This is a long drawn process. Even otherwise alternative classical theory focused on long run equilibrium in every field of activity. As Keynes quipped, "We all are dead in the long run".

Principle of Balanced Budgeting

Public budgets have been used as the instrument of implementation of economic and fiscal policies. But the process of the budgeting is not guided by theory alone it is greatly conditioned and influenced by political, social and economic objectives. Annual Budgets of the governments and their agencies are used as instruments of implementation of fiscal policy of the day. Resources are used for funding of all public expenditure but resources are also required and mobilised by instruments designed for the realisation of policy objectives other than funding of public expenditure.

Theories of public finance have been developed in the course of human development and evolution of civilisation through the ages. At each stage of evolution of new civilisation, concept and theory of state and its finances has been changing; these concepts and theories have been the base of policies of public finances for long. It is in view of this that one chapter of the book has been devoted to the analysis of the evolution of the concept of the State and the roles and functions of its government. Besides, at each stage of development, new concepts and means and ways have been evolved for the mobilisation of resources for funding ever increasing needs of public expenditure. The emergence of industrial age has been the bench mark in the history of human civilisation. The classical theory has been propounded to suit the needs of post first industrial revolution economies of the world. But the same theory cannot serve the needs of modern post industrial society.

But the balancing of the budget needs consideration of both public revenue and public expenditure, though the following four are major constituents of public finances: (i) public revenue; (ii) public debt; (iii public expenditure; and (iv) fiscal deficit.

As the source of funding of public spending are public revenue, borrowings and fiscal deficit, should one not be talking of balancing expenditure with the resources drawn from all these sources rather than balancing spending with revenue? But the classical theory stipulated equality between public expenditure and public revenue alone.

PR ~ PE.

The concept of revenue may coincide with the concept of public revenue. The principle/theory of balanced budget is based on the assumption that what holds true for households also holds true for governments. Just as households should not and cannot live beyond their means forever, governments should not and cannot spend more than their revenue from taxes, fines, penalties, donations, etc. Spending in excess of households' incomes and government's public revenue may, however, not be altogether bad in the short-run. For example, households' purchases on the basis of equally spaced payment of instalments increase savings of not only the households but also of the economy. It also enhances level and style of living which generates demand for goods which induces increased production; it promotes growth. If public spending in excess of revenue, which is financed either from fiscal deficit or debt or both is prudently directed to productive use, it shall be beneficial to the country and the people.

But the critical questions are how short should be the short-run? How low/high should be the shortfall in revenue? What are the limits to public borrowing and fiscal deficit? What are the ways and means of regaining budget balance in the long run of reasonable duration? In other words, how can it be ensured that the short run deficit is liquidated autonomously in the long run? It is difficult in practice to distinguish where do the short-runs end and long run begins; long-run is only an envelope of the multitudes of short-runs.

Example of erstwhile rural India may be cited to highlight the pitfalls of living beyond one's means. Rural society of India, especially farming community suffered from perennial indebtedness which was carried from one to other generations. In recent years, hundreds of farmers committed suicide due to their inability to repay the debt. Sub-prime crisis of the US also emanated from excessive private spending financed by bank credits. Euro-debt crisis has also affected World Economy adversely. But, suicide is not an option for the government. Above aberrations at the national and international level lend substance and empirical support to the public prudence embodied in balanced budgets rather than in year on year deficit public budgeting and carry forward of the burden of public loans and interest thereof.

But the question is if the concept of balanced budget is restricted to the balance between budgeted public revenue and public expenditure alone? More often than not, the actual revenue collected by the government is found to be more than the budgeted amount whereas the actual public expenditure may be more or less than the budgeted amount. Many departments of the Government of India used to find themselves with unspent budgeted allocation which used to lapse or in many cases it used to be spent recklessly just to exhaust it before 31st March. In view of the wastage in such spending, Government of India (GoI) changed the rules and now the unspent allocation is allowed to be carried forward to the next budget year.

The principle of balanced budgeting can logically be extended to the fulfilment of the requirement of striking a balance between different sources from which revenue is raised by taxation on the one hand, and balance between different lines of spending of the total budgeted expenditure on the other. Above discussion makes it clear that the concept of balance is quite hazy. This principle of balance may also imply equalisation of the burden of taxation on all segments of the population and equal distribution of expenditure among all lines of expenditure. The principle may also be interpreted to mean that the shares of different lines of expenditure should be proportional to the priority or importance attached to each line of expenditure. Alternatively, distribution of public expenditure may be envisaged to be proportional to benefits expected to be derived from each line of expenditure. Such ambiguity in technical terminology is not associated with a precise scientific principle. Similarly, all the assumptions underlying these twin assumptions of minimal government and balanced budget have been left unstated.

The theory of balanced growth, propounded much later than the classical principle of balanced budgeting may probably be taken as an implicit extension of the principle of balanced budgeting. The balanced growth theory has also been interpreted differently by different economists. A popular interpretation of the theory is to keep a balance between the aggregate demand and aggregate supply *a la* J.M. Keynes. Another school of thought stipulates balancing demand and supply of goods and services produced by each sector of the economy. Thus, allocation of total investment among different lines of production will be proportional to the target output of each good, while target output has to be proportional to the anticipated demand for each good and service separately as well as jointly. But this may require balancing not only final but also intermediate demand for each sector's output. This leads to the stipulation of all sectors to grow at the same constant rate. In this case, reciprocal of minimum positive Eigen root of the equation of input output dynamic growth model (For different version of the theory, see, for example, Nurkse (1953) and Mathur (1967, 1969). But the resource constraints of developing countries make the satisfaction of such conditions of balanced growth difficult in practice.

The resource constraints and other facets of under-development, coupled with the concepts of backward and forward linkages of input output modelling, led to the enunciation of the theory of unbalanced growth. Chief proponents of the unbalanced growth theory are Hirschman (1957), Prebisch (1950) , Singer (1989), Lewis (1963), Clarke (1954) and several others who emphasise industrialisation as the major factor of growth. The balanced growth theory may have been anticipated by the proponents of policy of industrialisation as the key to rapid growth of developing countries (See, for example, Kuznets, 1973, Second Five Year Plan of India). The balanced growth aspect of theory of the fiscal policy emphasized progressive taxation so as to ensure resource transfer from the rich to poor on the one hand, and mobilisation of maximum resources needed for planned development on the other. The policy of progressive taxation was also warranted by extremely low levels of personal incomes and low levels of living of the masses, they could hardly save anything. This canon was also in consonance with the economic theory of social welfare.

The theory of unbalanced growth could be inferred in an almost exclusive emphasis on rapid industrialisation and highest priority to investment in heavy and basic goods industries in developing economies like India. Among other aspects of the theory is that priority to investment in heavy and basic goods industries ensures that the producer goods produced by such industries cannot be consumed. This involves compulsory savings of that proportion of GDP which is accounted by the output of heavy and basic goods industries.

Economic Neutrality of Balanced Budgeting

Balanced budget is stipulated as the necessary condition for making fiscal policy economically neutral. Revenue collected through taxation leads to reduction in disposable income of the people. Therefore, public expenditure of an amount equal to public revenue amounts to giving back what has been taken from the people. Therefore, balanced budget is supposed to be neutral in its economic effects. The above logic is obviously fallacious; public revenue raised from direct taxes affects the purchasing power of those people whose incomes are above the income exempt from income tax; it does not necessarily lead to the shrinking of consumption of such people. In most cases, direct taxes affect savings more than consumption, since consumption is downward sticky and highly flexible upward. Therefore, reduction in disposable income is likely to affect savings more than consumption. But indirect taxes stand on a different footing. Generally, value added/sales taxes make buyers of taxed goods and services pay more for the given quantity of such goods as they buy and are subject to this taxation. Price rise due to such taxes may reduce demand, and hence, consumption rather than savings (also see, Tripathy 1972). The logic advanced above also overlooks the fact that more expenditure on one or some goods reduces total money in the hands of the households for spending on other goods as well as savings. So, the structure of consumption is also changed by indirect taxation.

Public expenditure on defence, law and order, general administration and justice do not add anything directly to people's incomes; its positive indirect effects are beyond doubt. Besides, public expenditure can never equal public revenue empirically due to leakages and seepages on the one hand and expenditure on administrative machinery on the other; both positive and inverse effects of expenditure multiplier on income and consumption can also not be over looked. Besides, expenditure, public or private, embodies multiplier effect on growth of income which appears to be assumed as zero in classical theory. Classical framework also assumed away the fact that an economic system is a whirlpool of mutual inter-dependences. Therefore change in value of any economic variable, resulting from fiscal policy, carries cascading effects on numerous parts of the economy. Assumption of static state underlying the principle of balanced budgeting is another limitation of the classical theory.

Above limitations of classical theory of fiscal policy also led to the negligence of the following inter-relations between different elements of modern public finance:

$PE > PR \rightarrow (PE - PR) = (PD + FD) > 0$;

where $PE - (PD + PR) > 0 = FD$.

This overlooks receipt and payment of grants in aid and income derived from government enterprises.

PR refers to public revenue raised by the government mainly through taxation, fees and fines. PE stands for public expenditure on all items, PD denotes public borrowings or debt and FD shows fiscal deficit. Public expenditure may broadly be classified into the following categories

(i) public administration;
(ii) welfare of the people;
(iii) growth of the economy;
(iv) grants and aid to other countries or the people affected by disasters or in distress.

Shortfall in PR relative to PE requirement is covered by public debt, that is (PE-PR)>0~PD. This shortfall necessitates the raising of public debt. But debt may also be supplemented by fiscal deficit-FD. Public debt is raised both from internal and external sources; national and international financial institutions, market and the people. Fiscal deficit is treated as the last resort for filling up the gap between public expenditure and sum of public revenue and public debt. If monetary and financial resources mobilised through public revenue and public debt fall short of expenditure requirement, then the government resorts to fiscal deficit. Fiscal deficit is the ultimate culmination of budgetary deficits of all layers of government and public enterprises. The subscript t, wherever affixed to a variable, stands for time, which is generally one calendar/financial/accounting year.

Assumptions of Classical Theory of Fiscal Policy

Following assumptions underlie above formulations:

(i) Pure competition in the market in the absence of government intervention ensures operational efficiency;
(ii) Exercise of full freedom by individuals in making choices results in maximum gains to all. No conflict in individual and social interest is postulated.
(iii) These assumptions imply that all forms and structures of governments are *ipso facto* inefficient, and hence, fail to ensure efficient (a) allocation of resources among different economic activities; and (b) full utilisation of available/allocated resources.

(iv) It is further implicitly assumed that there are no barriers to free market operations and there exist no constraints to full capacity utilisation for production. Thus, problems of mutual inconsistency in individual units' production programmes and freely exercised choices underlying purchase decisions of the households are assumed away. Besides, the existence of bottlenecks in supply chains in the economy is also overlooked.

(v) Freely operating market mechanism, based as it is on the decisions of atomistic units competing freely in the open market without the distorting, contaminating and corrupting influences of the government, is assumed to be superior to the government in decision making. Therefore, government's interference in the form of taxation and other policy constraints result in wasteful and unproductive spending of government's funds; this distorts and misdirects the market operations.

An important inference in-built in above formulations is that the reduction in tax rates and public expenditure will lead to production and supply of larger quantities of goods and services in the economy. This will promote both growth and welfare. Thus, the least public revenue and lower public expenditure constitute the classical concept and core of classical theory of fiscal policy and public finances, including public expenditure. So formulation overlooks the existing pattern of distribution of income and wealth and its impact on future distribution even if the argument is valid empirically. Hansen (1949: 115) opines that the classical concept and theory of fiscal policy coincides with the 'maxim that the fiscal policy is neutral' between the ends of the government, which requires it to meet the following two conditions: (i) reduction of public expenditure to the utmost possible limit, and (ii) adoption of that tax structure which least affects the operating pricing system; it also includes the pricing of factors of production. This policy is designed to keep the relative distribution of income intact; it would correspond to a tax free society. The thrust of the argument is the avoidance of indirect commodity taxation at all costs in order to leave prices to be determined by factor cost of production by the market in the long run. Besides, it needs the fixing of direct tax rates in a way that does not distort market based distribution of income among the agents of production.

The implicit assumption of balanced budgeting being a necessary condition for the attainment and maintenance of long run full employment equilibrium was devastated by the evidence thrown up by the Great Depression of late 1920s and early 1930s. As was highlighted by Keynes, it is possible for the economy to be in equilibrium at less than full employment. Adherents of functional finance also subscribe to the above Keynesian view. In fact, empirical evidence shows that the working of free market depicts the tendency to settle at less than full employment equilibrium under the impact of balanced budgeting.

Products of different sectors of the economy satisfy wants of different nature and also have different levels of saturation points for households belonging to different income groups. Therefore, disproportionate shares of households' budgets are allocated for the satisfaction of different goods which satisfy different types of wants. Thus, these structural differences warrant unbalanced rather than balanced budgeting at the households' as well as at national level. Similarly, at the national level, expenditure on different lines of national priorities warrants the unbalanced rather than balanced budgeting. For example, if revenue constraints so warrant, expenditure on defence and law and order may transgress all limits; national survival is the most important priority of all countries and governments of all hues. This aspect also makes war finance different from normal or general finance. This is obvious that balanced budgeting is an inept principle for restoration or maintenance of structural equilibrium in the economy.

As against the balanced budgeting based fiscal policy, unbalanced budgeting based fiscal policy restores the structural balance in the economy at full equilibrium. For example, Learner (1951) has very forcefully argued that an unbalanced budget is a necessary instrument of counteracting the tendency of the market economy to be stable at underemployment equilibrium. In our view, structural equilibrium has to satisfy the following necessary and sufficient conditions: (i) sum of output of all sectors should equal the sum of intermediate and final demand of all sectors at the aggregate level. This is the necessary condition; (ii) sector wise output should equal the sum of intermediate and final demand at the micro level. This is the sufficient condition. Therefore, allocation of budgetary resources should be so intricately interwoven into the resource requirement of each sector that resources allocated to each sector are just enough to satisfy total demand of each sector' after 'under employment equilibrium.

The classical theory of public finance in general and principle of balanced budget in particular is wrong in assuming zero multiplier effect of balanced budgeting of public revenue and public expenditure. Post-Second World War advances in theory of balanced budget multipliers show that balanced budget may have non-zero multiplier effect on income and its effect may either be positive, or negative. Income elasticity of balanced public budgets may be unit, or greater or less than unit according to marginal propensity to save and import by the private sector is equal to, greater than, or less than the government's marginal propensity to leak (Baumol et al. 1955: 143).[1] But the Keynes' concept of multiplier differs from the concept of growth multiplier. Keynes' multiplier is the reciprocal of marginal ratio of savings to income. But the growth multiplier equals the reciprocal of average savings ratio to income. Keynes multiplier is demand expanding, while growth multiplier is productive capacity expanding. Savings ratio embodied in growth multiplier manifests the resources made available for investment in the economy; it results in capacity creation. Keynes' multiplier depends on marginal propensity to consume. Keynes' multiplier is inversely related to savings, while growth multiplier is a positive function of average propensity to save.

Besides, principle of zero income multiplier effects of balanced budget is not supported by empirical evidence. May be the principle could have been supported by empirical evidence in early days of the first industrial revolution, but it is no more valid in contemporary world economy. Even otherwise the policy of balanced budgeting has

1. For contributions of economists like T. Haavelmo and H.C. Wallich, G. Haberler, Ralph Turvey, W.J. Baumol, M.H. Peston and Alan Peacock, See Harris (1947).

no relevance for developing economies, whose governments have to play a pro-active role in economic development. The unbalanced budgeting is a potent instrument of countering cyclical fluctuations even in the developed countries. Besides, there is trade-off between the maintenance of surplus in revenue budget and deficit in capital account budget as the surpluses of revenue account are used for making up the deficiency of financial resources in the economy for investment.

The fiscal policy based on classical theory ruled the roost during the 18th and 19th centuries, the period characterised by capitalism based on private enterprise and free and autonomous market mechanism which were in the centre of all economic operations. Though the population was increasing, yet more rapid growth of economy than population ensured that per capita incomes were also rising so as to conform to the basic objective of the generation of maximum surplus/profits. Since a large part of profits was ploughed back into investment and incomes of labouring classes were not adequate to contribute to savings and investment, since greater share of income was appropriated by the capitalists. It resulted in accelerating growth. Interestingly, wages and standard of living were deliberately kept low in USSR in order to ensure rising investment for accelerated growth.

Other Reactions to Classical Thought

As fiscal policy based on classical notions did not interfere with freely working economy and uneven pattern of distribution of income among the classes, harsh living conditions of the masses, especially the working classes, evoked great criticisms of classical thought as a whole. Low incomes of, and almost no savings, and hence, investment emanating from the working classes also adversely affected the economy. The classical economic theory reduced fiscal policy to almost being redundant and irrelevant for economic growth. People's welfare was not on anyone's radar. Consequently, market based economic system functioned as long as the going was good. The signs of crumbling of the system started appearing with the emergence of rigidities, imperfect flow of information and knowledge, manipulation of market mechanism by those, who have had control over disproportionately large share of total supply of goods to the market, while commodity markets were highly segmented by emerging monopolies or near monopolies. These features of the working of the economy resulted in the emergence of inefficiencies both in allocation and utilisation of resources among different lines of production. Besides, social stratification and accentuation of poverty, deprivation and immesirisation of the masses gathered massive proportions, especially during the trade cycles. In the midst of these conditions, failures of the market could not be hidden any more from the public gaze. The capitalist world economy had gathered dark clouds of doom and despair around itself by the end of the First World War. The emergence of Great Depression during the post-First World War period ultimately shattered the faith in the autonomous market mechanism. Observed facts of falling output, declining profits, abundance of unemployment, unsold stocks of goods and imbalances in the economy flew in the face of classical myths including self correcting and self balancing market mechanism ensuring full employment equilibrium. The efficacy of Say's Law of markets lay in the ruins of declining incomes and falling demand. The unrealistic nature of such assumptions as pure competition, no control of an individual over the market, perfect mobility of factors and free flow of full information were satisfied more in breach than practice; all these made the classical concept and theory all the more untenable in the light of new empirical facts. As Mathur (1967) highlights the fact that the world economy in the midst of Great Depression and thereafter offered the spectacle of economic theory which did not have facts to support it, whereas the empirical boxes filled up with the observed facts were gazing at empty boxes of theory compatible with these facts. This triggered revolution in the history of economic thought which was pioneered by great economists like Leontief (1966), Hicks (1966, 1973), Keynes (1935/1997), Srafa (1960), Samuelson (1962) and a host of others.

Emergence of New economic theories, which were embedded more in facts than abstract logic based on stretching imagination to its limits, resulted in the emergence of new economic policies, including fiscal policy all over the world. Besides, 1917 Bolshevik Revolution in USSR and the spectacular success of planned development of its economy added further fuel to the inefficacy and ineffective nature of the market mechanism. Meanwhile, political and administrative forays into economic affairs during the prevalence of depression and Second World War time and experience gained from regulation and control of the economic processes had thrown up new thoughts. New instruments of fiscal management, based on new theoretical paradigms were evolved. The dominance of Keynes' theory over economic thought of his times also contributed greatly to the demise of classical theory. These developments endowed the political class and bureaucracy with enough logical thoughts and confidence of being able to manage the economy by means and ways that were supposed to be better and more effective than the free market, especially policy of fiscal neutrality based on classical theory.

Keynes' Theory of Fiscal Policy

Keynes' General Theory of Employment, Money and Interest heralded the dawn of a new era of economic thought and theory, which stands in contradistinction to basic tenets of classical economic theory and its twin principles of fiscal policy. Though Keynes did not explicitly explain his concept and core paradigm(s) of fiscal policy, yet the Keynesian traits in fiscal policy may be traced and inferred from his analysis of the macro scenario in its totality. Even otherwise, a general theory is one which subsumes and replaces multiple theories of different aspects of the given phenomenon. Naturally, Keynes' General Theory subsumed and replaced a number of macro- economic theories in prevalence then.

Baumol et al. (1957) offered a formal concept of Keynes' fiscal policy which he inferred from Keynes' General Theory of Employment Interest and Money. He opines that Keynes 'used the term fiscal policy in the context of 'taxation on savings and government's investment expenditure financed from loans from the public'. But Keynes was doubtful about the extent to which it will be safe and effective for the state's policy to raise and supplement the inducement for private propensity to save and the extent to which the policy will represent the common will of the people effectively in the determination of stimulation needed for raising people's average propensity to consume. The direction of state's policy for increasing capital may be so designed as raises capital by public investment in the economy without adversely affecting inducement for private investment so that overall increase in capital takes place to the desired extent. Thus, Keynes does not advocate limitless public intervention in the economy by means of fiscal tools.

Keynes' theory of fiscal policy, in fact, treats it as 'a balancing factor' between public investment and private investment on the one hand, and as an instrument of bringing balance between 'propensity to consume and inducement for 'propensity to save and invest' on the other. The satisfaction of these stipulations necessitates the bridging of the gulf between aggregate supply and aggregate demand functions. The gap between aggregate demand and aggregate supply functions is accounted by the deficient operation of consumption and investment functions in the market economy. The filling up this gap will push the economy from under-employment equilibrium and output to higher equilibrium level employment and output. These postulates run counter to the later day socialist precept and practice of state capitalism.

Like the classical economists, Keynes also accepted the capitalist orientation of the market economy. He effectively refuted Say's Law of markets, which maintained that supply creates its own demand, and hence, economy converges towards full employment equilibrium in the long run. Keynes dismissed the idea of long run itself and quipped that 'we all are dead in the long run'. He inferred that (i) it is possible for demand to be deficient relative to supply; (ii) it is feasible for the economy to be in less than full employment equilibrium. It is in-built in the operational mechanism of the market to settle down in equilibrium at less than full employment level; (iii) deficient demand implies less than full capacity production of output in order to adjust excess of supply over demand; it is therefore, technically feasible and economically viable to produce more output without the creation of additional capacity to produce provided that income-private investment gap is filled up by public investment; (iv) preceding premise leads Keynes to infer that less than unit marginal propensity to save leaves a gap between income and private investment in the economy. This gap necessitates public intervention in the form of public investment; (v) market left to its own devices has a tendency to perpetuate stagnation. Classical theory assigned no role to consumption in growth of investment and output. As adjustment of market is slow in response to changes and involves time while public investment is determined by policy decision, Keynes overlooked private investment in the centre of his analysis. He implicitly postulated an active fiscal policy to bring about equality between aggregate demand and aggregate supply functions. He also emphasized the inequality reduction effect of public investment. Equitable distribution of income in his view will activate induced investment which may converge towards the filling of the gap between income and private investment. In other words, deficiency of private investment is required to be mitigated by public investment, which may be guided by promotion of peoples' welfare rather than enhancement of private profit. Keynes insightfully incorporated elements of dynamic analysis in his short run static analytical framework by bringing in growth effect of public investment. However, his conceptualisation of growth was restricted to the pushing of the economy from less than full to full employment equilibrium. Thus Keynes did not perceive that dynamic growth of the economy may lead it to ever rising full employment equilibrium. As Keynes focused on short run analysis with invariant technology, he over-looked productivity enhancing technological change which leads to the reduction of employment per unit of output. Besides, movement of an economy along its growth path enhances the production possibility frontier as the substitution of capital for labour occurs almost in a continuum within the given horizon.

It is noteworthy that Keynes' postulated fiscal policy as a balancing factor and as an instrument of economic growth within a limited compass. The fiscal policy deals with the means and ways of increasing/decreasing the growth of consumers' purchasing power so as to be in consonance with the rate of growth of the economy as a whole. Increase in purchasing power is warranted by the need for pushing the economy from under-employment to full employment equilibrium, which may generally be higher on a higher trajectory than the market determined less than full employment equilibrium.

But general question of economic growth relates to the determination of means and ways of raising the rate of economic growth to a level which is required to provide a reasonably highly satisfactory level of living to the people (Kaldor 1955). Keynes has envisaged fiscal policy to operate in a static frame-work in which the following factors and parameters are treated as given and fixed: (i) existing skills and quantity of available labour, (ii) existing quality and quantity of available equipment, current production technique, (iii) degree of competition, and (iv) the tastes and habits of consumers' (Keynes 1935/1997). All these conditions generally remain constant only in static state in the short run. But these are factors that also affect economic growth beyond the current scales of operations. Keynes advocates change in fiscal policy within these constraints so as to raise income and employment above the current equilibrium level so as to prevent the economy from slipping into stagnation.

Keynes advocates fiscal policy for strengthening effective demand in the economy for leading to growth of income and employment. Focus of his fiscal policy is thus short run economic stabilisation rather than long term growth; he postulates full utilisation of resources, especially human resources by stimulation of consumption for which public investment is emphasised. He did not focus on growth *per se* but growth creeps into his analysis as an instrument of full human resource utilisation. Domar highlighted this aspect of Keynesian theory as follows: "Growth is entirely absent from it because it is not concerned with changes in productive capacity." It may be further added that the assumption of constant technology, tastes and preferences also rules out growth as the objective of policy. His concern is full utilisation of current productive capacity rather than capacity creation. "This approach permits the assumption that employment is a function of national income, an assumption which can be justified in short period of time, but it will result in serious error over a period of a few years." Labour is the variable, while productive capacity (capital) is a fixed factor of production in the short run. Therefore, full utilisation of potential savings is as utilisation of invested capital relating to employment of labour, raw material and intermediate goods. This is designed to raise not only demand for labour but also various commodities produced by different sectors of the economy *a la Leontief*. Besides, as pointed out by Hicks (1957) demand for labour is the derived demand which directly depends on the demand for goods and services. Derived demand is a derivative of effective demand. This inference is in conformity with the fact that Keynes' model falls in the class of general equilibrium model in which all macroeconomic variables are mutually inter-related; this is in spite of his static analytical framework. But Walras' general equilibrium model has also been formulated in the static framework. Social Accounting system has made it feasible to quantify core variables of Keynes' general equilibrium model. Simon Kuznets paved the way for empirical implementation of Keynes' aggregate consumption function (1973). Keynes' model has thus furnished a base for the formulation of an operational fiscal policy for economic stabilisation, though attempts have also been made to use Keynesian paradigm for the formulation of macro econometric models and models of economic growth (Harrod, Domar, Solow).[2] This view is embodied in the fact that almost all the fundamental variables of macroeconomic system have been incorporated by Keynes in his analytical framework; without these variables formulation of macroeconomic, or econometric or economic growth models is not feasible. Forecasting of future movements of macro variables, including anticipation of different phases of business cycles or recovery from the recessionary phases cannot be thought of without taking all such variables into consideration. Commenting on this aspect of Keynes' theory of fiscal policy, Kurihara (1967) observes that:

> Keynes' national income analysis is a minimal base of reference for development programming and a technical basis for estimating savings, consumption, investment, employment, and other

2. Shri Prakash and Sharma (1998) have found Keynes' consumption model rather than Milton Friedman's permanent income hypothesis valid for Indian economy.

> operationally significant variables of economic development. One cannot begin discussing economic development in an operationally significant way without reference to the quantities and functional relations stressed in Keynes' General Theory, though these variables must be supplemented by what Harrod calls fundamental conditions, which are population, technology, and resources in any long run analysis.

Progressively high taxation of income, especially unearned incomes, and taxation of capital for this purpose is discriminatory in nature. It militates against savings and hence, capital formation and reduces the degree of inequality in distribution of income and wealth in the economy. But more equitable distribution of income will result in imparting strength to propensity to consume. Consumption multiplier in Keynes' static framework is reciprocal to marginal propensity to save. This has income generation effect. As against this, taxation of income reduces propensity to consume, and hence, consumption in the economy. It has twin direct effects: (i) More money comes into the hands of the government for investment, and (ii) it enhances propensity to save, and hence invest. This leads to capacity creation (Tripathy 1970, 1985). Tripthy's logic appears distorted. Any act of investment has two effects: it results in capacity and employment creation. Capacity creation is bound to raise output while employment creation results in generation of income, though the fructification of these two effects may follow the lead and lag structure rather than synchronise or coincide in time and space. As against this, capacity creation effect of investment results in larger output and income in the hands of producers and increased supply to meet increase in demand induced by income generation effect of investment (Shri Prakash 19922, 1992b). Taxation of consumption, as against this, stimulates inducement to invest to raise output in order to cater to the rising demand in subsequent periods. Investment resulting from this leads to capacity creation and income generation. Besides, consumption multiplier has been postulated by Keynes as an instrument of income generation and it neglects investment effect of multiplier out of raised incomes (Shri Prakash and Sharma 2013, 2014). Thus, as against the classical neutrality of fiscal policy, Kenyes' fiscal policy is pro-active.

Keynes focused on adverse impact of government's sinking fund for the liquidation of public debt out of common taxation on propensity to consume. According to Keynes, substitution of policy of borrowing for liquidating existing public debt by the policy of creating sinking fund tends to severely reduce propensity to consume.

The Keynes concept of fiscal policy as a balancing factor also stipulates the government's national investment programme which includes not only direct public expenditure but also government expenditure on measures designed to guide and direct private investment also. Thus, he emphasises direct government action in economic affairs of the country. He states (1936: 114) that "I expect to see the State.....taking an ever greater responsibility for directly organising investment." He also mentions that "a somewhat comprehensive socialisation of investment will prove the only means of securing an approximation of full employment" (p.378). This he designed to counter the market economy's tendency to settle down at under-employment equilibrium and even to slipping into stagnation. This postulation also highlights the limitations and failures of the market in real life economies of the world.

Some of these facets of Keynes' theory of fiscal policy are dubbed as anti-growth from the view point of developing economies. For example, Tripathy observes that a rise in investment requires reduction in consumption. In this respect, according to him, a developing economy resembles the classical model of full employment where rise in investment involves curtailing of consumption. However, Tripathy misses the basic point that an act of investment results in increase in income almost instantly as investment is translated into creation of employment and larger procurement of intermediate inputs, resulting in the rise in incomes of employees and suppliers. A part of the incremental income is absorbed in consumption *a la* Keynes' positive marginal propensity to consume, and other part is subsumed in savings. So, investment in such scenarios need not necessarily involve reduction in savings/ investment. This also implicitly underlies fiscal policy of switching from minimal government intervention and balanced budgeting to proactive policy according to the needs of the situation involving resort to unbalanced budgeting. Pursuit of this line of action had resulted in large scale public policy interventions in the economies of the world in an almost routine manner during the post Second World War period. Tripathi's contention relates to a static case at a point in time while growth involves two or more points in time.

Economic development of third world countries delayed for centuries by colonial exploitation through the draining of national resources to the ruling countries, as highlighted by Dada Bhai Naoroji's drain theory of underdevelopment of Indian economy. He also highlighted the dichotomy between precept and practice of colonial masters; they preached the virtues of free market operations but protected their own interest by Commonwealth Imperial Preferences in trade with Britain. The British Orthodoxy was seriously challenged by German Historical School; emergence of institutional economics and protectionism under the leading thoughts of Fredrich List who made the professional opinion to tilt in favour of active and corrective roles of public policy in economic affairs. Keynesian theory dawned as the bright star on the horizon of economic analysis.

Theory of Fiscal Policy and Functional Finance

Functional finance originated from the Keynes' theory of fiscal policy. Learner (1951: 57-58) used Keynes' theory to infer that the level of employment is a function of the rate of public expenditure. He opines that this postulate is universally valid in so far as it is applicable to the capitalist, socialist, planned, or mixed or unplanned economies, and irrespective of whether the policy interventions are designed to encourage or discourage private profits or for promoting peoples' welfare. He highlighted the following five components of total national expenditure: (i) government expenditure on consumption, (ii) public investment,(iii) investment by enterprises, public or private, (iv) Households' expenditure on consumption, and (v) Households' investment. This classification exhausts the disposal of entire national income; it also conforms to expenditure method of income accounting.

Theory of functional finance focuses on twin phases of business cycles: (i) inflationary phase; and (ii) recessionary/deflationary phase. But Learner misses the recovery phase from recession or deflation. Employment is greatly affected by all three phases. Inflationary phase is associated with rising employment, and hence, decline in un-employment. Obviously, zero unemployment denotes full employment in the economy. Incidentally, full employment is not always reached even in the inflationary phase. However, inflation becomes counterproductive if it crosses the limit of tolerance. That is why Joan Robinson once remarked that inflation is conducive to growth only if it remains within the limits of tolerance. The Committee appointed by the Government of India recommended that inflation beyond 4 per cent crosses the limit of tolerance in the Indian economy. But the authors' view is that the threshold of the limit to tolerance of inflation in an economy cannot and should not be determined without a reference to (i) current levels of GDP and per capita GDP; and (ii) prevailing rate of growth of GDP and per capita GDP if standard of living is to be protected from erosion by inflation. A rate of inflation that equals rate of growth of GDP will just keep the current level of real GDP intact; if it equals the rate of growth of per capita GDP, then it just about keeps the rate of growth of per capita GDP constant. These postulates are an extension of Fisher's inflation neutral growth rate of GDP.

If the incidence of poverty is less than what it is in India, then the limit to inflation may be at a higher level and *vice-versa*; inflation hurts the poor most. That is why an economist dubbed inflation as an 'invisible robber which robs the people in day light'. If inflation prevails in the economy and public expenditure is far too much in excess of what is warranted by supplies of goods, services and factors, then the remedy lies in the fine tuning of fiscal policy for reducing public expenditure by incorporation of measures for curtailing public spending. For example, expenditure on subsidies may be reduced and interest and commodity tax rates may be raised with a view to decrease excessive purchasing power in the hands of the public. But such simplistic remedies are not effective if inflation is structural rather than general. General inflation refers to increase in the general price level, whereas structural inflation begins from specific sector(s) though it may spread to other sectors subsequently. Structural inflation may be accounted by supplies of specific goods falling short of demand rather than money supply having been increased. For example, inflation in India has generally been structural rather than general. Historically inflation has been occurring in Indian economy due to crop failures (Swamy 1973, Mathur and Shri Prakash 1981, Shri Prakash 1981, Sharma and Shri Prakash 2013, Sharma 2014).

Traditional theory considers inflation as the consequence of excess supply of money, and hence, excess of general level of demand for goods and services relative to supplies. Therefore, problem of inflation may be approached either from the side of demand, or from the side of supply. In other words, inflation may either be treated as monetary phenomenon or as structural in nature and origin. Excess demand warrants reduction in total spending, including public spending in the economy. This requires reduction in money supply in the economy. Alternatively, it needs increase in supply, say, by imports in the short run. The raising of supply of goods and services is a long term affair, whereas inflation may be a short term phenomenon. Therefore, traditional thinking emphasizes demand management as the remedial measure for inflation. This is an easier route since it is relatively difficult to raise output, and hence, supplies Government has three different sets of measures for the curtailment of total spending: (i) direct reduction in the government spending by reduction or even total with-drawl of subsidies; (ii) slowing down the pace of expenditure on development projects; (iii) delaying the initiation of new development projects; (iv) reduction in pension rates and public contribution to the provident fund of government employees; (v) delaying the repayment of maturing public debt, etc. It may, however, be noted that some of these measures may prove to be harmful to the economy in the long run, since their impact will emerge in reduced supplies of goods and services, which will be inflationary besides being anti-growth; (vi) measures to reduce less money in the hands of the people by means of increased rates of commodity and other taxes, increased interest rates on borrowing by households and institutions, higher prices of public and merit goods etc. Some of these measures may accentuate rather than mitigate inflation in the economy. For example, withdrawal of subsidies on goods and services and enhanced tax rates on goods will result in adding to the already prevailing inflation rather than mitigating the same; and (vii) government may enter the debt/bond market for public borrowing and delaying of the payment of maturing public debt.

As against this, recessionary or deflation heralds the onset of the tendency of unemployment to rise and consequent decline in employment (Cf. Philips). If there is unemployment in the economy and it tends to rise through time, it is accounted by inadequacy of total expenditure; it warrants the spending to increase. It does not matter whether individuals or government or business houses or all of them spend more. In reality, expenditure incurred by all three entities is greatly related to each other. For example, increased government expenditure on education, health, irrigation, power and infrastructure provides stimulus to households and other entities also to spend more. Thus, the formulation and implementation of fiscal policy has to take into account the major determinants of public and private expenditure (Shri Prakash 1977, 1995).

Above discussion suggests that the government has three sets of measures to cope with deflation and inflation in the economy. In deflationary conditions, economy requires increased spending by all agents in the economy and the government has to lead to take the economy out of the woods and prevailing morass. First, government should increase its own spending by (i) raising its purchases of commodities and services, initiating projects of development and accelerating completion of on-going projects, raise the rates of subsidies or provide subsidies on additional items, raise the rates of pension and its contribution to provident fund, etc.; (ii) provide incentives for households and institutions to raise their spending. This may be done by raising purchasing power in the hands of the people by means of reduced taxation rates, reduction of prices of public and merit goods, etc.; (iii) government can enter loan/bond market and repay the pending loans before due date, lend money to institutions and individuals with newly issued currency to raise money supply in the economy and so on.

Major Postulates of Functional Finance

Following three are the major postulates of functional finance relating to fiscal policy:

Taxation

Taxation is the major instrument of mobilisation of resources in the form of public revenue. But according to the functional theory of fiscal policy; (i) alterations in taxation rates should not be used for raising more revenue. (ii) the functional theory of fiscal policy envisages taxation as an instrument of changing the behaviour of people so as to induce them to increase or decrease total spending according to the state of the economy. This is, however, a narrow view of taxation. Taxation is, in fact, an instrument of resource mobilisation for (i) growth of the economy irrespective of whether the economy is capitalist or socialist; planned or unplanned; (ii) Taxation may also be used as an instrument of redistribution of income and wealth in the economy in case income inequalities are markedly high; (iii) It is also a tool to reduce drastic differentials in the spending of different groups/classes in the economy. Those, who have the high propensity of spending cause distortion in the structure and pattern of production of various goods and services. Consequently, socially desirable goods may either be produced in less than desired quantities, or in certain cases, such goods may not be produced at all. Taxation may be used for furnishing incentives or disincentives for consumption of specific goods/services. The theory of functional fiscal policy does not suit the paradigms of contemporary theory of fiscal policy

Public Debt

According to the theory of functional finance, public borrowings are neither inflationary nor are these deflationary in economic effect. As public borrowing raises demand for loan-funds in the market, it tends to raise interest rate, which results in less private investment; but it furnishes funds to the government for filling up its expenditure-revenue gap. Thus, it may avert the need for fiscal deficit. But more often than not government resorts to both public borrowings and fiscal deficit. Public expenditure, based on borrowed funds, need not necessarily be used for public investment. Therefore, overall consequence of public borrowing is two-fold: more money with the government leaves less money in the hands of the people; hence, it crowds out private investment; and (ii) it more often than not results in lowering total investment in the economy. This is because it is seldom that the governments use total amount of public debt for investment.

Economic growth, irrespective of the status of the economy being developed or developing, necessitates continuous rise in consumption and investment, since consumption multiplier and investment accelerator are the twin wheels on which the band-wagon of growth moves forward. Growth and development have to move forward despite the bottlenecks created by business cycles business cycles are short term in nature as against growth which is a long term phenomenon. Growth moves forward in the continuum of time and space, acceleration or deceleration of growth in different phases of the cycles notwithstanding. Consequently, effects of business cycles have to be seen through and policy packages are available to mitigate the adverse effects of cyclical fluctuations.

The functional theory of fiscal policy is basically anti-cyclical rather than growth promoting. Inflation and recession, excess or deficient money supply, and over or under spending are all short run phenomena. A continuously growing market economy has to bear the pangs of inflation. However, monetary and fiscal stability cannot be treated as the substitute of economic growth. If the economy is growing in the midst of either fiscal or monetary volatility, it may not be a signal of ill financial health of the economy, since investment and consumption expenditure depend on investors and consumers perception about the prevalent state of the economy and expectation about its future course of movement. Incidentally, theory of economic growth historically emerged from the analysis of trade cycles (Shri Prakash 1992a, 1992b).

Fiscal Policy and Theory of Economic Growth

Post Keynes and post Second World War Period heralded the era of growth which was in the centre stage of economic analysis. Efficacy of policy based on Keynesian theory and the attainment of political freedom by a large number of Asian, African and Carribean countries furnished immediate impulses of growth to move into the fore-front of economic policy. It was further strengthened by the focus on reconstruction and re-development of the war ravaged and damaged economies of Europe and Japan (Shri Prakash 1995). This induced economists to come out with a galaxy of growth models. Emergence of Harrod-Domar model in the firmament of growth economics provided impetus either to its application in the formulation of plans of development, or it furnished inducement to economists to highlight its limitations (See, Solow 1957, Kaldor 1955, 1957, Shri Prakash and Sharma 1997, 1998). All these models accorded an extremely high priority to investment, including public investment in plan programmes of development (See, First and Second Five Years Plans of India). Harrod-Domar model focused exclusively on accumulation of physical capital and emphasized the need for keeping a balance between the capacity creation outcome of investment and its income generation effect. In other words, full employment equilibrium required the balancing of growth effects of consumption multiplier and investment accelerator. Keeping these twin facets in balance is defined as the 'Knife-Edge' problem which needs continuously rising investment over the limitless time horizon. Shri Prakash (1992a, 1992b) depicted theoretically/mathematically and empirically that mathematically endogenised inventory investment in Harrod's basic growth equation eats up 72 per cent of Harrod growth potential of Indian economy. Subsequently, Shri Prakash and Sharma (1995, 1998) endogenised inventory investment in two sector Mahalanobis model; they empirically showed that 66 per cent of growth potential of Indian economy was eaten away by excess inventory investment. All the same, focus of all these models and growth theory *per se* generally concentrated on investment and public investment in particular in developing economies, since industrialisation was postulated to hold the key to growth.

Neo-Classical Theory of Economic Growth and Fiscal Policy

Unlike Harrod-Domar and Leontief models, Neo-classical model treats capital-labour and capital-output ratios as the variables of growth, but it treats population as exogenously given. Producers are assumed to vary employment of labour and capital according to wages relative to price of capital; it is measured as the ratio of wages to interest rate. If accumulation of savings, and hence, capital increases more rapidly than labour (which depends on external growth of population), then interest rate will fall more rapidly than wage rate. Therefore, producers will employ more capital than labour. Consequently, technology of production will become more capital intensive than before. The catch in the logic is that, if both labour and capital rise at the same rate, or labour supply increases more rapidly than capital, which depends on the rate of externally growing population, then age structure of population also changes. No one enters the labour force immediately after birth. This brings unrealism in the assumptions underlying neo-classical growth model. Sen (1967) highlighted this aspect in his *Comment on Correa-Tinbergen Model of Education/Manpower*. He observed that the Correa-Tinbergen model equation for estimating manpower requirement was erroneous as it overlooks age structure of population. Shri Prakash (1976, 1977) commented on Sen's Comment and formulated an alternative equation for incorporating both age and gender structures of the population to highlight the importance of both age and gender structure of population in the estimation of workforce which is incorporated in growth models.

The Neo-classical theory use Cobb-Douglas production function with the specified assumptions; it stipulates that output is a function of labour, capital, and technical progress *a la* Solow. Solow modifies C-D function by dividing the equation by capital. Thus the transformed function treats output per unit of capital employed, that is productivity of capital as a function of labour-capital ratio. Then, he assumes that the estimated value of the intercept of this function captures the influence of technical change. But this model treats fiscal policy as irrelevant and redundant in the growth function of the economy. This may run counter to observed reality and some logical inconsistency. For example, intercept of a regression model is designed to capture the influence of all such variables as are excluded from regression. Capital per unit of output captures the essence of technology in use. Besides, the variables excluded from this function include managerial techniques, structure of organisation and composition of industries, institutions in operation and infrastructure. Since the dependent variable is not value added, intermediate inputs used in production process are also excluded. Cobb-Douglas production function does not capture the influence of organisation structure, techniques of management, and lower or higher prices of intermediate inputs which also affect output/value-added both directly and indirectly. How one can then impute total value of intercept to change in techniques of production? Besides, if the government furnishes incentives to immigrants to come for overcoming labour shortages in the economy, the assumption that labour is becoming continuously costlier than capital may not hold true. If population increases so rapidly that per capita accumulation of capital diminishes and per-person workforce rises, assumption of capital being cheaper than labour may also not be valid. If, however, unemployment persists despite slower population growth, and hence, rise in work-force does not keep pace with the growth of capital accumulation, government may impose tax on capital equipment, or may provide subsidy on wage-bill. Besides, marginal product of capital may be greater than marginal product of labour. Growth of output will, therefore, be attributable more to capital than to labour in terms of their marginal productivities. This argument differs from the argument that marginal product of labour will exceed the marginal product of capital, and hence, greater productivity of capital will be attributable to population growth. In all above cases, the fact of the matter is that growth of output will result from the contribution of both labour and capital, unless the marginal product of labour or capital becomes zero due to changing factor proportions. Supporters of neo-classical theory miss this important facet of growth process. The inference of fiscal policy being rendered redundant and irrelevant fails to satisfy the empirical evidence and it displays the gap in logic. But Gurley and Shaw argue that, if the government provides incentives for raising savings, as the government of India has been doing right from the inception of planning era, supply of savings will increase and the rate of interest will fall. Production becomes more capital intensive but marginal product of capital falls. Consequently, long term growth rate of the economy is determined uniquely by the growth of population and accordingly fiscal policy is of no consequence. Since the growth of population is exogenous and is not affected by fiscal policy, government's tax and expenditure measures have no impact on long run rate of growth of the economy. But the argument misses an important point and it is that, given the external rate of population growth, what would have happened to interest rate relative to wages if no tax was levied on capital (or interest rate was not raised to curb inflation. Capital formation will not remain unaffected by high interest rate and high inflation. It is taxation of capital formation which makes labour relatively cheaper which will facilitate substitution of labour for capital. But employment of more labour than capital will, in fact, reduce marginal product of labour more than that of capital. In any case, no economist by any stretch of imagination argues that substitution of labour for capital or capital for labour is taken to the point where marginal productivity of one or other factor is reduced to zero. The argument also misses the point that the cause of capital being substituted by labour is taxation. In view of the above how one can accept that fiscal policy becomes redundant simply because population is made exogenous to the model? If incentive is given to people to restrict birth rate, as it is done in India, then neither population nor its growth will be exogenous. This is the consequence of particular way of model specification. Therefore, fiscal policy cannot be dismissed as irrelevant (Cf. Peacock and Shaw 1971). This view runs counter to the view of Musgrave (1959), who postulates a decisive role of fiscal policy in economic dynamics, which has growth as its inseparable part. Musgrave (1959) refers to the rate of growth which as per Harrod's postulation is warranted by the maintenance of full employment in the economy as the required rate of growth. Musgrave postulates that the positive role of fiscal dynamics/policy is to secure a growing level of full production capacity output/income at stable prices. Thus, the problem of economic growth to be addressed by fiscal policy is the choice of an appropriate (optimum) from the alternative rates of economic growth, which are viable under the given economic conditions. Maintenance of price stability is another important function of fiscal policy.

Peacock and Shaw also admit that even if fiscal policy does not affect growth directly, policies of taxation, public debt and expenditure do affect consumption directly and indirectly. Then, consumption multiplier plays an important role in growth. In fact, consumption is both a cause and consequence of growth of output. Besides, marginal propensity to consume and marginal propensity to save are inversely related both theoretically and empirically to each other *a priori*. But additional released by the growth propelled by consumption multiplier in first round is further used partially for consumption and partly for investment; then these two marginal propensities reinforce each other at a continuously diminishing rate. The inverse relation then becomes direct (Shri Prakash and Sharma 2013a, 2013b, 2015). Therefore, any fiscal measure that influences consumption is bound to influence investment.

Approaches to Public Budgeting and Composition of Public Budgets

Government budgets are the pivots of public finances. Besides, public budgets incorporate all the essential parameters and variables involved in the formulation and execution of fiscal policy. Budgets, in fact, are the instruments of implementation of fiscal policy; consequently, budgets reflect broad contours of fiscal policy and execution of policy design. Public/government budgets comprise income/revenue and capital accounts; budgets have four heads: (i) public revenue; (ii) public expenditure; (iii) public debt, and (iv) fiscal deficit. This excludes item of grants-in-aid received and paid and interest payment and receipts on public debts taken and given.

Besides, each layer of government from centre to state, from state to local bodies and public enterprises, educational, health and commercial institutions also make their own budgets. Overall picture of finances of the country may be viewed from top to down and down upwards. Under the first approach, aggregate of budgets of all governments and their enterprises/institutions may be decomposed to reach to the micro level budgets. In the reverse approach, budgets of individual units may be aggregated to arrive at the macro picture. This becomes essential as the central government shares resources with state governments which, in turn, share their resources with local governments. Then, there exist public enterprises and other institutions both in state and union domain. Naturally, lower micro units incorporate centre's grants and subventions in their credit side of the budget.

Types of Public Budgets: Deficit/Surplus Budgets

Public budgets may be classified into the following three categories: (i) balanced budget, which the classical economists emphasised as neutral in economic effects. The *per se* neutrality may or may not be feasible in practice, since the sacrifices of the people involved in tax payment may far outweigh the benefits conferred by the public expenditure due mainly to leakages and seepages and a substantial proportion of public revenue being subsumed by administrative expenditure.

Balanced Budget

It may be assumed for theoretical analysis that public expenditure under balanced budget comprises following items/heads: (i) consumer goods and social services, (ii) administrative services, (iii) investment. Total public revenue raised from taxes is totally exhausted by expenditure on these heads. So far as budgeting of expenditure is concerned, these items also constitute total public expenditure under deficit or surplus budgeting, except for repayment of public loans and interest thereof.

Government can promote economic growth by expenditure on consumption and investment. Proportion of total expenditure incurred on administrative services is, by and large, growth neutral. But larger the proportion of expenditure incurred on administration, lower shall be the expenditure on consumption and investment which will lower growth rate below the level warranted by revenue raised from taxes. Similarly, if larger proportion of total expenditure is incurred on investment, growth shall be accelerated. If expenditure on administration and consumption is kept constant, then additional revenue, raised from enhanced tax rates, will be spent on investment which will promote growth. If, however, expenditure on administrative services rises and that on investment remains constant, while extra expenditure is financed out of enhanced taxation growth rate may be adversely affected relative to total public expenditure. Financing accelerated growth from balanced budgeting may be conceivable theoretically but it is not possible in practice due to stickiness of public expenditure in general and administrative expenditure in particular. Besides, operation of Wagoner's Law also militates against growth being financed from balanced budgeting.

Surplus Budget

Surplus budget is that budget in which public revenue exceeds public expenditure. Question is why does government raise more revenue than what it needs for financing public expenditure? Answer is that the economy comes under high inflationary pressures in boom phase of the cycles and excess liquidity may heat up the economy too much. Surplus budgeting in such cases is used as an instrument of mopping up excessive purchasing power in the hands of the people. But the objective of withdrawal of excess money supply from the public is merely to raise more public revenue and the objective of liquidity control may be achieved by reducing bank credits by means of hikes in interest rates, and/or alterations in repo-rate and cash-reserve ratio, or reduction in public expenditure. Thus, budgetary surplus may be achieved either by reduction in expenditure, or increase in public revenue, or both. Government may also go for enhanced public borrowings which will also reduce money in the hands of the people.

The surplus budgeting obviates the need for fiscal deficit which is supposed to be inflationary in nature in monetary theory of inflation; it differs from structural approach to inflation. Thus, surplus budgeting is designed for contra-cycle fiscal policy in upward phase of the cycles. The surplus budgeting may also be used for countering falling exports due to high prices and falling value of the national currency in exchange market and consequent deteriorating exchange reserves.

Deficit Budget

Surplus and deficit budgets are parts of contra-cyclical fiscal policy measures to be used alternatively during boom and recession phases of the business cycles.

Public expenditure far exceeds public revenue in a deficit budget. Deficit budgets are an essential component of fiscal deficit. The deficit is defined as public expenditure net of the sum of public revenue, receipt of grants in aid, public borrowings, sale proceeds from bonds etc., in the current financial year. Fiscal deficit is generally covered by issue of more currency, which is considered generally inflationary in effect. Deficit budgets are used to specially counter recession. But, counter-cyclical budgeting is only a short term measure, and it is not a part of long term fiscal policy, if the country has any such policy. If budget after budget carries deficit, then deficit budgeting has to be a part of long run fiscal policy. This is used both in developed and developing economies. But United Nations maintains that "As a general rule, the main responsibility for contra-cyclical finance in under-developed countries now rests with fiscal policy, supplemented to an increasing extent by monetary measures." It is further stated that,

> As in developed countries, contra-cyclical policy in under-developed countries will essentially take the form of budgeting for overall budget surpluses in a boom and for deficits in recession, and the pursuit of appropriate debt programmes. How the surpluses and deficits achieved, whether through changes in total expenditure or in total revenue; what effects the changes may have on the structure of revenue and expenditure; how the deficit is financed, whether through credit from banking system or from non-bank sources; and how the changes in revenue and expenditure occur, whether automatically or through discretionary policy decisions of the government- these are all important aspects of contra-cyclical fiscal policy... (p.40).

Sequence of Determination of Budgetary Components

Since the budgets are formulated on the eve of new financial year, budget proposals are anticipatory in nature, and hence, there is certain element of uncertainty about the realisation of targets fixed in the budget proposals. More often than not, public revenue exceeds the expected figure while public expenditure many times falls short of the targeted expenditure. Such surpluses may be carried forward and may be reflected in the next year's budget proposal. The proposed targets reflect the advance plan of expenditure and the raising of resources needed for funding the expenditure. Assuming that public debt is designed, and hence, public debt policy is formulated and activated to cover the gap between expected public expenditure and public revenue, importance of the determination of the sequence of fixing of the targets of public revenue, public debt and public expenditure acquires both theoretical and practical importance for public policy dealing with public finances. The question to be addressed is the sequence of determination of needs for (i) public revenue and public debt; and (ii) requirement of public expenditure. Public revenue and public debt are raised for financing public expenditure while the residual is covered by fiscal deficit. Unless the magnitude of public expenditure is known, target for public revenue and public debt cannot be determined. As has already been discussed, public revenue depends largely on tax bearing capacity of the people which varies directly with personal incomes. Greater the GDP, greater is the tax bearing capacity and it indicates more scope both for taxation and public borrowings. But the budgetary proposals contain anticipated rather than actual value of GDP. This suggests that first variable to be determined for budget preparation is that of GDP followed by targeted public expenditure, public revenue, public borrowing and fiscal deficit. Fiscal deficit is obviously the residual of the equation.

Fiscal Deficit

Fiscal deficit is the derived variable; it is the residual of the following equation:

PE-(PR+PB)

Where PE shows public expenditure; PR stands for public revenue; and PB displays public borrowings. The extended form of above equation is as follows:

PE -{(Net Grants in Aid + Net Interest Receipts in the Year+ PR + Net PB the Year}.

Public debt is generally liquidated at the end of its duration, while new loans may be raised from various sources. Similarly, interest payment is made on cumulated public debt and interest is also earned by the government on its deposits with banks and other institutions and loans advanced to others. Each government receives grants in aid and also gives grant in aid to others. There may be some overlap if the fiscal deficit is used for making such payments.

There are two alternative streams of thought about budget making. One stream of thought emphasizes that all budgetary proposals are anticipatory/planned, which are formulated for the fiscal year at its beginning. But public revenue is first charge and budgetary proposals are prepared for it. This is in disregard to Zero-budgeting which, however, is seldom practiced in an economy. Taxation is the major source of public revenue. Can the government raise as much money by taxation from the people as it desires? This is a relevant question to ask. But the answer to this question may not be as simple as it looks on the surface. Maximum amount that the government can take from the people as taxes is total income in their hands though it is not a practical proposition. Next possible approach is to mop-up entire surplus over consumption expenditure of each household. This will leave nothing to save with any household and the individuals' savings will be zero. This is not practical since it is not feasible to devise such a scheme of taxation unless the taxable capacity rises with the rise in national income; growth of national income results in increasing personal incomes over the years. But at any given point in time, tax bearing capacity of the people is limited by their current incomes and payment of taxes is a disagreeable proposition to all individuals irrespective of whether the economy is developed or developing, capitalist or socialist. Imposition of high taxation rates is also the source of generation of discontent against the government. Therefore, government has to keep in view its political compulsions and economic rationality in a tight balance. The prevailing tax rates come into consideration as the platform to move from onwards in a careful manner. The finance minister has to identify revenue elasticity of different taxes and the range of taxes in which elasticity varies through time and across taxes. So, budgeted public revenue and public expenditure and their actual values in the preceding year become the reference frame at the outset. The excess or shortfalls in public revenue from different sources and future targets may be used as guide-posts in the determination of proposed tax rates on different items/sources. Then, future perspective over a span of few years is taken into consideration; it furnishes the base for policy formulation for at least a period of couple of years if not for the long run.

In case of the planned economy, fiscal policy horizon may be coterminous with plan horizon. Growth targets to be achieved within the financial year furnish important guide posts. These targets are three folds: (i) incorporation of shortfalls of preceding years to be made good in the coming financial year; and (ii) ongoing development and welfare programmes to be continued; and (iii) initiation of additional projects and programmes of growth and welfare. Past levels and patterns of expenditure and anticipated inflation become the base for the estimation of expenditure. Level and pattern of public revenue and expenditure are determined sequentially.

Just as money is required for spending for performing the functions of a club, association or society, State and its governments also need resources for spending. Clubs, associations, societies are formed by the people, who come together to realise well defined objectives on the basis of voluntary decision without any legal authority, though each club/society has its own rules and regulations to run its affairs smoothly. These rules may be codified in the form of a constitution or memorandum of association. The constitution or memorandum of association defines the roles and functions and rights and responsibilities of the members and office bearers. But this does not have any legal base in the narrower sense of the term. These entities cannot use coercion or force. The running of the machinery of the government and discharge of the duties/responsibility and performing the mandated functions, government needs resources. The resources are mobilised and acquired and/or appropriated by the government for spending on designated set of activities.

Public expenditure is incurred on the maintenance of administrative machinery and its expansion through time due to enlargement of scope of state's operations. Types: (i) routine administrative expenditure, (ii) expansion of size of administration in terms of personnel and posts, area of operations, increase in number of departments and institutions. But development administration differs from general administration. Development administration comprises following categories: (i) maintenance of assets and keeping them running; (ii) initiation of new programmes and projects of development; and (iii) expansion and diversification of functions and the areas/fields of development.

General Theory of Public Expenditure

General theory of fiscal policy should be based on following two parameters of public finance: (i) level of tolerance of society to bear the pangs of sacrifices they are called upon to make in terms of transfers of one part of individual resources/income and wealth to the government; and (ii) capacity of the economy for absorption of benefits flowing from government expenditure and other transfer payments. The values of both these parameters are fixed at every point in time but the values vary inter-temporally. Values of both these parameters depend upon size of the economy which itself depends on population size, its age and gender structure, level of GDP and general level of living of the people. Therefore, both the bearing capacity of the people and absorption capacity of the economy are defined by per capita GDP. Expression of GDP per capita frees GDP from the size effect of population and level of GDP at the given point in time. But both these factors tend to change with time as economic growth and social transformation occur. As public expenditure is an important part of public finance and all financial variables are intricately inter-related, above parameters need consideration in the formulation of fiscal policy in general and policy of public expenditure in particular.

As public expenditure and its theory are a part of general theory of public finance, theory of public expenditure should also be based on the nature of the parameters of theory of public finance. But public expenditure is the pivot of public finances and their inter-temporal and inter-spatial differences of behavioural traits. Besides, theory of public finance is only one component of economic theory and policy. Interestingly, science of economics in its infancy was named 'Political Economy' as it focused almost exclusively on the level and growth of finances of the state. Elaboration of this wider canvass will furnish a deeper insight than what is possible to have if the theory of public finance or public expenditure is considered without the backdrop of an appropriate economic theory. An important feature of the theory of public finance, unlike classical economic theory, is that theory of public finance has generally been evolved on the basis of its inter-face with empirical evidence. As the facts continue to change through time and vary over space, theories of public finance and public expenditure have also been revised and updated so as to match the precepts with practices. It means that the theory of public finance has generally been matched by observed facts. This aspect compromises universal character of Theory of Public Finance in general and public expenditure in particular. Consequently, theory of public finance in general and public expenditure in particular is inductive and empirical in nature. An important limitation of induction as against deduction is that it is next to impossible to have exhaustive and mutually exclusive data/empirical evidence to match any theory. Limitations of time, resources and mental horizon of even the best minds make it impossible to conceive and perceive all the facts. Therefore, it has not been possible to enunciate an empirical theory of public finance which will hold true across time and space. The socio-economic and political conditions within and between the nations change swiftly which makes it difficult to enunciate a pure general theory of public expenditure. Above facets have to be kept in view in order to comprehend and appreciate the complexities involved in what follows in ensuing pages.

Approaches to Theory of Public Expenditure

The theory of public expenditure may be enunciated either from macro or from micro view point, or purely on the basis of deductive logic, or alternatively, theory may be erected on the basis of empirical evidence by inductive logic. The theory of public expenditure, enunciated deductively with logically consistent arguments and assumptions, may be called Pure Theory of Public Expenditure. The theory based on inductive logic which is consistent with extensive empirical evidence, may be defined as Applied Theory of Public Expenditure (cf. Shri Prakash and Chowdhury 1995: 37-42).

The following differences in the approaches to theory of public expenditure are important from the analytical view point:

(i) Level of total public expenditure is taken into account at a given point in time without reference to the behaviour of any other variable of the system under consideration;

(ii) Inter-temporal growth or decline in public expenditure is considered as the given parameter;

(iii) Level of public expenditure and its growth are considered as essential components of economic growth of the country; it keeps the rise or fall in public expenditure related to the rise or fall in national income/GDP and its growth;

(iv) Public expenditure as a proportion of GDP/NNP at the given point in time and changes in the same through time are considered as important factors in the determination of overall public expenditure. Analysis of public expenditure per unit of GDP reveals not only relative position of these two variables but their inter-temporal changes are also linked together which highlights direction and magnitude of their inter-dependence irrespective of lead or lag structure of their relationship. Besides, public expenditure as a proportion of GDP makes it appropriate for inter-temporal and inter-spatial comparison;

(v) Public expenditure and its growth may be analysed with reference to the objectives of economic policy in general and fiscal and monetary policies in particular. This approach takes public expenditure out of the narrow confines of growth of national income alone. It is widely recognised that economic development does not and should not be taken to mean the growth of income or per capita income alone. Socio-economic objectives of growth go much beyond the level and growth of income. It is not to deny the fact that human and social development are closely related to the level and growth of income;

(vi) Inter-temporal changes in employment or unemployment rate and degree and structure of inflation also play an important role in political economy of the country. Economic stability in general and price stability in particular are important factors to be kept constantly under surveillance;

(vii) Composition of public expenditure and growth of its constituent elements may be as important as the growth of total public expenditure. If differential rates of growth of components of public expenditure lead to distortion of overall priorities, it shall become counter-productive in relation to the objectives of economic policy in general and monetary and fiscal policies in particular. For example, objective of price stability may not be realised if the economy is dominated by food inflation, while rest of the economy is in a state of recession. Therefore, the theory of public expenditure has to satisfy twin criteria of being in sync with economic theory in general and monetary and fiscal policy in particular. Keeping the balances among different directions of allocations is also an important objective of growth. Another objective may be to determine the pattern of allocation of resources for the optimisation of value of the objective function under consideration. This necessitates the analysis of public expenditure to be approached from the micro view point of the constituents of the total expenditure without losing its macro focus. Even otherwise a system cannot be in equilibrium even if one of its components displays imbalance.

Pure Theory of Public Expenditure

Construction of pure theory of public expenditure has revolved round the consideration of (i) size and range of variation of public expenditure both in absolute and relative terms; (ii) allocation of the given total public expenditure among different functions/activities of the State; and (iii) sources of financing public expenditure. Objectives of public expenditure on different State activities are an instrument of (i) influencing minds of the people and touching their hearts; (ii) promotion of economic growth and welfare of the people.

Public expenditure may also be used to realise the political objectives of the government of the day; but political objectives may be governed by ideology and social constraints of the times. Expenditure on merit and public goods and infrastructure promotes both growth and welfare. With the rising importance of public provision of merit and public goods and services has enhanced the importance of both the level and structure of public expenditure theoretically as well as practically. Total public expenditure depends on political ideology, number, nature, scale, reach and scope of public activities, stage of economic development, social liabilities and number and scale of operations of public enterprises and utilities (Shri Prakash and Chowdhury 1995: 38).

The pure theory of public expenditure has not attracted much attention of economists due partly to the classical assumption of *laissez faire* which assigned minimum well defined functions and roles to the state due partly to the influence of the thought that the determination of public expenditure is more a practical than theoretical proposition. 'The indifference of the analysts may be explained by the uncritical acceptance of the philosophy of *laissez faire* and firm faith in the efficacy of the market mechanism leaving the state with the performance of minimal necessary functions. Hence the chief problem of public finance is envisaged to determine the most efficient method of raising the requisite amount of resources/revenue. The allocation of public resources posed hardly any problem while the size of expenditure was automatically determined by the operational scales of the minimal functions that the state had been assigned' (Shri Prakash and Chowdhury 1995: 37). This apathy was broken by the incorporation of the problems of welfare, growth, planning, regional and personal disparities of income and wealth, distributive justice, merit and public goods as important elements of economic analysis. All these elements have now become inseparable part of general economic theory. So, theory of public finance can no more afford to keep such elements out of reckoning in its theory/

paradigms. However, the building blocks of pure theory and models of public expenditure were provided by such economists as Wicksell and Lindhal. These buildings blocks were transformed into sophisticated theoretical apparatus by Samuelson, Wiseman and Peacock.

But it has to be kept in view in the formulation of pure theory of public expenditure that economic analysis seeks to determine the conditions of equilibrium of the economic system and its constituent parts concurrently or simultaneously. Even if a single element/component of the system is in a state of disequilibrium, the system as a whole will be in disequilibrium. Therefore, the equilibrium of the economy requires its fiscal and monetary sub-systems also to be in equilibrium with other sub-systems of the economy. But a system is said to be in a state of equilibrium if it has attained its most desired position. Most desired position is that which either confers maximum gains/benefits with the utilisation of given resources; or alternatively, the system reaches/realises given state/outcome with the minimum resource cost. It requires the balancing of two sets of factors/forces operating on the side of cost, and the factors/forces operating on the side of benefits. If outcomes of operations of two sets of factors are in balance, then a change in this condition will not increase total benefits or gains. Thus, this is the state in which the system has also minimised the resource cost of the given outcome/benefits; or it has realised the maximum gain from given resource cost. Therefore, pure theory of public expenditure also enunciates the conditions under which given resource cost of given level of public expenditure yields maximum benefits to the economic-social-political system of the country.

Allocation Pattern and Public Expenditure

Pure theory of public expenditure may first determine total expenditure envisaged to be incurred during the financial year; or it may treat total expenditure as sum of expenditure on different public activities. Total public expenditure may thus be determined either as the sum of line/item wise public expenditure; or on the basis of allocation of pre-determined total public expenditure among different lines or items of expenditure. Frisch, Tinbergen, Hicks, Samuelson and Theil have developed sophisticated macro models of determination of aggregate public expenditure. These models have gained great deal of importance over the years. Both these approaches shall briefly be examined hereunder.

Construction of pure theory of public expenditure has, however, revolved round the consideration of (i) size and range of variation of public expenditure between the years and among the uses both in absolute and relative terms; (ii) allocation of total public expenditure among different functions/activities of the State; and (iii) sources of financing public expenditure. Objectives of public expenditure on different State activities is an instrument of influencing minds of the people and touching their hearts and it is an instrument of promotion of economic growth and welfare of the people. Public expenditure may also be used to realise political objectives of the government of the day; but political objectives may be governed by ideology, philosophy of ruler(s)/ruling party and social constraints of the times. Expenditure on merit and public goods and infrastructure promotes both growth and welfare. Increasing importance of public provision of merit and public goods and services has enhanced the importance of both level and structure of public expenditure theoretically and practically. Total public expenditure depends on 'political ideology, number, nature, scale, reach and scope of public activities, stage of economic development, social liabilities and number and scale of operations of public enterprises and utilities (Cf. Shri Prakash and Chowdhury 1995: 38).

Principle of Maximum Social Advantage as Base of Pure Theory of Public Expenditure

General theory of public expenditure is stipulated to be an integrated paradigm which determines (i) size and pattern of public expenditure at the given point in time and over a period of time; (ii) public revenue in general and tax revenue in particular; (iii) requirement of public borrowing along with need for fiscal deficit, if any. Samuelson highlighted difficulties encountered in the evolution of operational mechanism which is needed for generation of true preference ordering of society which may be used to determine the objective function of social welfare sought to be maximised by public expenditure. He further points out that even if an appropriate mechanism is developed for determining the scale of social preferences, signals may be incomplete, or inconsistent, and at times the signals may even be confusing. Kenneth Arrow also discussed such classic difficulties of fixing scale of social preferences which prompted him to formulate his impossibility theorem (Shri Prakash and Chowdhury 1995: 41-42). John R. Has, however, developed the conditions of maximisation of social welfare function.

Total Public Expenditure as Sum of Item/ Activity-Wise Public Expenditure

Incorporation of pattern of allocation in the theory of determination of total public expenditure enhances the range and scope of pure theory of public expenditure. In this case, determination of total expenditure and its allocation among different uses is simultaneous or concurrent rather than sequential. The problem of determination of total expenditure on the basis of level and pattern of allocation among different uses may first be prioritised according to the location of each use in the public preference scale along with the targets/objectives to be attained and constraints to be faced in each direction. Then, the level and pattern of allocation will be determined with a view to maximise the sum total of social benefits conferred by each line of expenditure. Ratio of marginal social benefit of each use will have to be equal to the ratio of the marginal cost of each line of expenditure a la Hicks.

One may also consider Pareto's optimality condition that the level and pattern of allocation of public expenditure shall be the maximum if it is not possible to make even one person better-off without making one or more persons worse off than before the change in the pattern of allocation.

Expenditure may be classified in two categories of (i) transfer payments as subsidies, grants, scholarships, etc., and (ii) expenditure on activities which directly promote growth of output. Transfer payments are generally related to consumption of goods and services, and therefore, such expenditure does not promote production, and hence, growth directly. The objective or criterion for its decision may be to maximise aggregate social satisfaction for which the social marginal (opportunity) cost and marginal social benefit may be equalised. However, consumption at the given level or its expansion in the given year over output of the preceding year indirectly contributes to the growth of production/output. However, it may be argued that if transfer payments were not made. Output of such goods would have to be decreased subsequently. Therefore, transfer payments contribute to the maintenance of output at the given level. Besides, as consumption activates multiplier of growth, it may be erroneous to classify transfer payments as ineffective in promoting growth.

Conventional analysis considers deriving maximum social benefit from the given public expenditure as the base of allocation decisions. The allocation decisions have two layers: First, allocation of total public expenditure is determined between production and distribution of public and private goods; and second, pattern of allocation of total expenditure on public goods is determined to maximise social benefits. But this thesis considers total public expenditure as given or having already been determined. It is also implicit that total discretionary income of the economy has first to be divided between the production of public and private goods. This allocation may be decided according to the principle followed in the determination of allocation of private goods, that is, equalisation of ratio of sacrifices involved in the last unit of expenditure on public and private goods to the ratio of their respective marginal returns.

But first thing for consideration is the total public expenditure incurred during the preceding period on the activities undertaken by the government. This may be treated as the bench mark. Public expenditure like family consumption expenditure is downward sticky. If the projects or programmes related to these activities are incomplete, continuation of expenditure on their completion will be essential. If, the projects have been completed, then expenditure on such projects will fall under expenditure on the maintenance of operations. Hence, preceding period's expenditure may be taken as the bench mark, since outcomes/output of preceding period is generally treated as the minimum acceptable in current year, unless there is some change in policy. Total social benefit conferred by total public expenditure in the preceding period becomes the minimum necessary acceptable outcome in the current year. Additions to preceding period's total expenditure will then depend on the initiation of new programmes/projects planned to be undertaken in the current period, current prices and expected change therein will constitute the base of estimation of the costs.

Lindhal's Hypothesis

Lindhal proposed the theory of pricing to recover full cost from the beneficiaries of public and merit goods and other public services rather than putting forward any pure theory of public expenditure *per se* which is required to determine the absolute level or size of public expenditure or to determine its size relative to GDP or private expenditure. But he has not explained whether he considers average cost plus or just average cost pricing of merit and public goods and utilities. His thesis may imply that sale proceeds of total quantum of goods and services supplied by the government should equal total cost or total expenditure incurred on the same. But total cost of supplies may include administrative and delivery costs also. As he has not thrown light on such facets, there remains some ambiguity in his postulations.

As the public and merit goods and services are used by many beneficiaries, he suggested that beneficiaries may be charged prices according to their scale of preferences which may, among other things, vary with incomes of beneficiaries. It amounts to price discrimination. As he has not specified the degree and nature of discrimination among the beneficiaries, his thesis may be compatible either with first degree price discrimination according to which each beneficiary is charged that price which s/he may be willing to pay. This will leave no one with any consumer surplus. In such cases total sale proceeds are likely to exceed total cost of supply, yielding profits to the government. However, this may not be the intended idea of Lindhal. This may also run counter to the basic objective of public policy. This pricing procedure is quite impractical and may put it under Arrow's impossibility theorem.

Therefore, separate prices may be determined for each income group to which the beneficiaries belong. The maximum price that the least affluent beneficiary of each group is able and willing to pay will equal the price determined for every member of that group (Cf. Shri Prakash and Chowdhury 1995: 38-39). Besides, it may also be surmised that total cost of public goods and services may be allocated on the principle according to which private resources are allocated among different uses or agents. Therefore, optimal pattern of allocation of public goods among different segments of beneficiaries in the state of equilibrium will be one in which ratio of marginal cost of supply to marginal social benefit as a whole equals the ratio of individuals' marginal sacrifice or price paid to last marginal individual's benefits. Consequently, state discriminating monopoly is envisaged to incur no loss in the production and distribution of merit and public goods and services. According to Hirshleifer (1987: 260) perfect price discrimination combines inter-personal discrimination of market segments with intra-personal discrimination of multi-layered pricing procedure. It implicitly assumes zero income elasticity of demand for public and merit goods irrespective of differentials in nature of different goods under public domain as well as differentials of preferences for such goods in the scales of individuals. It means that the quantities taken but used later at lower prices are independent of quantities taken and used at higher prices for initial units. Above two are different parts of Lindhal's theory; both these parts have been supported by economists of education and health subsequently in the implementation of programmes of globalisation. Practical difficulty of implementation of such discriminating monopoly has not been taken into account. Incidentally, discriminating pricing of tickets of different classes by Indian railways and Air India could not save these public sector organisations from incurring losses year after year.

Applied Theory of Public Expenditure

Unlike pure theory of public expenditure, applied/empirical theory of public expenditure has been enriched by contributions of many economists. The empirical theory has been guided and governed by observed facts which have been chancing from time to time. Impact of economic growth on facts and impact of change in social and political philosophy on public policy in general and economic policy in particular, has been the base of evolving new theories of fiscal policy; it directly affected the policy. Facts have been changed due to the effects of policy; facts in their turn led to evolution of new applied theory of public fiscal policy in general and policy of public expenditure in particular. But there are two major applied theories of public expenditure: (i) Wagner's Law and Wagner's Squared Hypothesis; and (ii) Peakok-Wiseman Hypothesis. Other economists have either extended or modified these two hypotheses on the basis of empirical reality.

Wagner's Law

Wagner is probably the first ever political economist who propounded the law of public expenditure. Wagner used the following psychological, demographic and growth premises to propound his law; the law has held its ground over a long period of time: (i) Administrative head (Bureaucrat) of every public activity has a psychological urge to be important and relatively more powerful in bureaucratic hierarchy. This necessitates multiplication of number of subordinates working under his/her immediate command. It may be added that every newly appointed person creates space for her/himself. It results in expansion of not only bureaucratic hold but also in creation of or other type of work; (ii) as the population increases, scale of public operations increases in volume and area of operation needing more persons and spatial area under the given activity. This requires involvement of ever increasing numbers engaged in the given activity; (iii) economic growth results in an increase in the spending power of the government and the tax burden bearing capacity of the people; it results in rise in expenditure in quantitative terms. The delivery mechanisms tend to become more intricate and sophisticated. Besides, Wagoner had also observed the outbreak of First World War, which resulted in massive increase in government's activities across the sectors of the economy and segments of the people. All these factors taken together culminate in raising division of labour and consequent acquisition of specialisation in a narrower filed over the years.

Wagner (1890) used his observations of facts across the countries to formulate his Law of Government's involvement in social, political and economic activities. He postulated that the government's activities have an inherent and latent tendency of expansion in intensity and scale due to ever increasing involvement of the government in a variety of fields. He observed that the growth of GDP and public expenditure are so closely linked as makes the growth paths move together in sync. But public expenditure increases more rapidly than GDP. Consequently, public expenditure relative to GDP increases through time.

Analysis of extensive data of the US Germany, Japan and India shows that (i) absolute public expenditure rises secularly through time; (ii) second degree convex parabola approximates these data extremely closely; (iii) signs and statistical significance of the coefficients of growth curves indicate that growth of public expenditure has been accelerated from lower to higher stages of economic growth; (iv) public expenditure rises more rapidly than income/GDP in the process of growth but it stagnates for a while at the mature stage of growth; and (v) public and merit goods emerge as superior goods in growth; (vi) public expenditure as a proportion of Net National Product increases by one percentage point per year. These inferences lend credible support to Wagnor's Law of public expenditure (for detailed analysis of data of 90 countries, see, Shri Prakash and Chowdhury 1995).

But Wagner did not clarify whether he formulated the law for the growth of absolute public expenditure, or public expenditure relative to income, or relative size of public sector in the economy. Musgrave interprets Wagner's law as applicable to the size of public sector relative to size of economy as a whole. Relation between Net National Product (NPP) to total size of the economy has been analysed by Shri Prakash and Chowdhury and they examined the Wagner's proposition with different layers and levels of data. Wagner's law is universally applicable to the public expenditure, irrespective of its measurement in relative or absolute terms or in terms of growth rates (Shri Prakash and Chowdhury 1995).

Squared Hypothesis

Buchanan and Tullock (1977) used data of US economy for evaluating empirical validity of Wagner's Law. They, however, related public expenditure to production of public goods alone. Discrepancy between the growth of output of public goods and growth of public expenditure on these goods prompted them to designate discrepancy in two growth rates as Wagner's Squared Hypothesis. They inferred the hypothesis from two observed facets of (i) more rapid growth of public expenditure on administration than the output of government's activities; (ii) rising proportion of population covered by social security and other transfer payments of the government.

The above theses have certain limitations. Output of public goods is quite precisely measurable as the product of quantities and prices. Prices of public goods are, however, administered and include an element of subsidy. If the state has the monopoly over production of these goods, it is not possible to determine their market price. At the most, the prices may be based on average cost of production which is generally higher than prices at which public goods are supplied. But output of a set of public goods should either be considered relative to their cost, or to output of administrative activities, which is neither tangible nor measurable. Cost of public expenditure is quite obvious and may be measured in terms of expenditure incurred in the performance of administrative services. At the most, output of administration is also attributable to expenditure.

Peacock differs from Buchnan and Tullock's (1977) twin theses. He advances following arguments: (i) individuals do not weigh the sacrifice involved in their tax payments to the government against the benefits they may derive from public provision of public goods and other services; (ii) individuals try to maximise their gains/shares from the public services at the level of taxation they are subjected to. But electorates demand greater provision of public services when they are contacted for votes before the election. The contestants generally do promise increase in future supplies of public services for which the electorates have to bear larger burden of increased taxation. But the tax liability of beneficiaries need not increase in proportion to additional benefits they would derive in future. The tax burden need not fall on most of the beneficiaries even at all. Who would bear the tax burden and who will benefit from increased public expenditure depends on which segment of population or sector of the economy tax is levied and for which section of the society public expenditure is incurred. But the main thrust of the argument is that both people and politicians, who run the government, desire public expenditure to rise year on year. The cost or productivity of public expenditure seldom comes into reckoning in the decisions to raise public expenditure inter-temporally. It is a commonly observed fact that much less care, if at all, is exercised in decisions relating to public than private expenditure.

Wiseman-Peacock Hypothesis

Wiseman-Peacock's hypothesis is derived from the analysis of 65 years data of UK from 1890 to 1955 of public expenditure. This thesis asserts that public expenditure increases by jumps and jerks rather than smoothly in step-wise fashion in the continuum of time. If revenue receipts constitute the constraint to public expenditure, its growth will be slowed down. Thus, revenue is treated as the main determinant of public expenditure during normal times. But this trend is periodically disrupted by occurrence of socio-political and economic turbulences and natural disasters. These upheavals make public expenditure transgress the revenue constraint; since such upheavals are redressed by abnormally high public expenditure beyond the bounds of revenue of normal times. More revenue is raised for redressing pains and pangs inflicted upon the society by disasters and its economy has to bear the burden of increased taxation. New tax rates then become the future bench mark, since public expenditure, like private consumption expenditure is upward flexible but downward sticky. The enhanced expenditure displays the inadequacy of revenue of normal times for meeting rising public expenditure requirement. This may, however, be applicable to successive increases in tax revenue in developing countries in order to meet the ever rising public expenditure for investment required for economic growth. Wiseman-Peacock defines this displacement of revenue and expenditure curve from normal path to push it on an upward movement as an 'inspection effect'. Limits to 'Tolerance of Taxation' are thus periodically raised by such disturbances in the normal functioning of fiscal policy. The hypothesis thus emphasises that growth of public revenue follows the leads of growth of public expenditure. As public expenditure stabilises at rising level, revenue also tends to stabilise at the corresponding higher level. This hypothesis may imply that even though immediate public expenditure requirements caused by natural and other disasters may be met by public loans and/or fiscal deficits. Ultimately, public expenditure has to be financed out of public revenue.

Besides, each disturbance and disruption in the normal balance between public revenue and public expenditure leads to the coverage of larger set of public activities, net result of rising expenditure-revenue is increased degree of concentration; it refers to relatively greater increase in expenditure of central than state and local governments. Reason is that the tax raising and expenditure capacity of the central government is much wider in space and larger in population base than those of the state and local governments.

Even though disasters and upheavals, natural or man-made are random in nature in occurrence, resultant rise in public expenditure depicts temporal regularity and spatial pattern. A larger or smaller part of temporal regularity and spatial pattern are in-built in the growth of economy, especially of planned economic growth and social development of developing economies like the Indian or Tanzanian ones.

Public Expenditure, Disasters and Policy Change

Public Expenditure is highly sensitive to occurrences of natural, social and political or other disasters in the economy and the change in policy, especially switching from one policy regime to another. Greater the frequencies of such occurrences, greater shall be the volatility of policy relating to size and composition of public expenditure. Such changes generally refer to the switching away from *laissez faire* to controlled and regulated regime of an economy or *vice versa*; or from an open mixed economy to a greatly controlled mixed economy. For example, during and after the occurrence of a disaster, disaster management emerges as first national priority. Disasters normally inflict great loss of property and human life, production facilities may be partially or wholly destroyed or disrupted, supplies routes may be blocked or restricted. Such consequences are very different from the normal occurrences in society or its economy. These disasters require immediate response from government which involves unprecedented quantum of public expenditure, nature and composition of which greatly differ from normal pattern of expenditure and among disasters and disruptions of different types. Aid by other countries and U.N. agencies enables the country affected by natural or man-made disasters to transgress its limit of public income to public expenditure.

First priority is generally the rehabilitation of people and sectors of the economy and segments of spatial units affected adversely by such happenings. Second priority is the restoration of supplies of essential goods, which have to be arranged immediately. Then normal production facilities have to be restored to their normal level. Expenditure on such priorities is generally not the part of normal budgeting since such needs arise only after the event. Besides, the magnitude and structure of public expenditure are changed radically. In several cases, expenditure on the prevention of recurrence of similar disasters in future is also undertaken. For example, in the aftermath of floods, such measures as dredging and/or bonding of the river banks are undertaken. Total public expenditure crosses the earlier peak of budgeted public expenditure and it creates a new benchmark till it is crossed again by another disaster of the same or different genre and the extent of damage inflicted on the socio-economic systems is comparable. This also results in the creation of new long run bench mark for tax revenue. This is because, like the living standards of individuals, public expenditure is greatly downward sticky and highly upward flexible. Such occurrences may also impart short run volatility of public expenditure in so far as the expenditure incurred on the management of consequences of such occurrences coupled with normal expenditure make public expenditure to rise to an abnormally high level (Cf. Musgrave 1959, Peacock and Wiseman 1961, 1967).

Clark's Hypothesis

Clark (1954) propounded the following inter-related twin hypotheses relating to (i) critical limit of the economy and people's tolerance and ability to bear the burden of taxation; and (ii) inflationary impact of rising public expenditure, irrespective of its nature and cause(s) in a market economy. His thesis of inflationary effect of rising public expenditure shall not be valid if most of the prices are publicly administered as is the case in socialist economies. His twin thesis are based on an extensive analysis of inter-war period's data of several Western economies. He opines that 25 per cent share of public activities in the total economy is the critical maximum limit. Increase in public revenue to finance public expenditure above this limit tends to adversely affect the productivity of tax payers, since they are left with less money to finance private investment, while productivity of public investment tends to be lower than that of private investment. The productivity differentials between private and public investment may generally be attributed to the nature and direction of public investment. Public investment may generally be concentrated in such lines of production as have low returns and need huge investment beyond the reach of private investors. Besides, involvement of long lead times in capacity creation and generation of additional income by public investment may also account for such productivity differences. Negligence of composition and nature of investment between public and private enterprises may conceal rather than reveal this facet. But Clark hypothesises that supply side effect of growth of public expenditure beyond 25 per cent of GDP may be negative and the demand side effect of public financing of expenditure beyond the critical limit is generally inflationary.

The validity of Clark's hypothesis is very sensitive to the assumptions on which these hypotheses have been based. Incentives for private investment may be squeezed even at lower or higher levels than critical maximum of 25 per cent of GDP; it depends on lower or higher per capita incomes at different levels of growth and nature and pattern of income distribution; it impinges upon the tax revenue raising capacity of the government of the country. Past conditioning of the people to bear the tax burden also plays an important role in people's taxable capacity which is not just material but it is greatly psychological also. That is why people willingly part with greater proportion of their earnings out of the given income levels during war and times of natural disasters. In fact, Clark's critical maximum limit has already been crossed in several market economies without there being inflationary pressure. Besides, investment incentives need not necessarily be monetary or financial always. For example, entry preventing extra capacity creation by oligopolists or investment for cornering larger share of the market is not directly related to greater returns. As Baumol points out in managerial theory of the firm, corporate executives' objective may be sales rather than profit maximisation. Similarly, Williamson's hypothesis that executives focus more on growth and diversification of the company rather than the maximisation of profits highlight non-monetary objectives of private investment.

Brahamanand's Hypothesis

Brahamanand (1977) analysed growth of expenditure, including public expenditure, in relation to the growth of real national income of India. He found the growth of these two variables to be closely related to each other. For evaluating inflationary effect of growth and expenditure, he brought money supply into the centre stage of analysis. This resulted in focus being shifted more to inflation and money supply than the inter-relation between public expenditure and growth of income.

Growth of Public Expenditure and Output of Manufactures in India

Shri Prakash (1982) treated growth of industrial output as a function of public investment; he used the data Indian economy which covered the period from 1950-51 to 1973-74. The positive relation between growth of output of manufactures with public expenditure has been postulated on the basis of three premises: (i) Industrialisation in post independent era of India was been initiated and nurtured by public investment; (ii) Role of public administration in the maintenance and propelling of economic growth has been rising consistently, especially from 1956, the year of commencement of Second Five Year Plan. The objective was to have greater control and regulation over the expanding private sector; and (iii) Inadequacy of private investment and scarcity of enterprise in the initial stages of growth of Indian economy has to be covered and even augmented by public policy in the economy.

His findings showed that (i) both preceding and current period's public investment augmented output of manufactures, though the lead-lag structure of relation between output and investment made the contribution of preceding period's public investment greater than that of current public investment; (ii) income/GDP was found to be uniquely related to the optimum size of public investment; and (iii) but there existed a saturation point beyond which growth of public investment, especially non investment part of public expenditure tended to adversely affect growth of income; and (iv) minimum level of public expenditure and its growth might have been autonomous and independent of the level of GDP/income. It implies that public expenditure may grow ahead of income/GDP at a rate greater than the rate of growth of GDP. But GDP tends to be affected by public expenditure. These findings may facilitate proper explanation of the growth of income, and growth effects of public expenditure.

Growthless Capital Stock, Public Expenditure, Stockless Money and Inflation

Public policy was designed to propel public sector to acquire the commanding heights of the Indian economy by means of rapid capital accumulation in public sector; consistent growth of public investment during the era of planned economic development of Indian economy from 1951 to 1989-90 accounted for this phenomenon. But high growth of public investment resulted in the creation of productive capacity which was under-utilised over a considerable period of time due mainly to scarcity of imported and domestically produced intermediate inputs. Paucity of foreign exchange and cornering of large stocks of these goods by importers, having direct import licenses and permits for scarce domestic goods resulted in the emergence of the flourishing black market. Thus, huge inventories/ stocks of intermediate and scarce finished goods were piled up in the midst of under-utilised productive capacities. Consequently, abnormally high capital-output ratios in public enterprises raised the overall cost, especially the capital cost, and accumulated inventories resulted in the locking of capital in inventories. Shri Prakash (1992a, 1992b) developed a mathematical model for the analysis of this facet of Indian economy; the model incorporated inventory investment in Harrod's key growth equation and applied it to Indian data. He theoretically and mathematically highlighted that excessive inventory investment reduces the growth of an economy in proportion to the excess of inventory investment. His results show that as high as 73 per cent of total growth potential of Harrod Growth model was lost in inventories. This resulted in a peculiar situation of growthless capital stock in a capital scarce economy, where public investment accounted for the major proportion of total investment.

Shri Prakash and Sharma (1998) incorporated inventory investment in Two Sector Mahalanobis Growth Model of Indian economy. They applied the modified and extended Mahalanobis model to Indian data. It was found that the inventory investment ate up almost 67 per cent of total growth potential of the economy. Thus, a great deal of public investment was mal-allocated and misdirected which adversely affected the growth performance of India economy during a prolonged period.

Conclusions

Theory of fiscal policy has basically been empirical in orientation and time-space specific in nature. The theory of fiscal policy has, therefore, been evolving over a long period of time and it continues to be extended or modified in time-space domain till now. Theory of policy of public expenditure has also been evolving over the years. But public expenditure has emerged as the driving force of public finances. Analysts have developed both pure and applied theories of public expenditure, though pure theoretical back-up of the policy of public expenditure still remains a bit thin relative to applied theories of public expenditure. Wagoner's Law has been in the centre stage of the evolution of new directions and dimensions of applied theory of public expenditure. However, literature has largely been dominated by Keynes' General theory for pretty long. A fascinating feature of the theory of fiscal policy in general and theory and policy of public expenditure in particular, has borne the periodic swings in favour or against or for more interventions by the government in economic affairs.

6

The Status of Tanzanian Economy Before and After Globalisation

Introduction

The status of Tanzanian economy is analysed in this chapter to highlight the major changes associated with shift in policy since independence in 1961 to 2012. Three important phases during this period are distinguished. First phase commenced when the nation attained its political independence in 1961 and it lasted till 1985. This phase is referred as 'Ujamaa Socialism'. This phase is subdivided in the following three sub periods: (i) 'Pre-Arusha' Declaration period, (ii) "Pre-crisis" period. This period runs from 1968 to the collapse of coffee boom in 1978; and (iii) 'Crisis' period started with the Uganda War in mid 1978 and subsequent OPEC oil price shock in 1979. It runs until the resignation of President Julius Nyerere in 1985. The second phase begins with the adoption of major International Monetary Fund (IMF) and World Bank SAPs (structural adjustment programmes) in 1986 and runs till 1992. This period is called the 'reform' period. The third phase is the post reform period which runs from 1993 to 2012 (Bigsten and Danielson 1999). Each of these phases is discussed briefly next.

Phase I: Ujamaa Socialism

From Independence to Pre-Arusha Declaration Period, 1961-1967

The Government of Tanzania since Independence was concerned more with structuring of public sector as a measure to stimulate growth of the economy and improve social welfare of the poor Tanzanians. Tanzania followed multi-party democratic system during the period; political democracy was accompanied by economic democracy. Hence, market led economic policies with minimal government intervention were pursued (Adam 2014).

The government did not do much to change economic policies which had been pursued by the colonial power. The tax system and allocation of public expenditure were designed to assist the operations of colonial plantations during the colonial period. However, a large proportion of public expenditure was devoted to road construction to link the raw materials producing areas like the sisal, cotton and coffee plantation estates, and other raw materials, which were required by the colonial power, to the ports and harbours for shipment. This is similar to the policy followed by the then British Government of India. Expenditure on education, health and other social welfare activities was relatively low and it was designed to further the interest of colonial rulers. This situation prevailed even after political independence up to 1967 when the government adopted the so called 'Ujamaa Socialism' through Arusha Declaration. However, the government still encouraged peasant agriculture with the policy of import substitution in industry by relatively small enterprises; this largely depended on private ownership of major means of production and partly on public sector (Cliffe 1972).

The main reason for adopting socialist system based on planning was to address the economic and social problems of high level of poverty and large income inequality among the Tanzanians which were caused by market oriented policies adopted even after the attaining of political independence (Bigsten and Danielson 1999). Besides, process of growth was extremely slow and low. Soviet Model, which attained that level of success in few decades which was attained in few centuries by market based economies (Shri Prakash 1994). The market led policies resulted in marginally improved economic performance during the period 1961-1967.[1] Per capita income grew by an average of 1.9 per cent per annum, while inflation, population and gross capital formation as a share of GDP grew at 4.9, 2.9 and 13.7 per cent respectively (see Table 6.1). This implies very low output per unit of capital employed

1. This is much greater than the annual compound rate of growth for the whole period.

and dissipation of most part of the growth in nominal terms. Besides, 91.7 per cent of total labour force was employed in agriculture and the economy depended greatly on this sector in terms of export earnings. Further, its average value added was 53 per cent as compared to 5.3 per cent for manufacturing sector (Fan et al. 2005). This also reflects the poor output per unit of labour and capital in manufacturing. But the government achieved sound macroeconomic stability with relatively low inflation rate in the planning era. This is evident from figures reported in Table 6.1.

Table 6.1

Average Growth Rate of Tanzanian Macroeconomic Indicators, 1991-2012

Economic Indicators	*Percentage*
Real GDP Growth Rate (annual growth %)	5.24
Per capita income growth (annual growth %)	2.40
Population growth (annual growth %)	2.90
Gross capital formation (% of GDP)	24.95
Inflation (annual growth %)	14.24
Fiscal Deficit (% of GDP)	8.10
Domestic Saving (% of GDP)	10.73
Exports (% of GDP)	19.87
Imports (% of GDP)	33.55
External balance on goods and services (% of GDP)	-13.68
Trade (% of GDP)	54.05
Agriculture, value added (% of GDP)	36.28
Industry, value added (% of GDP)	20.20
Services, etc., value added (% of GDP)	43.52
Public Revenue (annual growth %)	22.75
Recurrent Expenditure (annual growth %)	25.56
Development Expenditure (annual growth %)	65.66
Public Expenditure (annual growth %)	26.56
Recurrent Expenditure (% of Public Expenditure)	76.92
Development Expenditure (%Public Expenditure)	23.08
Public Expenditure (% of GDP)	17.68

Source: Authors' Own Compilation.

Pre-Crisis Decade of 1968-1978

This period differed from the preceding one because a sharp increase in public expenditure to support internal and external responsibilities of the government occurred. The period is marked by abnormally high hikes in international oil prices in 1973-74 and 1978-79; it resulted in internationally high inflation jointly with recession. This is the first time in history when inflation and recession, two opposite phases of business cycles, came to exist together in most of the economies of the world (Shri Prakash 1981). High prices of oil and other imports created inflationary conditions in Tanzania also. Inflation was further accentuated by the rapid growth in public expenditure due to sluggish exports of coffee and other primary Tanzanian products. Exports of Tanzania were adversely affected by recessionary conditions abroad. Public expenditure also grew to support administration of the newly formed ministries, defence and those areas which were neglected during the colonial period like secondary and university education and health. Heavy taxation to finance the increased public expenditure resulted in further accentuation of recession. Establishment of large number of new public enterprises, including heavy industry group to loosen the grip of foreign owned enterprises on Tanzanian economy also accounted for rapid growth of public expenditure.

The political independence of Tanzania in 1961 is the key factor of change in the roles and functions of state in general and public expenditure in particular. Adoption of the socialism and economic planning in 1967 under the Arusha Declaration resulted in a policy of more egalitarian public expenditure, especially rapid increase in public spending on health, education and other social services. Large public expenditure led to large fiscal and BoPs (balance of payments) deficits.

The Arusha Declaration in 1967 was also the watershed in political and economic history of Tanzania. President Nyerere and his ruling party launched the strategy of 'African socialism' in this period, when the government took control of the economy. Privately owned institutions were nationalised. During the early 1970s, banking and large portions of industrial sector had been nationalised and all major investment programmes were under the state control. The major concern was to create an internally integrated economy that was free from too much external dependence and achievement of maximum possible self-reliance. This change was facilitated by increased state control of the economy and acquisition of ownership of all former major private enterprises. From then, the government became the major player in addressing social, economic and political problems of the society. Economic transformation had a positive impact on the performance of the economy. However, this success was short lived because of the negative consequences of two oil price shocks in 1973-74 and 1979, the breakup of East African Community in 1977 and Tanzania-Uganda war of 1978 (Wenzel and Wiedemann 1989; Ndulu 1994).

However the growth of per capita GDP during this period declined to 1.08 per cent which is much smaller than that of pre-Arusha Declaration period. The average size of public expenditure as a share of GDP was 28.3 per cent as compared to 18.3 per cent during the pre-Arusha Declaration. The period was also associated with an increase in growth rate of GDP as well as an increase in gross capital formation as a percentage of GDP with an average of 5.9 and 24.1 per cent respectively. The growth was probably led by increased investment in such sectors as education, health, etc. Sizeable contributions came from agriculture and manufacturing sectors. Tanzania's exports dominated by traditional agricultural goods such as coffee and cotton, stagnated (See Table 6.1).

Crisis Period, 1979-1986

The 'crisis' period started in 1979 after the Tanzania-Uganda war. This period witnessed increased fiscal deficit due to high public expenditure relative to public revenue. The year also coincided with the international oil crisis. The crisis period was associated with rapid decline in economic growth and other macroeconomic variables (Wobst 2001). A combination of a slowdown in economic growth and rising population growth resulted in a decline in growth of per capita GDP which resulted in negative average rate of -1.47 per cent. But the rate of growth of GDP averaged 1.1 per cent per annum. Fiscal deficit rose to 11.5 per cent which resulted in inflation with an average of 31 per cent per annum (Nord et al. 2009). Population growth was relatively high as compared to economic growth. This resulted in high unemployment and runs counter to Phillips' thesis about positive relation between inflation, growth and employment. Besides, it is also contrary to Keynes' thesis that increased expenditure, especially public expenditure, boosts aggregate demand function which pushes the economy towards full employment equilibrium. The economic decline might partly be attributed to economic shocks like the Uganda war, drought and oil crisis. This may also be attributed partly to the failure of the government of President Nyerere to accept such macroeconomic policy reforms as a 15 per cent devaluation which were recommended by the World Bank and IMF (World Bank 2000). This implies that economic crisis in Tanzania emanated from the failure of socialist policies of central planning of economic system which was implemented after the Arusha Declaration. However, the government might have considered price inelasticity of exports and imports in international and domestic markets. Devaluation would have merely escalated import bills without countervailing increase in export earnings. Besides, increased prices of imports would have accentuated inflation in the economy.

The government in 1981-82 decided to implement its own home led economic reforms which were called 'National Economic Survival Programme' and 'Structural Adjustment Programme' aimed at addressing poor economic performance. This was sought to be achieved by increasing production of both cash crops to increase export earnings and food crops to eliminate food shortages. However, these home driven reforms were not successful in mitigating the prevailing economic crisis; failure of these reforms may be due to government's failure to accept the conditionalities imposed by the donors. These conditions related to exchange rate over valuation, cost sharing in education and health services, privatisation of public owned enterprises (Chaligha et al. 2002), tight monetary policy, introduction of multiparty system and liberalisation of agricultural marketing in order to acquire financial support necessary for implementation of such programmes (Adam 2014). Most of the donors started to withdraw their support to the government in 1983 because of the negative effects of Ujamaa Socialism on economic efficiency.

Tanzania's economic performance indicated a continuous deterioration and highly inefficient economy in the 1980s as a result of the crisis. So, the government had to seek an alternative policy to replace the Ujamaa socialism policy. Moreover, the economy experienced an extremely overvalued exchange rate, which ultimately decreased the country's competitiveness in traditional export markets of agricultural commodities, thereby diminishing export earnings. In addition, Tanzania's terms of trade deteriorated severely during the same period (early 1980s) because of the collapse of prices in world market. Consequently, the trade deficit increased, foreign capital inflows decreased, and overall indebtedness exceeded critical levels (Bigsten and Danielsson 1999). However, it is probable that the poor performance of the economy of Tanzania is solely attributable to excessive government intervention and it ultimately led to the rapid growth of black market with the inefficiencies that go with the open market operations. The slowdown of growth rate of GDP together with slower growth of per capita income and the high inflation rate brought about a reduction of real income of people living both in rural and urban areas. Government expenditure on services of health, education, water and other social services will also be reduced.

Reform Period, 1986-1992

The reform period in Tanzania commenced in 1986 when agricultural sector, the largest part of the economy, was the main priority. The Government of Tanzania embarked on the Economic Recovery Programme (ERP) during the sub-period from 1986 to 1989. This programme included a number of policies based on trade and exchange rate liberalisation and macroeconomic stabilisation to stimulate domestic savings, and restoring fiscal sustainability. Apart from the above reforms, the government also included reforms in the banking system, agricultural marketing, the parastatal sector, government administration, and the civil services, together with the targeting of social sectors which had deteriorated substantially during the crisis (Bagachwa 1992). In later stage of reform process, the government was mainly engaged in reforming structure of the economy by: (a) reducing size of public sector and its expenditure through fiscal policy of contraction, (b) reduction in the size of civil services, (c) closing or selling of loss-making public enterprises, and (d) initiation of financial sector reforms. Besides, cost sharing in education and health services was introduced and subsidies to agriculture were eliminated. With these reforms many people lost their jobs and privileges in the government and the parasatals. This was the period when the government moved from state led economy towards market led economy as a way to secure financial assistance from the IMF and the World Bank. The private sector was encouraged to play an active role in economic growth of the country which was contrary to Arusha Declaration period. In 1992, the Government of Tanzania established Presidential Parasatal Sector's Reform Commission (PSRC) in order to privatise the SOEs (state owned enterprises) and thus expand the role of private sector in the economy (Waigama 2008). Consequently, a large number of SOEs, particularly the loss making ones, were privatised and they are now privately owned. Up to 2003, a total of 281 public units were already privatised, including 50 which were under Loans and Advances Realisation Trust (LART) (URT 2008).

The period was followed by some marginal improvement in the performance of various economic variables. For example growth of GDP moved from 1.1 per cent in the crisis period to 3.6 per cent, while growth of per capita GDP increased from -1.5 to 1.2 per cent, fiscal deficit decreased to 5.9 from 11.5 per cent. The share of public expenditure in GDP also declined from 29.9 to 18.5 per cent, while inflation decreased from 31.0 to 26.5 per cent.

Post-Reform Period, 1993-2012

Despite economic reforms that took place in mid 1980s, around 1993-94 the government again started experiencing a new crisis with the donors; it emanated from poor fiscal control, particularly the large scale tax exemptions granted by the Ministry of Finance, which resulted in a severe decline in tax revenue. Besides, the existing economy was still characterised by large public monopolies of enterprises with poor performance, poor management of public funds, larger fiscal deficits, high inflation (double digits), and large debt burden (Nord et al. 2009). The government had to revert to borrowing from the central bank as a way to finance fiscal deficit. The donors also felt that corruption and tax evasion was rampant, and that the government was not committed to dealing with these issues, (Mutalemwe et al. 1998: 10).

The new government under third president of Tanzania, Benjamin Mkapa, in 1995 focussed on macroeconomic stabilisation and economic reforms to restore the international donor community's confidence in Tanzania's commitment to such reforms. In 1996, the government launched the 1996-97–1998-99 Economic Recovery Programme (ERP) under the three year Enhanced Structural Adjustment Facility (ESAF). This enhanced the relations with the other donors. In 2000, the International Development Association (IDA) and the IMF "agreed to support a comprehensive debt reduction package for Tanzania under enhanced Heavily Indebted Poor Countries (HIPC) Initiative." Assistance was to be provided under severe conditions, which included the adoption and implementation of a participatory poverty reduction strategy paper (World Bank 2000). The Government of Tanzania was again constrained by the World Bank and IMF to implement economic reforms under SAPs by opening and integrating its economy with the rest of the world. These economic reforms concentrated on trade liberalisation, privatisation of SOEs, public sector reforms, liberalisation of financial sector, creation of market driven regulatory framework and encouragement to FDI (foreign direct investment) (Nord et al. 2009). These reforms have largely affected Tanzanian economy because instead of doing right liberalisation and privatisation, the government ended with the so called "foreignisation". Most of the key sectors of the economy were put in the hands of the foreigners and this could not generate long-run growth and economic independence of the nation. Historical experiences indicate that there is no country in the world which implemented the IMF and World Bank policies and reached high level of economic growth (See Mathur 1991). This support the concept propagated by Stiglitz regarding IMF and World Bank policies that "one size does not fit all", meaning that the policies designed for developed nations might not fit the developing economies and vice versa. Besides, the strategy of growth that succeeded in one country may not succeed in another country. Similarly, the strategy of growth that delivered in one country at some time need not succeed in that country at another time. The very success of strategy of growth results in changes, which render some of the past policies redundant (Shri Prakash 1995). The IMF and World Bank policies have not succeeded to address the economic problems of the Tanzanian society such as poverty, ignorance and diseases; but have resulted in increased dependence on donors politically, socially and even economically.

Empirical Evidence

The above postulations and contentions need empirical support. Table 6.2 shows the growth of several key macroeconomic variables during the post reforms period from 1991 to 2012. The post-reform period shows a better economic performance as compared to the reform period. The average rates of growth of GDP and per capita GDP increased to approximately 5.5 and 2.6 per cent respectively. These growth rates show convergence towards the growth rates of first two periods. It highlights the fact that post reform period has enabled the Tanzanian economy to recover some of its lost ground. While the rate of growth of population has declined substantially which resulted in an improvement in the rate of growth of per capita GDP and capital formation has touched the new high of about 24 per cent growth.

Inflation, like population, also decreased to 12.4 per cent but still remained in double digits. This is pretty high in magnitude and quite beyond the limits of tolerance. Persistence of the inflation will harm the future growth of the economy. One reason of high inflation seems to be continual increase in fiscal deficit again to 8.1 per cent. However, the ratio of public expenditure to GDP marginally declined to 18.1 per cent from 18.5 per cent in the preceding period.[2] This is an indication that despite an increase in GDP, the revenue collection, most of which is tax revenue, was not buoyant enough to meet the

2. Neither fiscal deficit nor public expenditure is inflationary per se; both fiscal deficit and public expenditure may promote growth if resources generated by these financial instruments are used productively

demand for public expenditure; it may also be a factor behind the rising fiscal deficit. Tax revenue did not show desired growth despite the efforts made by the government to broaden the tax base by introducing the Tanzania Revenue Authority (TRA) in 1996 and VAT (value added tax) in 1998. Increased fiscal deficit indicated that the government still financed it by printing more money. Agricultural sector continued to plays dominant role in economic performance as it employs approximately 77 per cent of the entire labour force. This however is a testimony to the failure of the economy to industrialise itself. But other sectors like tourism, manufacturing, mining, transport and communication have gained relatively more importance than before. Thus, tertiary sectors in Tanzania seem to have got an upper hand just as these sectors have usurpted the dominant position in Indian economy.

Table 6.2

Comparative Figures of Sub-Period Wise Selected Macro Variables

Economic Indicators	*Pre-Arusha (1961-1967)*	*Pre-Crisis (1968-1978)*	*Crisis (1979-1985)*	*Reforms (1986- 1992)*	*Post-Reforms (1993-2012)*
Real GDP Growth Rate	5.70	5.90	1.10	3.60	5.50
Per capita income growth %	1.93	1.08	-1.47	1.19	2.60
Population growth %	2.90	3.03	3.19	3.13	2.90
% of labour force in agri-culture	91.66	88.80	85.50	84.68	77.5
Gross capital formation as % of GDP	13.70	24.11	26.07	24.30	24.10
Inflation %	4.93	14.00	31.00	26.50	12.40
Fiscal Deficit as % GDP	-	10.70	11.50	5.90	8.10
Public Exp/ GDP (%)	18.31	28.27	29.88	18.52	18.14

Source: Authors' Calculations.

Overview of all the Sub-Periods

Table 6.2 shows the period wise values of important macro variables. A perusal of the table reveals that:

(i) Rates of growth of GDP during the first two sub-periods almost match each other. But the rate of growth of GDP declined radically in subsequent sub-periods and recovered some lost ground during the last sub-period.

(ii) Population increased consistently from the first to the last period, when it ultimately declined by slightly more than two per cent.

(iii) As a consequence of declining rate of growth of GDP and high but increasing rate of growth of population per capita GDP also declined period after period till it also rose in the last period of observation.

(iv) Fiscal deficit and public expenditure rose consistently from one to another sub-period. Unlike other variables, fiscal deficit and public expenditure grew even more rapidly during the last period. Fiscal deficit and public expenditure have thus been reinforcing the growth of each other in every sub-period.

(v) Sustained increase in public expenditure, fiscal deficit and taxation, including indirect taxation, led to continuous growth of inflation in the Tanzanian economy.

(vi) Labour force employed in agriculture has declined continuously from the first to the last sub-period; its value has gone down from 92 per cent to 78 per cent in the post reform period.

(vii) Gross capital formation has been rising continuously from the first to the third period where from it started declining till the last sub-period. But growth of gross capital formation ahead of the growth of GDP implies continuous decline in productivity of capital. It also implies more capital being available per unit of labour; it also means the decline in labour productivity. Growth of Tanzanian economy cannot be sustained over the long period with declining capital and labour productivities. Inefficient use of human and physical capital has to be weeded out wherever it exists.

Tests of Staionarity of Main Economic Variables

In this section, some empirical analysis of change in various economic variables before and after globalisation is undertaken. The study uses multiple methods and models for data analysis. The objective is to rule out the probability of acceptance of any otiose type result(s) embodied in a specific model/method. The results of various methods and models are outlined briefly hereunder. Because of the nature of time series data used in this study, first the analysis of the properties of stationarity of the variables is done in order to avoid spurious results. The study uses three tests for analysing stationarity nature of the data, namely: (i) Dickey-Fuller (D-F), (ii) Augmented Dickey-Fuller (ADF) and (iii) Phillips-Perron (PP) tests. Regression results of these variables may be accepted as genuine even at level. The results of D-F test are presented in Tables 6.3.

Table 6.3

Results of Dickey-Fuller Test of Unit Root

	No Constant	*With Constant*		*With Constant and Stochastic Trend*		
Variable	*Slope*	*Intercept*	*Slope*	*Intercept*	*Slope*	*Trend*
GDPt	0.0553	-248013.512	0.0839	-249458.3	0.109	-7511.882
	(17.2201)	(-6.0514)	(15.9335)	(-6.360)	(8.827)	(-2.229)
PRt	3.4949	1007914	1.5240	479516.8	1.0341	24044.26
	(3.5368)	(14.4714)	(3.5078)	(4.9224)	(3.1948)	(6.3378)
PEt	3.7969	1416880	11.356	568322.9	1.1102	38711.65
	(2.9889)	(11.356)	(3.788)	(2.9459)	(3.2323)	(5.1250)
INVt	-0.8349*	316157.32	-0.9181 *	-120587.2	-0.9498*	19279.68
	(-11.295)	(6.4277)	(-16.7096)	(-2.0154)	(-27.9263)	(8.4614)
PVTCt	0.0279	318543.27	-0.0187	554859.78	-0.2897*	57474.26
	(1.3219)	(0.9543)	(-0.3517)	(1.6970)	(-2.4869)	(1.6969)
FSDt	1.1711	439379.1	0.8676	75122.51	0.7148	16094.45
	(3.0108)	(6.6019)	(3.0868)	(0.6317)	(2.8204)	(3.5303)
POPt	0.0294	0.2011	0.0220	0.082	0.037	-0.010
	(15.9159)	(1.5105)	(4.2211)	(0.238)	(0.929)	(-0.379)
SUBt	0.2368	83.3456	0.2364	70.4659	0.2363	0.7036
	(77.4207)	(0.2380)	(68.0696)	(0.0977)	(47.5823)	(0.0205)

Source: Authors' Computations.

Random Walk Model

Table 6.3 contains OLS estimates of three versions of Random Walk Model (RWM) fitted to all eight variables and results of application of D-F test for evaluating the value of the root of regression functions. Six out of 8 variables are found non-stationary in all three versions of RWM; but investment/savings series is shown stationary by all three versions of RWM and third version of RWM reveals private consumption expenditure as stationary. The coefficient δ, attached to lagged $PVCE_t$ and INV_t is negative and statistically significant at 0.05 probability level. Therefore, the root, ρ of these functions is less than one.

ADF and Phillips-Perron Tests of Unit-Root

Results of ADF and PP tests of unit root are reported in Table 6.4. All variables except population and investment are found to be non-stationary at level. This inference is derived by comparing the computed test statistics of both tests with corresponding critical values at 1 and 5 per cent probability.

All these variables, except population and investment, are subjected to unit root test at first differences because of the existence of unit root at level. Both ADF and PP test statistics have been estimated with the constant and constant and trend. Results of the test of differences reveal that all variables are stationary at the first differences and are well integrated at I (1). These results pave the way for estimating the appropriate regression functions of the variables under consideration. But before that, results of descriptive statistics are also examined. Our experiments show that, if the time series is stationary at level, its regression does not require incorporation of lagged value of the dependent variable; if the series is stationary at first difference, then its regression needs incorporation of its first lag of the dependent variable. In general, if a series is stationary at m differences, then its regression requires incorporation of m lags.

Table 6.4

Augmented Dickey-Fuller and Phillips-Perron Tests

	Augmented Dickey-Fuller				*Phillips-Perron*			
	Level		*First Difference*		*Level*		*First Difference*	
Variable	*Inter-cept*	*Inter-cept & trend*	*Inter-cept*	*Inter-cept & trend*	*Inter-cept*	*Inter-cept and trend*	*Inter-cept*	*Inter-cept and trend*
Ln(FSD/GDP)	-2.643	-2.632	-6.883*	-6.803*	-2.537	-2.525	-8.657*	-8.527*
lnGDP	2.120	0.371	-3.32**	-4.010**	2.376	0.561	-3.249*	-4.001*
Ln(GDP/Pop)	1.698	0.679	-3.44**	-4.075**	2.184	0.706	-3.43**	-4.12**
Ln(PE/GDP)	-1.2292	-1.5621	-7.621*	-7.532*	-2.336	-2.702	-9.112*	-9.003*
Ln(PE/POP)	-1.6243	-0.4607	-8.624*	-6.480*	-1.582	-1.508	-8.570*	-8.565*
LnPCE	1.0833	-0.6939	-5.215*	-5.491*	0.682	-0.956	-5.287*	-5.491*
LnPE	1.2504	0.1121	-6.699*	-7.170*	1.654	0.367	-6.747*	-7.172*
LNFSD	-1.0172	-1.8577	-5.728*	-5.680*	-1.035	-1.825	-5.723*	-5.672*
LNINF	-2.2930	-2.3369	-7.515*	-7.423*	-2.269	-2.314	-7.786*	-7.676*
LNPOP	-2.1438	-4.773*	-	-	-2.382	-4.712*	-	-
LNINV	-3.746*	-4.212*	-	-	-3.746*	-4.212*	-	-

Note: The critical values are -3.58 and -2.93 at 1 and 5 per cent respectively when the regression has a constant term and -4.15 and -3.50 at 1 and 5 per cent when the regression has a constant and trend term; * and ** indicate significance level at 1 and 5 per cent respectively.

Source: Authors' Computations.

Descriptive Statistics

The tools of descriptive statistics are used as a preliminary step to examine the nature and status of distribution of values of selected macroeconomic variables. Symmetry and equality of mean and median are the two most important features of normal distribution. These properties also free the distribution from the scale effect and the unit of measurement of values of variables from being skewed or highly concentrated in the narrow space around the mode. Besides, if the

Table 6.5

Results of Summary Statistics, Descriptive Statistics Before and After Globalisation

	Before Globalisation (1966-1985)									*After Globalisation (1986-2012)*								
	POP	*INF*	*PR*	*PE/GDP*	*PE*	*PVCE*	*INV*	*GDP*	*GDP/POP*	*POP*	*INF*	*PR*	*PE/GDP*	*PE*	*PVCE*	*INV*	*GDP*	*GDP/POP*
Mean	3.19	17.65	4.88	3.21	6.38	4.80	13.22	3.12	0.06	2.94	16.79	5.67	1.83	6.96	4.85	20.12	4.98	2.21
Standard Error	0.02	2.39	2.54	4.84	4.95	1.91	10.62	0.56	0.58	0.05	2.07	2.71	3.29	3.52	2.59	16.09	0.41	0.43
Median	3.17	15.60	5.93	3.51	6.60	3.13	22.42	3.06	-0.17	2.99	12.80	7.65	-0.64	5.77	4.54	3.41	4.93	2.83
Mode	#N/A	#N/A	#N/A	#N/A	#N/A	#N/A	#N/A	#N/A	#N/A	#N/A	#N/A	#N/A	#N/A	#N/A	#N/A	#N/A	#N/A	#N/A
Standard Deviation	0.07	10.41	11.06	21.09	21.59	8.31	46.31	2.45	2.54	0.28	10.77	14.10	17.10	18.31	13.44	83.60	2.15	2.22
Sample Variance	0.01	108.36	122.4	444.8	466.3	69.11	2144.5	5.98	6.43	0.08	115.96	198.9	292.42	335.24	180.64	6988.50	4.63	4.93
Kurtosis	-0.01	-1.28	-0.68	2.65	2.33	-0.68	0.30	-0.11	-0.03	-0.96	-1.41	3.46	0.92	1.02	5.38	11.73	-0.87	-0.84
Skewness	0.33	0.33	-0.15	0.85	0.83	0.42	0.41	-0.49	-0.08	-0.12	0.40	-1.51	-0.06	-0.18	-0.96	3.03	-0.53	-0.29
Range	0.28	32.65	37.34	96.96	98.83	28.73	179.79	9.08	9.76	0.95	31.09	68.71	82.12	89.81	75.44	440.37	7.43	8.19
Minimum	3.06	3.49	-13.97	-34.21	-32.62	-9.41	-56.48	-2.36	-5.32	2.47	4.74	-39.6	-41.64	-40.6	-40.80	-71.4	0.40	-2.37
Maximum	3.34	36.15	23.37	62.74	66.21	19.32	123.31	6.72	4.44	3.42	35.83	29.08	40.48	49.23	34.64	369.01	7.83	5.82
Sum	60.54	335.41	92.71	61.06	121.15	91.18	251.26	59.26	1.18	79.40	453.39	153.15	49.37	188.01	130.92	543.37	134.4	59.72
Count	19	19	19	19	19	19	19	19	19	27	27	27	27	27	27	27	27	27

Source: Own Compilation.

mean and variance of a series are constant, series may be treated as stationary. Hence, standard deviation/variation is another important parameter of any distribution. These parameters of descriptive statistics are used in data analysis. The summary of descriptive statistics of growth rates of selected economic variables is presented in Table 6.5. Based on the assumption that mean and median of the observed distribution must be equal if such distribution is normal, it is found that the observed distribution of all variables both in pre and post globalisation period diverges significantly from the normal curve. Besides, the distribution of the variables is skewed and highly peaked. This indicates that there is high degree of inequalities and concentration in one or the other period.

Gross Domestic Product

This study uses economic growth which indicates the rising of a country's national and per capita incomes. The data of GDP (gross domestic product) are used as the proxy of economic growth. GDP is estimated from the contribution of three main sectors in Tanzania: (a) service sector; (b) agriculture sector; and (c) industry and construction sector. The agriculture sector consists of forestry, hunting, and fishing, as well as cultivation of crops and livestock production. Service sector is the largest in Tanzania and it includes value added in wholesale and retail trade (hotels and restaurants), transport and communication, and public administration, financial intermediaries, professional, and personal services such as education, healthcare, and real estate and business services. It also includes the imputed bank service charges, import duties, and any statistical discrepancies noted by compilers of national income as well as discrepancies arising from rescaling. Industry and construction sectors comprise value added in mining and quarrying, manufacturing, construction, electricity, water supply, and gas. Value added of the service sector as a share of GDP averaged 43.5 per cent as compared to 36.3 per cent of agriculture and 20.2 per cent for industrial sectors from 1991 to 2012. These shares highlight the contribution of different sectors to the economy. Besides, the shares also highlight the declining importance of agriculture relative to tertiary sector. This economic structure is associated with the developed rather than the structure of developing economies. Business outsourcing has taken care of manufacturing sectors of the developed economies. So, they want tertiary sectors of the developing economies to be opened up. This skirts the historical pattern and stages of growth traversed by the economies of the developed countries. Indian economy has had also gone through the same process. Sum of total income and employment is exhausted by the shares of these sectors. Policy makers can also observe the historical trend of changes in the contributions to GDP made by different sectors in different stages of growth of developed countries. The received knowledge tells us that developed countries had increased the share of secondary sector in GDP to lift the economy from the clutches of under-development. Only at mature stages of growth, the share of tertiary sector became the dominant contributor to GDP in the developed countries of the world (for example, See Kuznets 1973, Lewis 1963, Clarke 1954). But both India and Tanzania have skipped this first stage in order to move away from the domination of primary production to the domination of tertiary domination in the process of growth. Moot point to be noted is that narrow commodity production base cannot sustain the domination of economic structure by tertiary activities.

It should be noted that GDP in absolute value does not provide a good economic indicator of growth; it conceals more than what it reveals about the YoY (year on year) oscillations in output and income. Annual compound rate of growth of any variable differs sharply from YoY growth rate of the same. The YoY growth rates provide valuable information about the pattern of change over the years. This is the rationale for treating growth rate of real GDP as an important indicator for economic analysis. It is, however, advisable to use real GDP per capita rather than GDP for inter-temporal and inter-spatial comparison.

In order to analyse the growth of Tanzanian economy, data of GDP at constant prices is considered. All data series are in Million TZS. We have collected absolute values of GDP at constant prices from which YoY growth rates are calculated:

$$Ry_{GDP} = \{(GDP_t - GDP_{t-1})/GDP_{t-1}\}*100$$

Ry_{GDP} is the YoY growth rate of real GDP. Results presented in Table 6.5 show the descriptive statistics for the selected variables for pre and post globalisation periods. It is found that growth rate of GDP at 3.12 per cent and growth rate of per capita GDP at 0.06 per cent are much lower and slower during the Pre-globalisation period than the rates of growth of 4.98 and 2.21 per cent in post globalisation period. This highlights an increase in the pace of growth during the post globalisation period. Incidentally, YOY growth rates show volatile oscillations.

Public Expenditure

Growth of public expenditure and its components, which are considered relevant for the study, are also discussed. The study focuses largely on public expenditure rather than public revenue because of the argument given from Neck and Getzner (2007) that the ratio of public expenditure to GDP is important for getting the true picture of the growth of size of public sector. Besides, needs of public expenditure influence the determination of public revenue. The ratio of public expenditure to GDP provides a better picture than the ratio of public revenues to GDP and the ratios of resources allocated by the government to various sectors of the economy.

A striking feature of the Tanzanian public expenditure is its continuous growth since independence, especially after the government adopted the so called 'African Socialism' in 1967. The government struggled to establish a welfare state based on planned socialist policies, which were also designed to promote economic growth and reduce poverty after the attainment of independence from the British Rule in 1961. Consequently, a continuous average rate of growth of around 6.38 per cent of public expenditure has occurred before globalisation as compared to 6.96 per cent in the post globalisation era. It only means that the growth of public expenditure lagged behind the growth of GDP. Thus, growth of public expenditure accelerated a bit at slower pace in the post globalisation era. This runs counter to the paradigm of free market economy. This, however, supports our thesis that public expenditure is downward sticky and upward flexible. This thesis is supported by the analysis of Indian data also. But, the ratio of public expenditure to GDP was as high as 3.21 per cent before globalisation compared to 1.83 per cent after globalisation. Growth rate of public revenue has been much slower than that of public expenditure; growth of public revenue was 4.88 and 5.67 per cent in pre and post globalisation eras respectively (see Table 6.5).

Table 6.5 shows the descriptive statistics of other selected economic variables before and after globalisation. The table shows the growth rates of (a) inflation (INF), (b) population (POP), (c) private consumption (PVCE), and (d) saving/investment (INV). The growth of investment and private consumption is much higher in the period after globalisation than the period before globalisation. But population and growth of inflation has declined in the post globalisation period. Principally, growth of inflation and public expenditure has shown very marginal change after globalisation in relation to Pre-globalisation period. Average inflation rate decreased marginally from 17.3 to 16.8 per cent, while public expenditure increased from an average growth of 6.38 to 6.96 per cent. The increase in public spending after globalisation depicts the importance of government intervention in promoting a healthy economic growth particularly in a developing economy like that of Tanzania. This may also reflect either the dearth of enterprise and entrepreneurs or capital or both which makes the economy largely dependent on the government. But this runs contrary to tenets of LPG. Above all, pattern of growth of public expenditure shows that Tanzanian economy has been absolutely dominated by the development expenditure both in pre and post globalisation periods. Growth of the recurrent expenditure in both these periods has been significantly slower than that of development expenditure but both layers of public expenditure are exhibiting acceleration from pre to post globalisation era. Acceleration of growth of administrative expenditure along with development expenditure is accounted by the multiplication of roles and functions of the government along with development. Rate of growth of recurrent expenditure from 1966 to 1985 was 5.5 and it rose to 6.2 per cent after globalisation as against 11.3 and 36.2 per cent of development expenditure. Shares of these two types of public spending in total GDP is also different. The share of recurrent spending in GDP has increased from 67.5 per cent to 76.6 per cent but that of development expenditure decreased from 12.02 per cent to 5.81 per cent from before to after globalisation. It implies unbridled multiplication of bureaucracy.

Private Consumption Expenditure

Private consumption expenditure is defined as the market value of all goods and services purchased by households at different points of time during the year. The average rate of growth of households' consumption expenditure has increased nominally from 4.8 per cent before globalisation to 4.9 per cent after globalisation. This acceleration of growth of private final consumption expenditure may be the result of base effect; smaller the base value, larger is the growth rate. Base value in the post-globalisation period is larger than that in pre-globalisation period. However, it cannot be denied that the small increase in rate of growth of private consumption is just an in-built trend that has taken place in the Tanzanian economy from pre to post globalisation period. But it may have nothing to do with the policy of reforms (globalisation).

Does more rapid growth of GDP than private consumption imply more rapid growth of investment? Answer seems to be affirmative which may be inferred from the growth of investment.

YoY Growth of Macro Variables of Tanzanian Economy

For better understanding of the pattern of public expenditure and the factors underlying its growth, YoY pattern of growth along with the growth of those macro variables associated with the growth of GDP are considered.

Basic features of YoY growth rates of various variables are discussed briefly hereunder.

YoY Growth of Public Expenduture

A perusal of Table 6.6 reveals the following features of YoY growth of public spending:

(i) The YoY growth rates of public spending oscillate a great deal.

(ii) Fifteen of the 45 fluctuating YoY rates of growth of public expenditure are negative; 30 out of these 45 fluctuating YoY growth rates of public expenditure are positive. Thus, there is one trend reversal in so far as the direction of change is concerned. But increasing or decreasing trend has changed direction several times.

(iii) Positive YoY growth rates of public expenditure vary from 1.63 per cent to 66.21 per cent. As against this, negative YoY growth rates of public expenditure vary from 0.95 per cent to 45.58 per cent. Thus, the range of oscillations of negative YOY rates is much larger than that of positive rates.

(iv) Drastic reduction in YoY growth rates in 1970s, especially in 1974 and 1978, might be explained by the occurrence of worldwide oil price shocks, drought, balance of payments crisis in 1974-75 and the Uganda-Tanzania War in 1977-78.

(v) But the trend growth rates of public expenditure during the pre and post liberalisation periods are 30.7 per cent and 66.2 per cent respectively. Thus, there is substantial increase in the growth of public expenditure from pre to post globalization period.

(vi) All the years following the general election of Tanzania like 1990, 1994-95 and 2000 have shown more rapid growth of public expenditure. Growth of public expenditure has shown rapid growth as compared to the growth of public revenue.

(vii) Implication of this is that the country is experiencing large fiscal deficit, which is financed either through printing more money or through internal and external borrowings. Neither very high levels of fiscal deficit are sustainable nor is the heavy loan burden can be carried forward by the economy for ever; it is because inflation tends to increase over the years along with the rising fiscal deficit and public debt. Besides, domestic investment is also crowded-out by the increased interest payment; adversely affecting the growth of the economy (see Table 6.6).

YoY Growth of Public Revenue

Table 6.6 reveals the following main features of YoY growth rates of public revenue raised by the Government of Tanzania over the years:

(i) YoY rates of growth of public revenue of the Government of Tanzania depict a great deal of variation between the years. The variation is not confined to only the magnitudes but the signs have also been turning from positive to negative to positive again.

(ii) As many 11 YoY growth rates of public revenue are negative, which leave only 33 positive rates of growth. Turning of positive into negative growth rates of public revenue is associated with 8 trend reversals during the period of four and a half decades. Most of these trend reversals have occurred during late 1970s to mid-1980s.

(iii) Positive YoY rates of growth of public revenue varied between 1.54 per cent and 23.6 per cent. As against the positive rates, the negative rates of growth varied between 1.78 and 39.63. Thus, the range of variation of negative YoY rates of growth of public revenue is much greater and wider than that of positive rates.

(iv) The range of variation of YoY rates of growth of public revenue is much lower than the range of variation of YoY rates of growth of public expenditure. This may be accounted by upward stickiness of tax rates, proportion of population subjected to direct taxation and tax bearing capacity of the people.

(v) Trend reversal in YoY growth rates of public expenditure has coincided with the trend reversal in the YoY growth rates of public revenue in most of the years covered by the study. This suggests a direct relation between public revenue and public expenditure.

YoY Growth of Private Consumption

Table 6.6 shows the following important features of the growth of private consumption in Tanzania:

Table 6.6

Year on Year Growth Rate of Macroeconomic Variables

	POP-GR	INF	PR-GR	PR/GDP-GR	PE/GDP	PE-GR	PVCE-GR	INV-GR	GDP-GR	GDP/POP-GR	FSD-GR
1967	3.07	12.2	13.85	9.43	12.73	17.28	2.01	25.83	4.04	-1.25	16.99
1968	3.06	15.6	6.61	1.36	-3.37	1.63	17.52	24.96	5.18	4.35	-26.4
1969	3.13	16.4	10.37	8.37	16.42	18.56	-3.71	22.42	1.84	0.03	36.75
1970	3.11	3.49	22.53	15.82	10.65	17.07	18.69	22.51	5.80	3.09	-0.70
1971	3.24	4.78	3.28	-0.87	13.82	18.58	3.70	-4.28	4.18	0.91	75.02
1972	3.28	7.64	5.93	-0.74	-12.19	-6.28	13.59	73.34	6.72	4.44	-35.7
1973	3.31	10.4	16.58	13.12	13.45	16.92	0.76	-56.48	3.06	0.40	21.13
1974	3.34	19.6	2.88	0.37	4.43	7.04	7.30	-37.2	2.50	-0.21	21.08
1975	3.23	26.1	14.69	8.29	23.39	30.68	4.73	43.20	5.91	2.10	62.05
1976	3.19	6.86	-13.97	-19.2	-26.5	-21.8	-9.41	123.3	6.41	-0.73	-29.3
1977	3.21	11.6	2.75	2.34	13.66	14.12	-1.09	55.50	0.40	-2.62	52.40
1978	3.17	6.57	23.37	20.80	62.74	66.21	19.32	-52.81	2.13	-1.26	151.7
1979	3.13	12.9	-11.97	-14.05	-34.21	-32.6	-1.14	35.08	2.42	-0.32	-53.1
1980	3.20	30.20	5.94	2.87	3.51	6.60	13.22	-36.25	2.99	2.31	-6.88
1981	3.16	25.7	-5.94	-5.46	2.92	2.40	-3.24	46.98	-0.50	-3.18	9.22
1982	3.22	28.9	-7.43	-7.97	-1.54	-0.95	-4.09	-0.94	0.59	-2.55	-0.47
1983	3.17	27.1	9.98	12.64	-8.29	-10.45	6.90	-40.42	-2.36	-5.32	-37.0
1984	3.17	36.2	-11.10	-13.99	-13.93	-11.03	3.13	-9.04	3.36	-0.17	-21.0
1985	3.16	33.3	4.36	-0.22	-16.58	-12.75	2.98	15.58	4.59	1.14	-46.6
1986	3.11	32.4	-7.54	-9.26	-11.98	-10.32	6.51	52.34	1.89	0.47	-23.6
1987	3.06	29.95	-1.78	-6.39	0.12	5.05	1.67	130.6	4.93	1.62	41.26
1988	3.06	31.2	18.71	13.67	-17.00	-13.32	30.14	-71.36	4.43	3.04	-117

1989	3.18	25.9	29.08	25.85	6.99	9.74	24.04	369.0	2.57	-0.63	411.8
1990	3.20	35.8	16.77	9.93	40.48	49.23	34.64	62.98	6.23	3.30	-121
1991	3.38	28.70	2.38	-0.39	-9.46	-6.95	-6.18	-51.63	2.78	-0.06	-250.4
1992	3.42	21.9	-39.63	-40.71	-41.64	-40.58	-40.80	-34.92	1.82	-0.99	35.85
1993	3.38	25.28	-24.66	-24.96	29.46	29.98	1.63	-1.81	0.40	-2.37	-755.5
1994	3.23	34.08	13.32	11.76	7.68	9.19	2.53	-5.69	1.40	-1.40	-0.47
1995	2.99	27.43	7.65	3.83	-19.33	-16.36	3.29	-56.67	3.68	0.81	-60.45
1996	2.81	20.98	14.25	9.65	-14.42	-10.83	4.30	38.62	4.20	1.32	-134.6
1997	2.63	16.1	6.28	2.88	-1.17	2.10	5.61	-12.70	3.31	0.23	75.18
1998	2.50	12.80	-5.98	-9.58	18.39	23.11	7.48	-8.54	3.99	0.88	-274.1
1999	2.47	7.89	2.09	-2.62	-4.13	0.51	3.77	3.41	4.84	1.70	-5.39
2000	2.53	5.92	3.44	-1.42	27.56	33.85	5.30	118.3	4.93	1.79	225.2
2001	2.59	5.15	-6.62	-11.90	-17.71	-12.78	-16.48	-37.00	6.00	2.83	-8.72
2002	2.61	5.32	4.75	-2.25	-2.11	4.90	2.81	17.43	7.16	4.93	7.03
2003	2.65	5.30	7.64	0.71	17.06	25.13	3.62	28.39	6.89	4.81	73.24
2004	2.75	4.74	11.99	3.86	9.63	18.21	3.52	14.98	7.83	4.71	30.80
2005	2.78	5.03	14.21	6.37	10.02	18.13	6.31	-12.88	7.37	4.61	25.17
2006	2.89	7.25	13.78	6.60	8.93	16.27	8.78	5.15	6.74	2.96	17.24
2007	2.95	7.03	18.29	10.40	-1.06	6.02	7.76	-12.12	7.15	5.01	-7.25
2008	2.99	10.3	20.84	12.47	-1.60	5.72	5.04	12.82	7.44	4.22	-18.3
2009	3.05	12.1	9.71	3.48	13.56	20.39	4.54	2.77	6.02	2.87	39.11
2010	3.05	6.20	1.54	-5.14	6.04	13.51	2.29	19.81	7.04	3.90	35.48
2011	3.07	12.69	9.59	2.96	-0.64	5.77	12.46	-33.31	6.45	3.35	-2.44
2012	3.09	16.0	13.05	5.72	-4.28	2.35	6.33	5.36	6.93	5.82	-16.5

Source: Own Compilation.

(i) Private consumption has also shown a very large degree of variation in YoY growth rates both in magnitudes and direction of change.
(ii) Nine out of 44 YoY rates of growth of private consumption have turned out to be negative; thus, 35 years covered by the study have recorded positive YoY growth of consumption. On the whole, the trend of growth of private consumption highlights that the living standard of the people of Tanzania has been rising consistently and the consumption is, by and large, downward sticky.
(iii) Negative growth of private consumption has also been shown largely by the latter years of 1970s and 1980s. It implies that the world wide recession caused by unprecedented rise in oil prices has affected not only the government finances and expenditure but these twin maladies greatly affected the lives of the people of Tanzania also.
(iv) Six reversals of trend from positive to negative have occurred during the entire period.

YoY Growth of Fiscal Deficit

A perusal of YoY growth rates of fiscal deficit depicts the following main features of the growth of fiscal deficit in Tanzania:

(i) As many as 25 out of 45 years covered by the study have recorded negate rates of growth of fiscal deficit in Tanzanian economy. This represents the attempts of the government to bring about balance between the public income and public expenditure. However, 19 years have recorded positive YoY rates of growth of fiscal deficit.
(ii) The magnitudes of the YoY rates of growth have run even into three digits. In fact, the negative rates of growth of fiscal deficit varied between 0.47 per cent and 755.0 per cent. As against this, positive YoY growth rates of fiscal deficit varied from 7.33 per cent to 411.8 per cent. Thus, the range of variation of negative rates of growth is much greater and wider than that of positive rates.

(iii) Inter-temporal variation of fiscal deficits relate not only to changes in magnitudes between the years but these also characterise the change in direction from positive to negative and from negative to positive growth. Such changes are expected to affect the values of means and variance both being the feature of non-stationary time series.

(iv) The time series of fiscal deficits have experienced as many as 13 trend reversals.

(v) An important feature of the trend reversal is the bunching of negative or positive YoY growth rates of fiscal deficits together over a couple of years.

YoY Growth of Inflation

The inter-temporal feature of the time series of inflation in Tanzanian economy differ a bit from the features of other macro variables discussed in the study; Following are the major features of the time series of inflation in Tanzania:

(i) Inflation has not only continuously persisted but it has consistently and continuously increased in the economy. Therefore, inflation has not recorded any reversal in the positive trend in the Tanzanian economy ever since it attained independence.

(ii) However, the rates of YoY growth of inflation have varied greatly between the years.

(iii) The minimum YoY growth rate of inflation has been 3.49 per cent whereas the maximum YoY growth rate of inflation is 32.7 per cent. Thus, the magnitude of range of variation is as high as 36.2 per cent.

(iv) The growth of inflation has remained below two digit level when it varied between 3.5 to 7.8 per cent in 15 out of 45 years. As against this, growth of inflation ranged between 10.3 per cent to 19.6 per cent in another 11 years. It ranged between 20.8 per cent to 29.95 per cent in 11 years. The highest range of growth of inflation has been from 39.2 per cent to 36 per cent in 7 years. Thus, two third of the total period covered by the study has been engulfed in moderately high to extremely high inflation in Tanzania.

(v) Rates of growth of inflation have been clustered in the specific range of variation most of the times.

(vi) An interesting aspect of inter-temporal changes in inflation seems to have remained disjoint with the growth of public expenditure and fiscal deficit. This may, however, need empirical testing rigorously.

YoY Growth of Investment

Following are the important features and facets of YoY rates of growth of investment in Tanzania:

(i) The YoY rates of growth of investment in Tanzanian economy have been negative in 19 years. The YoY rates of growth of GDP are expected to have been adversely affected in these years.

(ii) The range of variation of the rates of negative YoY changes in investment has been 0.94 per cent to 71.3 per cent. But the YoY rates of decline in investment have remained between 0.94 per cent to 12.8 per cent in 9 years. During the remaining years of the study YoY rates of decline in investment remained in the range of 33 per cent to 74 per cent. It runs counter to the policy of globalisation.

(iii) YoY rates of growth of investment have been positive and the range of their variation is from 2.77 per cent to 369 per cent. YoY growth rate of investment has been above three digits in 4 years and below two digit level in 8 years. Positive YoY growth rates of investment have been in two digit level during the remaining years.

(iv) The overall growth of investment has put the Tanzanian economy on a long run growth path.

Empirical Results of Testing of Hypotheses (i) to (iv)

The above discussion of empirical findings relating to inter-temporal behaviour of macroeconomic variables has paved the way for evaluating the results of empirical testing of the hypotheses stated earlier in the chapter.

However, there are alternative ways of evaluating effect of change in economic system. Outcomes of the impact of policy on the economy are also discussed. The following methods are used for the analysis of the results:

(i) Dummy variable for different time periods and prevailing economic conditions is used.

(ii) For evaluating statistical significance of the slope coefficients of each regression for two periods (pre and post globalisation) t-test is employed.

(iii) McNemar test of effect of change in selected variables is used to supplement the results of t statistics, and

(iv) Significance of difference between the parameters of two periods taken as a whole is evaluated. Obviously, this is a more comprehensive test. This study has applied three of the above tests and the results are reported hereunder.

Significance of Differences of Means of Two Periods

Important question in the above context is whether the difference between the means of two variables of two periods (pre and post globalisation) is statistically significant. The t-test is used to evaluate the mean differences for two periods; results are reported in Table 6.6. The value of t-test statistics is determined as follows:

$$t = [(\overline{X}_1 - \overline{X}_2)/\sigma]\sqrt{n-2}$$

and $\overline{X}_1$ $\overline{X}_2$ are the means of pre and post globalisation period respectively. As the calculated values of t statistics of 10 out of 11 variables are greater than the critical value of 1.96 at 0.05 probability level, it is inferred that the differences of the means of these two periods differ significantly. Significant difference between the means and variance of two periods suggest that the series are non-stationary. But stationary facet of time series is examined by the more powerful D-F, ADF and PP tests. The growth of GDP, public revenue, public expenditure, private consumption, fiscal deficits, population, and per capita GDP highlight the fact that the economy of Tanzania has broken away from stagnancy of colonial period and it has recorded substantial growth both in pre and post globalisation periods. But the growth of inflation during two periods does not differ significantly from pre to post globalisation periods. This implies that the policy of economic reforms in Tanzanian economy has significantly accelerated the growth of GDP, public expenditure, private consumption, public revenue, investment, per capita GDP and fiscal deficits in absolute terms. As inflation is a concomitant of economic growth, continuous rise in inflation needs to be kept within the limit of tolerance. Limit to tolerance of inflation is directly related to growth of nominal income, change in the pattern of income distribution and change in general price level. It may, however, be proposed as a general rule that the rate of growth of per capita nominal income should be 2-3 per cent greater than the rate of increase in general prices.

Table 6.6 also shows that all variables except inflation, public expenditure as a share of GDP and fiscal deficits are positively skewed and peaked. This implies that there is high inequality and concentration of high values in the distribution in the period. The distribution of most economic variables diverges from normal distribution. Tanzanian economy has moved out of colonial low growth performing economy into a modern planned developed moderate growth performing economy. Thus, in the post globalisation era, most of these economic variables have indicated higher growth than that in the pre-globalisation period. This makes the distribution not only diverge from normality but it also suggests the distribution to converge towards non-stationarity. But the growth performance is generally assessed by the results of the OLS estimate of growth curves of the relevant variables. Results of descriptive statistics are reported in Table 6.7.

Growth Curves without Policy Dummy

OLS estimates of growth curves are presented in Tables 6.8 and 6.9. The estimated values show that the growth curve without policy dummy fits the data of (a) GDP, (b) population, and (c) consumption, as the proportion of GDP well; total variation explained by the growth functions ranges from 89.2 to 99.5 per cent. Besides, the coefficient of determination is significant. But the proportion of total variation of investment, public revenue and public expenditure by the growth curve ranges from 28.6 to 62.6 per cent though investment, public revenue and public expenditure are the functions of several variables, including consumption and policy. But the coefficients of determination are significant. Besides, intercepts and slope coefficients in all these functions are significant also. The growth curve, however, does not fit the data of fiscal deficit and inflation well; intercept of the function, the coefficient of determination and slope of time are not significant. It implies that systematic factors, that time embodies, explain the growth of all variables well except fiscal deficit and inflation. Fiscal deficit seems to be subject more to public expenditure, fiscal policy, economic and political exigencies' random influences than systematic factors. These inferences also lend credence to the earlier inference that inflation in Tanzanian economy does not seem to be related to domestic factors.

Table 6.7

Test of Differences of Descriptive Statistics of Two Periods

Variables	*Mean diff*	*t*	*Std Dev diff*	*F*	*Skewness*	*Kurtosis*
INF	-0.469	-0.1509	0.48425	1.0964	-0.0215	-0.2049
PR	546814	4.1438*	447637	10.6172*	2.0724	1.2216
PR/GDP	-4.9930	-5.5763*	1.09443	2.0568*	1.5686	1.7841
PE/GDP	-9.5975	-5.4391*	-2.8879	2.8765*	-0.79159	-3.3935
PE	707424	2.8156*	764430	7.5392*	0.8917	0.0893
PVCE	4643538	10.7504*	1237342	6.4500*	0.8808	0.7101
INV	501965	4.0698*	349279	6.2742*	1.2844	6.6763
GDP	5648357	6.9332*	3405230	31.3914*	1.3249	0.9726
GDP/POP	40554.7	3.4558*	46235.9	21.0710*	1.2873	1.2226
FSD	3361.87	2.0955*	5366.67	10.1048*	-1.21553	-6.287
POP	15.8459	10.5556*	3.69253	4.6733*	0.01668	9.47E-06

Note: * means significant at 5% level; The t and F-tests are used to test the significance of the mean variance and standard deviation respectively.

Source: Own Compilation.

A perusal of the elasticity coefficients, calculated as the ratio of appropriate estimated growth rates (Table 6.9) reveals that public revenue (PR), public expenditure (PE), private consumption, investment, population and fiscal deficit rise at the rates ranging from -0.24 to 2.6 per cent in response to one per cent increase in the rate of growth of GDP. Thus, the intensity of growth of public expenditure is greater than that of GDP. Public expenditure, in fact, emerges as the most sensitive variable to any change in GDP. A unit change in GDP results in an increase of 2.6 per cent change in public expenditure. It means that public expenditure tends to rise 2.6 times more rapidly than GDP in the process of economic growth. The greater than one value of elasticity coefficient of public expenditure reflects more than proportional increase in public expenditure with respect to growth of GDP. The intensity of growth of such variables as investment/savings, public revenue, private consumption and investment is less than that of public expenditure when GDP grows. These variables are less sensitive (inelastic) to change in GDP. One per cent change in GDP results in less than unit change in all these variables. Another important finding is that, while private consumption is growing at the same rate as GDP, other variables are growing at much lower and slower rates than GDP. Responsiveness of inflation and fiscal deficits to change in GDP is not significant; it implies that GDP of Tanzania does not determine changes in the rate of inflation and growth of fiscal deficit.

Table 6.8 contains the results of OLS estimates of the growth curves of the above variables.

The above discussion has cleared the way for the discussion of the results derived from the OLS estimates of growth curves with policy dummy.

Growth Curves with Policy Dummy

The results yielded by OLS estimates of these growth curves with policy dummy are reported in Table 6.9. The policy dummy determines the impact of change in policy. Careful evaluation of the results reveals that:

(i) Growth curve with dummy fits the data better than the growth curve without dummy. The value of the coefficient of determination has increased in all cases. Besides, the coefficients are highly significant statistically.
(ii) The slope coefficients of all variables are significant at 5 per cent probability.
(iii) But the effect of globalisation differs between the macroeconomic and financial variables. For example, GDP,

public revenue, per capita GDP, inflation and fiscal deficit have been significantly affected by the change in policy (globalisation).

(iv) Three of these five variables have significantly decreased over time as a result of globalisation.

(v) But inflation and public revenue depict a positive and significant growth effect of globalisation. It means that the opening up of the Tanzanian economy had substantially raised the imported part of inflation whereas public revenue also seems to have increased as the economic reforms focus on reducing fiscal deficit and public debt.

Table 6.8

OLS Estimates of Growth Curves without Policy Dummy

Variable	*Intercept*	*Slope*	*R2*	*F*	*P**	*CAGR (%)*	*E-Growth Rate*
$InGDP_t$	14.8134*	0.0363*	0.9574	1011.871	1.73E-32	3.6997	1.000
	(470.498)	(31.8099)					
$InPR_t$	13.2204*	0.0250*	0.6260	75.3150	3.63E-11	2.5311	0.684
	(166.497)	(8.6784)					
$InPE_t$	13.4798*	0.0274*	0.5129	47.3881	1.52E-08	2.7755	2.604
	(122.952)	(6.8839)					
$InPOP_t$	2.4219*	0.0296*	0.9954	9638.444	0.0000	3.0002	0.811
	(291.765)	(98.1756)					
$InPVCE_t$	14.6552*	0.0348*	0.8915	369.6763	2.49E-23	3.5367	0.956
	(294.083)	(19.2270)					
$InINV_t$	12.8961*	0.0220*	0.2862	18.0464	0.0001	2.2272	0.602
	(90.2138)	(4.2481)					
$InFSD_t$	6.1791*	0.0099	0.0007	0.0323	0.8581	0.9917	0.268
	(4.0842)	(0.1798)					
lnGDP/ POP	12.3491*	0.0080*	0.4991	44.8333	2.88E-08	0.8036	0.217
	(374.758)	(6.6958)					
INFt	2.8289*	-0.0089	0.0306	1.4217	0.2394	-0.8877	-0.240
	(13.7212)	(-1.1923)					

Note: *(**) denotes rejection of the null hypothesis at 5%(1%) level of significance.
Source: Own Compilation.

(vi) Coefficient of investment is positive but not significant.

(vii) Growth of variables like population and public expenditure do not seem to have been significantly affected by globalisation. But the slope coefficients have a negative sign.

(viii) An important aspect of growth of Tanzanian economy, revealed by these growth curves, is that (a) public expenditure, fiscal deficit, public revenue, inflation and savings/investment have increased at greater rate than GDP; (b) fiscal deficit has also increased at the rate higher than that of public expenditure and nearly seven times more than that of GDP. This result runs counter to the paradigm of globalisation that recommends reduction in fiscal deficit and inflation.

(ix) Financing of growth of public expenditure partially accounts for growth of inflation though unproductive public expenditure and expenditure on projects involving long lead times also explain inflation.

(x) Public expenditure has also grown more rapidly than public revenue which also furnishes the rationale for such growth of public revenue.

(xi) Rate of growth of fiscal deficit is the highest growth rate relative to the rates of growth of all other variables. It may be the base effect. Fiscal deficit is followed by the growth of investment and public expenditure in that order. These inferences are also supported by the geometric means (reported in last column) of YoY rates of growth of these variables.

(xii) Value of R-squares and F-statistics indicate that the model fits the data well (see Table 6.9).

YoY growth rates, shown by the value of the geometric means, indicate that investment and fiscal deficits have recorded the highest YoY growth rate followed by consumer price index/inflation, public expenditure and public revenue. The rest of the variables (GDP, per capita GDP and population) have indicated a smaller YoY growth rate less than 4 per cent. The average YoY growth rate of GDP and the YoY growth rate of all variables have positive significant values (See Table 6.10).

Table 6.9

Growth Curves with Policy Dummy

Variables	*Intercept*	*Time (T)*	*Dummy (D)*	R^2	F	P*	*CAGR (%)*	*Geomean*
lnGDP	14.7855	0.0423*	-0.2088*					
	(554.275)	(22.922)	(-4.2230)	0.9709	718.267	9.16E-34	4.321	3.5142
lnPOP	2.4202	0.0297*	-0.00033					
	(270.128)	(48.749)	(-0.0205)	0.9953	4524.881	1.02E-50	3.015	3.0316
lnPR	6.1248	0.1919*	0.5176*	0.9928	2957.438	9.02E-47	21.155	8.7146
	(79.16)	(36.219)	(3.6490)					
lnPE	6.3700	0.2123*	-0.0495					
	(77.723)	(38.128)	(-0.3318)	0.9928	2727.353	5.08E-46	23.652	10.7122
lnFSD	4.5466	0.2677*	-1.6565*					
	(24.302)	(20.1933)	(-4.6659)	0.9595	510.082	1.12E-30	30.965	29.0063
lnInv	5.6899	0.1935*	0.5112	0.9422	350.156	2.45E-27	21.349	23.1588
	(24.937)	(12.4841)	(1.2312)					
lnPVCE	14.692*	0.0282*	0.2106*					
	(292.286)	(8.4168)	(2.2929)	0.9031	204.954	5.04E-23	2.858	2.7629
lnGDP/POP	12.3105*	0.0149*	-0.2210*					
	(409.330)	(7.4392)	(-4.021)	0.6337	38.053	2.54E-10	2.8581	1.4717
lnINF	-2.0743	0.1388*	1.2404*					
	(-22.686)	(22.3376)	(7.4554)	0.9868	1601.691	4.21E-41	14.889	13.7658

Note: In the parenthesis () are the t-values.
Source: Authors'own calculations.

Difference of Two Regressions of Two Periods

Results of two sets of growth curves with and without policy dummy have been compared cursorily in a robust way. This comparison does not reveal the statistical significance of the differences of growth rates of different variables during the pre and post globalisation periods. Therefore, new set of regressions has been estimated from the differences of paired values of the variables for the two periods (See, Rosander 1965). The significance of the coefficient of these regressions shall indicate whether the individual slope coefficients of growth curves of the two periods are statistically different or not.

The results of the regressions of differences of values of all variables of study for two periods, reported in Table 6.10, indicate that only the rates of growth of GDP, inflation and population have changed significantly from one to the other period due to the adoption of the policy of globalisation. Growth of the rest of the variables has remained practically the same from pre to post globalisation period. This implies that the process of globalisation has significantly affected the growth of only GDP, inflation and population. These findings stand in contradistinction to the earlier results of two separate regressions for two periods as well as the growth curves having the dummy variable.

Table 6.10

Regressions of Differences of Two Data Sets of Two Periods

Variable	*Intercept*	*Slope*	*R2*	*F*	*P**	*CAGR (%)*
LNGDP	14.4079 (111.3334)	0.0646 (5.9766)*	0.6649	35.7192	1.18E-05	6.670
LN(GDP/POP)	-0.6051 (-0.1315)	-0.0603 (-0.1568)	0.0014	0.025	0.877123	-5.848
LNPR	8.4511 (1.5971)	-0.2797 (-0.6332)	0.0218	0.401	0.534589	-24.398
LNPE	8.4275 (1.4223)	-0.5637 (-1.1396)	0.0673	1.299	0.269393	-43.089
LNPOP	2.2627 (55.4122)	0.0289 (8.4839)*	0.7999	71.977	1.05E-07	2.934
LNFSD	3.6753 (1.6482)	0.2254 (1.2110)	0.0753	1.466	0.241574	25.285
LNINF	-4.4778 (-6.3301)	0.3969 (6.7213)*	0.6993	45.176	2.66E-06	48.721
LNINV	-12.899 (-2.423)	0.704 (1.585)	0.122	2.512	0.130	102.240
LNPVCE	-15.104 (-89.601)	-0.006 (-0.397)	0.009	0.158	0.696	-0.558
LN(PE/GDP)	0.5177 (0.7265)	0.1126 (1.8926)	0.1660	3.582	0.074603	11.916

Source: Own Compilation.

But the policy dummy is a qualitative variable in nature and has only 0 and 1 as admissible values. The coefficient of the dummy represents the difference of two intercepts of two periods. Therefore, it cannot capture the magnitude of differences of the values of two periods precisely. In case of the regression of differences of values of variables in two periods, magnitude of effect on differences is captured. This is a more powerful test. Hence, conclusions of this regression model are accepted.

These results are further supplemented by the application of McNemar test of effect of change. This is a test developed for the analysis of change. Change itself is a qualitative variable though its effect can be measured quantitatively very precisely.

Results of McNemar Test of Change

Results of application of McNemar test are reported in Table 6.11. The calculated value 3.86 of x^2, of McNemar test for the impact of change in policy on the growth of GDP is greater than the critical value of 3.841 at 0.05 probability level. Null hypothesis that the change in policy has not affected the growth of GDP stands rejected It is, therefore, inferred that the policy change (LPG) has significantly affected the growth of GDP. But the calculated values of x^2 for all other variables are much smaller than the critical value. So, the null hypothesis that the globalisation has not affected the growth of the variables of this study except GDP is accepted. The values of x^2 are reported in Table 6.11. Results furnished by McNemar test lend credible support to the inferences drawn from the application of other tests. Thus, the results of the study may be taken to be quite conclusive rather being in-built in a specific method/model used in the study. This is an important aspect of empirical research, since the power and sample spread of different statistical or econometric methods/models differ sharply from other.

The growth of PE and other variables of the study except those mentioned above, have not changed significantly from pre to post reform period. This runs counter to LPG. Results furnished by McNemar test lend credible support to the inferences drawn from the application of above test. Policy of globalisation has only affected the growth of GDP significantly.

Table 6.11

McNemar Test

	GDP-GR	(GDP/P)-GR	TR-GR	PE-GR	Pop-GR	(PE/TR)-GR	(PE/P)-GR	(PE/GDP)-GR
χ^2-test	3.857	0.7273	1.1905	0.4286	0.0588	0.1818	0.0435	0.0476

Note: Critical value of $\chi^2_{0.05}$=3.841.

Source: Own Compilation.

A pertinent question is "why has GDP behaved differently from other variables during the period of globalisation?" The question gains weight from the fact that several variables, included in the study, have been found to have significant relation with GDP. Another important question is "can public expenditure, investment, public revenue, ratio of public expenditure to GDP, per capita GDP and consumption remain immune to the significant changes in GDP, if yes, why?"

Answers to both these questions are attempted hereunder. First, the graphic portrayal of moving averages of GDP is examined for pre and post globalisation periods. Six out of first 7 observations depicts decline in YoY rates. This means that the trend during these years has been negative. In the second set of observations, 6 out of 8 YoY values show decline; but there is a consistent rise thereafter. Therefore, the overall trend of change in GDP is expected to be negative during the Pre-globalisation period. This has been examined by the trend of YoY growth rates during the pre-globalisation period. The estimated regression function is reported hereunder:

RY_{gdp}= 5.1657 -0.205T, R^2=0.2219, F=4.848; P=0.0418

T is time and RY_{gdp} depicts increase in YOY rate of growth of per unit time. The fit of the function is not good in so far as the value of the coefficient of determination is concerned. The function explains only 22.19 per cent change in inter-temporal variation in rates of growth of GDP. Since the function captures change of rate of change, 22.5 per cent explained proportion of total variation is not negligible. However, the coefficients of determination and slope are statistically significant. There is significant decline, on an average, by 0.21 points in YoY growth rate. This supports the inference about GDP and its trend growth in Pre-globalisation period. Thus, trend reversal has taken place during the post globalisation period. This is supported by the regression of YoY growth rate on time for the post globalisation period.

$R_{gdp} = 2.1633 + 0.201T$, $R^2 = 0.5500$, $F = 30.559$; $P = 9.57E\text{-}06$

Figure 6.1

Moving Average (GDP-GR) for Pre-Globalisation Period

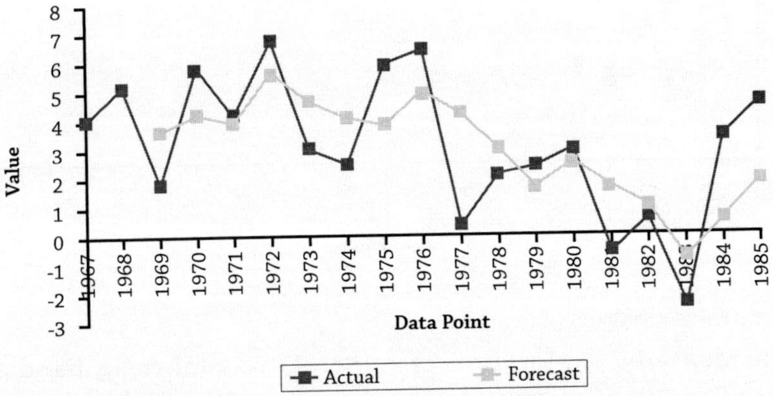

Source: Own Compilation.

In this case, the trend turns out to be positive. The positive and significant change in YoY is 0.2. Thus the acceleration in the growth of GDP during the post globalisation period may partly, if not wholly, be attributed to change in policy. Thus, the inference about reversal of negative trend of Pre-globalisation during the period of economic reforms is empirically supported. These results are further evaluated graphically before being accepted finally.

During the first 7 years after the adoption of policy of reforms, trend of Pre-globalisation is exactly replicated. During this phase, globalisation does not seem to have worked positively. Trend reversal has occurred only thereafter. Incidentally, no country can afford to continuously experience the negative trend growth of GDP irrespective of policy regime. The trend reversal in the second phase of post globalisation period may thus be called course or error correction of the past. This inference also gets strength from the fact that as many as seven macroeconomic variables have not been affected by globalisation during this period. The result seems to be the dilution of the effect of change in GDP on other macroeconomic variables.

Figure 6.2

Moving Average (GDP-GR) for Post-Globalisation Period

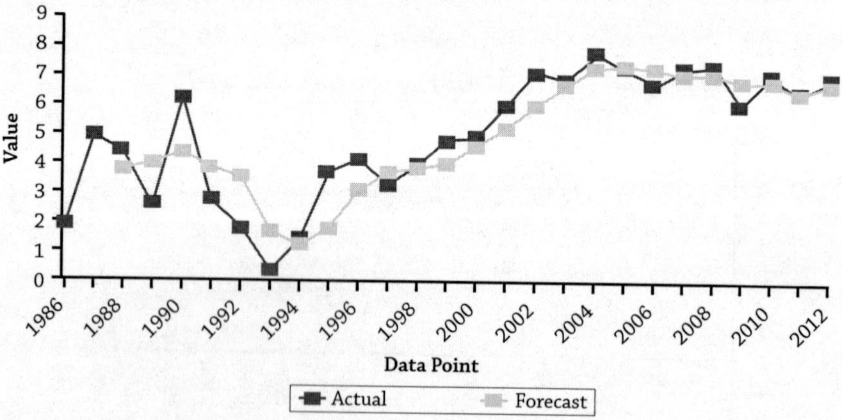

Source: Own Compilation.

Incidentally, exploration of minerals was taken in hand in 1970s. Consistent efforts of exploration resulted in discovery of commercially vital reserves of valuable minerals like natural gas, Gemstones,oil, gold and diamonds. These discoveries and income thereof have nothing to do with globalisation. Growth of other variables has not been affected significantly since incremental GDP seem to have been spread over large heads.

Augmented Engle-Granger (AEG) Test

Above graphical portrayal of data and significance of differences between means and variances are examined. On the basis of the 3 versions of RWM (no trend, no intercept; with intercept, no trend; and with intercept and trend), ADF and PP tests are applied. Results show all the variables to be non-stationary except population and investment. So, ADF unit root test was applied to the residuals of the regression equation containing variables time series of which is non-stationary.

However, application of the unit root test to the residuals (AEG test) of Model 1 and 2, null hypothesis of non-stationary or no co-integration is rejected for each of the equation showing that the residuals are stationary at order zero I(0). This suggested that GDP, investment (INV), private consumption expenditure (PVCE) and public expenditure (PE) as shown in model 1, are co-integrated. This implies that there may exist long term relationship between policy and economic growth. Authors, however, differ from this interpretation, since long run relation is nothing but an envelope of short run equilibria. Besides, incorporation of estimation errors of the model does not mean that the relation is long run; what it means is that the short run values of the coefficients are made more precise than before.

The same procedures are applied to the rest of the models and the empirical results reveal the results are limited to those of model 1. This implies that, though all the variables under this particular investigation are individually non-stationary at level, yet they tend to move together in the long-run. The results are indicated in Table 6.12.

Table 6.12

Summary of Augmented Engle-Granger (AEG) Test Results

	Model	*Coefficients of* $\hat{U}_{t-1}$	*tau-statistic*
Model 1	GDP_t=f(INV_{t-1},$PVCE_{t-1}$,PE_{t-1},D)	-0.5809	-4.2881*
Model 2	PE_t=f(GDP_{t-1},FSD_{t-1},D)	-0.6781	-4.2414*

Note: The critical values are -2.62 and -1.95 at 1 and 5 per cent respectively.
Source: Own Compilation.

Engle-Granger Error Correction Model

It is important to apply the error correction models (ECM) in this study because it helps in estimating directly the speed at which the dependent variable can adjust or return to equilibrium after the change in the independent variable caused by some structural breaks or shocks occurring in the economy. Above all, the ECM can be used to capture both short-run and long-run effects of one variable on another (Mehmood and Sadiq 2010). For example, the short and long-term effects of variable X on variable Y can be captured.

The findings that the residuals (U_t) of each regression model are stationary I(0) or co-integration obtained from the application of model 1 and 2. It leads to the second step of estimating the ECM. The ECM uses residuals of the estimated long-run equations (See Model 1 and 2). The ECM measures short-run dynamics of economic relationship among the variables and the Model 1 and 2 can be rewritten as follows:

$$\Delta InGDP_t = \alpha_0 + \alpha_1 \Delta InPE_{t-1} + \alpha_3 \Delta InPVCE_{t-1} + \alpha_3 \Delta InINV_{t-1} + \alpha_4 D + \lambda ECT_{t-1} + \varepsilon_t \quad .....(1)$$

$$\Delta InPE_t = \eta_0 + \eta_1 \Delta InGDP_{t-1} + \eta_2 \Delta InFSD_{t-1} + \eta_3 D + \lambda ECT_{t-1} + \mu_t \quad .....(2)$$

ECT_{t-1} is the lagged error correction term or lagged residual computed from estimates of co-integrated model 1 and 2 and λ and γ are the parameters/coefficients of speed of adjustment of model 1 and 2 respectively. In order to validate existence of long-run association amongst the variables through ECM, sign of the coefficient of the lagged residuals (ECT) is required to be negative and statistically significant and its value has to be between -1 and 0 in order to avoid an explosive process. The results of equation 1 and 2 and their respective diagnostic tests are reported below.

$$\Delta lnGDP_t = 0.029 + 0.0147 \Delta lnPE_{t-1} + 0.011 \Delta lnPVCE_{t-1} + 0.007 \Delta lnINV_{t-1} + 0.018D + 0.052ECT_{t-1} \quad (3)$$

t=(5.603) (0.538) (0.341) (1.100) (2.893) (1.636)

Regression equation 3, based on AEG test, reveals that though the variables indicated existence of co-integrated relationship, ECM re-affirms that there is no existence of any long-run relationship in the model. In other words, though equation 3 reveals no convergence among the variables in the long-run, yet the policy of globalisation is shown to have a significant positive effect on GDP of Tanzanian economy in the short-run. The coefficient of the dummy variable is positive and statistically significant at 5 per cent probability. The coefficients of rest of the variables are not statistically significant, so, they represent no significant impact on growth of GDP in the long-run as well as in the short-run. It is because the coefficient of ECT is neither negative nor significant. Consequently, the economy cannot correct itself from preceding year's disequilibrium. Authors have followed the standard procedures of econometric modelling with certain reservations. Above interpretations suffer from some technical limitations, embodied in the specification of the functional relations of the values of variables involved. Log linear functions capture the relation of rate of change of the values of independent with the rate of change of the values of dependent variable of the function. But the first differences of the log values of the dependent variable used in the function relate the first differences of log values of the independent variables which dilute the magnitudes. Such functions capture the relations of rates of change of the rates of change of the variables involved. Therefore, the non-significance of the regression coefficients of such values of the variables cannot be taken to represent the relation at level or even the relation of rate of change with rate of change. Such functions relate the acceleration/ deceleration of the rates of change. Besides, more often than not independent variables like public expenditure, consumption and investment are multi-collinear. So, the non-significance of the coefficients may also be due to multicollinearity.

Diagnostic Checks of Residuals

The study uses three tests to check robustness of model 1 and the results are shown in Table 6.13. The results of Breusch-Godfrey Lagrange Multiplier (LM) indicate that the model has no problem of serial auto correlation because the null hypothesis of no serial correlation in the residuals is not rejected. Similarly, Breusch-Pagan-Godfrey test of heteroskedasticity reveals that the residuals are homoskedastic. Lastly, the Jarque-Bera test of normality points out that the residuals are normally distributed as the probability of Jarque-Bera is greater than 5 per cent level of significance.

The following regression equation may also be examined.

$$\Delta \ln PE_t = 0.0016 + 1.414 \Delta \ln GDP_{t-1} + 0.029 \Delta \ln FSD_{t-1} - 0.041D - 0.481 ECT_{t-1} \ldots (4)$$

$$t = (0.023) \quad (1.0772) \quad (0.4196) \quad (-0.657) \quad (-2.601)$$

Equation 4 depicts the existence of long-run relationship among the variables. The coefficient of error correction term (ECT_{t-1}) is negative and highly significant; it implies that the system corrects the preceding period's disequilibrium at a speed of 48.1 per cent annually. However, the rate of adjustment is too low and slow to be completed in a reasonable period of time in a dynamic state in which even before the dependent variable is adjusted to the preceding period's change up to 65-75%. new forces emerge which make this adjustment meaningless. So, the above mechanical interpretation needs to be taken with a pinch of salt. Lagged change in the rate of change in GDP and public expenditure have significant impact of the change in the current rate of change in public expenditure in the long-run. Conversely, short-run changes in preceding period's GDP and fiscal deficits indicate no impact on short-run changes in public expenditure because their coefficients are not statistically significant. Besides, policy dummy (globalisation) depicts no significant impact on GDP. This contradicts earlier result which depicts positive impact of public expenditure on GDP.

Table 6.13

Residual Diagnostic Test for GDP Equation

Breusch-Godfrey Serial Correlation LM Test			
Obs*R-squared	1.7645	Prob. Chi-Square	0.4139
Heteroskedasticity Test: Breusch-Pagan-Godfrey			
Obs*R-squared	5.2129	Prob. Chi-Square	0.3905
Normality Test			
Jarque-Bera	1.6783	Probability	0.4321

Source: Own Compilation.

Table 6.14

Residual Diagnostic Test for PE Equation

Breusch-Godfrey Serial Correlation LM Test:			
Obs*R-squared	3.0216	Prob. Chi-Square	0.2207
Heteroskedasticity Test: Breusch-Pagan-Godfrey			
Obs*R-squared	5.7602	Prob. Chi Square(4)	0.2178
Normality Test			
Jarque-Bera	0.9847	Probability	0.6112

Source: Own Compilation.

Analogous Diagnostic Checks

Analogous diagnostic checks were applied to results of model 2 of public expenditure and the results are reported in Table 6.14. The findings reveal that the model is robust as there is neither serially correlated errors nor are the error variances heteroskedastic.

Finally, the normality test points out that the residuals of the model are normally distributed. Therefore, the results reported above are valid and suitable for consistent economic analysis.

Conclusions

The chapter examines the status of Tanzanian economy before and after globalisation period on the basis of time series data. The study covers the period from 1966 to 2012. Pre-globalisation period is taken from 1966 to 1985 (1966-1985) and the post globalisation period is from 1986 to 2012 (1986-2012). The study employs the D-F, ADF and PP tests to determine stationarity of time series and Augmented Engle-Granger test of co-integration is used to probably show the long-run relationship among the variables under the study. Besides, the growth curves with and without the dummy variable are used to analyse the changes in various economic and financial variables before and after globalisation.

The results show that: (a) the policy of globalisation has not affected Tanzanian economy significantly, and (b) all variables (public expenditure, public revenue, private consumption expenditure, per capita GDP and fiscal deficit) have shown similar level and pattern of growth over time from pre to post globalisation period. GDP is a marginal exception. But, the significant growth of GDP in post globalisation period due to trend reversal is attributable to long-run trend rather than policy. The study has traced the historical changes over a long period from 1966 to 2012.

7

Economic Growth and Public Expenditure

A Comparative Analysis of India and Tanzania

Introduction

Economic growth has been treated mainly as a function of investment. But several studies highlight consumption multiplier as an equal if not more important factor of growth. As public expenditure comprises both investment and consumption, public expenditure has also been used as determinant of growth in this study. Both investment and consumption have two components: (i) public and private investment; and (ii) public and private consumption. Public expenditure is incurred largely on investment and consumption, though expenditure on social welfare also constitutes a large proportion of total public expenditure.

Approach to Balanced Budgets

Two alternative approaches are generally used in theoretical analysis of public expenditure. Just as households cannot live on deficit budgets forever, public budgets cannot be kept unbalanced forever. So, public budgets should be balanced to avoid more spending than public revenue. States and their governments, like households, cannot live beyond their means forever. This concept of budgeting argues that public expenditure is constrained and limited by government's income in general and public revenue in particular. So the government should plan its budgetary expenditure within the bounds of public revenue expected to be raised during the financial year.

Public expenditure, and hence, government's budget has three distinct features: (i) public expenditure is generally downward sticky but up-ward highly flexible; (ii) total public expenditure has a committed part similar to that of households, institutions, and business houses; and (iii) a discretionary part. Public expenditure on salaries of officials and other employees and maintenance of administrative services are difficult to compromise with. Expenditure on on-going projects and programmes has invariably to be incurred otherwise expenditure already incurred till date will go waste. Expenditure on on-going projects includes expenditure required for completion of incomplete work and time and costs over-runs due to delays in completion. These are parts of committed expenditure. Public expenditure on growth and welfare falls in the category of essential needs of the government though it is a part of discretionary expenditure.

Public revenue is raised for all above components of public expenditure. Existing sources of revenue are generally used more intensively to increase public revenue and new sources of raising revenue are also explored. However, public revenue is constrained and limited by (i) GDP and its expected growth in the coming fiscal year, and (ii) total tax- bearing capacity of the people and degree of this capacity already exploited. Therefore, public revenue cannot grow without the growth of GDP; tax bearing capacity of the people is directly related to peoples' gross incomes and their levels and styles of living. Incidentally, peoples' consumption levels are also upward flexible but generally downward sticky. Therefore, tax revenue has its own limitations. Shortfalls in revenue relative to public expenditure are often made good by public debt and fiscal deficit. Fiscal deficit and public debt are generally extremely low under this approach. According to the monetary approach, inflation generally remains low. under this approach.

Public Expenditure Needs as Determinant of Public Revenue

As against the above approach, alternative theoretical thrust emphasises needs of public expenditure as the determinant of public revenue required to be raised during the financial year. Greater the needs of public expenditure, greater shall be the public revenue required in the coming financial year. Besides, in case public revenue falls short of public expenditure needs, gap is filled up by fiscal deficit and/or public debt. Need for public debt is thus related to needs of public expenditure and the peoples' capacity of bearing tax burden at any given point in time. In a democratic polity, political class keeps the peoples' reactions and views in mind in the policy of taxation. Incidentally, difference between these two approaches does not lie in the mechanics of raising revenue and/or the order of sequencing in the determination of revenue and expenditure. Need for fiscal deficit and public borrowing generally remains high under this approach. Consequently, inflation tends to be high in this policy regime according to the monetarists' argument. However, fiscal deficit and public revenue are not necessarily attributable to the approach of public expenditure needs being the determinant of public revenue. Level, structure and growth of public expenditure may be governed and guided by the growth and welfare needs of the society also.

These two approaches are organically different in so far as their theory and philosophy are quite different in thrust and orientation. Though the budgets are made for one financial year yet an essential feature of public budgeting is its futuristic orientation, and hence, any year's budget is in the long chain of links. Public budgets are not just a statement of revenue and expenditure alone, the budgets have to be a part of future scenarios. Annual budgets pave the way and chart out the road map for the realisation of envisaged future growth scenarios of national economy and its business. Public budget is, however, an instrument of realisation of important social, political and economic objectives that political class of the country envisions in the given socio-political-economic context of the country. In fact, budgets of a country are the manifestation of (i) national economic and fiscal policy as a whole and (ii) objectives of social and economic development and the strategy formulated for the realisation of the same.

The government first fixes the objectives and targets to be achieved during the financial year through operating the instrumentality of budgeting. Realisation of these objectives and targets forms the basis of fixing the target of public spending and allocation of resources for public spending among different lines of expenditure. Broadly, three important lines of expenditure are distinguished in this context: (i) administration; (ii) peoples' welfare; and (iii) economic growth. Maintenance of administrative structure and its shortfalls observed in the preceding period(s) are kept in view in order to keep the government running without compromising basic objectives of governance. But there is a thin line which distinguishes public expenditure on welfare from public expenditure on growth. For example, public expenditure on health and education may be viewed as the public spending on social infrastructure or spending on social welfare or for the promotion of consumption of health and education services. But it may also be viewed as public investment in long-term growth of the country (Among others, see Shri Prakash 1976, 1977, Shri Prakash and Chowdhury 1995, Bowen 1966). It has now been globally recognised that human capital plays an important role in the growth of an economy as physical capital. Whereas machinery and equipment are the carriers of hard technology, human capital is an embodiment and carrier of soft technology (Shri Prakash and Balakrishnan 2008). Public spending and its allocation is guided and governed by multiple considerations and facts. Provision for subsidies is made with a view to control inflation or to stabilise prices or to promote consumption of particular goods. Subsidies may also be granted for the promotion of output of socially desirable goods and services, and the subsidies also promote welfare and growth. For example, minimum support price policy for agricultural goods seeks the stabilisation of food prices on the one hand, and it provides an incentive to farmers to invest in agriculture for its growth. It is difficult to define and determine where welfare stops and growth begins; or growth stops and welfare begins in the context of public expenditure. However, welfare and growth conceptually are distinct and different, though these two are inseparably inter-linked in practice.

It is not only the level of public spending that affects growth, its structure is also important. Public expenditure promotes growth both directly and indirectly. In several cases, indirect effect of public expenditure is not only much greater than its direct effect, but it is also catalytic in spreading the momentum of growth across the sectors and spatial units of the economy/country. Linkages between sectors and spatial units are the catalyst of spreading the momentum of growth from one to another sector and one to another region.

Economic Growth and its Propellants

Economic growth moves on two legs: consumption and investment. Expenditure on consumption promotes growth through its multiplier effect. A unit of spending on consumption raises output/income by multiple times of one unit. Consumption represents effective demand which induces producers to increase the supply/output. Production of additional output requires investment in working and fixed capital on the one hand, and hiring of larger number of human resources and use of more material goods than before on the other. Increased output of one good to satisfy its greater demand involves increase in output of several goods through linkage effect. Increased productivity is also an inseparable instrument of rapid growth. Growth of productivity also means more output/income per person and per unit of capital.

Output can be raised by (i) Increasing the rate of production of existing units per unit of time. This is possible by making more intensive use of existing resources, including installed capacity to produce. This results in higher production and productivity; (ii) Increasing the number of production units to increase output without affecting productivity, (iii) expansion of the capacity of production of existing units. New productive capacity may embody better and more advance technology than before. All three ways of increasing output/supply require investment. Investment is obviously the key or pivot of growth. Investment contributes to growth through accelerator, which is ignited both by consumption and production.

Investment emanates both from private and public sources and it falls either in the category of autonomous or induced investment. Private investment minimises the need for public investment in capitalist market oriented economies. As against this, public investment in health, education, infrastructure, irrigation, transport, communication, etc., promotes private investment not only in these but in other sectors also. But public investment in planned socialist economies and it crowds out the private investment.

Sources of Data and Period of Study

All data relating to India and Tanzania have been taken from IMF-World Bank web-site in constant US dollars with 2005 as the base year. Data relate to the period from 1990 to 2013.

Choice of Pre-Determined Variables

General conception of growth is that investment is prime mover of economic growth. This study partially diverges from this conventional wisdom in so far as it takes private consumption rather than private investment into account as one of the two major determinants of growth of GDP of India and Tanzania. This approach is based on the premise that despite the adoption and implementation of the policies of liberalisation, privatisation and globalisation in 1986 in Tanzania and 1990 in India, both these economies have still retained the remnants of socialism, especially controls and licenses and the governments of these two countries still play critical role in the growth of many sectors of the economies. Therefore, public expenditure, comprising both public consumption and public investment accounts for the major proportion of total investment in these economies. Besides, explicit incorporation of private consumption as the determinant of GDP takes care of investment induced by consumption multiplier and its income effects both on consumption and private investment over the period covered by study. Recent studies by Shri Prakash and Sharma (2013, 2015) show that the growth effect of initial private consumption expenditure in Indian economy lasts over as many as 17 years, indirect income effect of consumption, further supplemented by induced investment based accelerator, accounts for much greater proportion of growth than the direct effect of consumption or investment. In view of the above, it is surmised that negligence of private investment in the study will not affect empirical results substantially.

Empirical Results

Results of empirical analysis are presented sequentially according to variables, countries under study and order of the listing of models used in the analysis of data. Since the time series models are used, it is incumbent on all the researchers to examine whether the data constitute stationary series or not. Results of application of Random Walk Model with the inferences based on Dickey-Fuller's test of unit root of regression equations are discussed first.

Results of Random Walk Model (RWM)

Following three versions of Random Walk model are estimated for India and Tanzania as a preliminary step. The models are given hereunder.

$\Delta Y_t=\delta Y_{t-1}+U_t$.........................(1)

$\Delta Y_t=\beta_0+\delta Y_{t-1}+U_t$....................(2)

$\Delta Y_t=\beta_0+\delta Y_{t-1}+\beta_1 T+U_t$............(3)

Root, ρ, of above equations is required to be less than 1 for the series to be stationary. This condition will be met if δ is negative and generally less than one, since

$1+\delta=\rho$.

RWM is applied as a preliminary step to evaluate if the time series of all variables of the study are stationary. OLS estimates of 3 versions of RWM of GDP, Public Expenditure and Private Consumption Expenditure of Indian economy are reported hereunder in Table 7.1 with a view to evaluate whether the root of these regression functions differ from unit. The results for Indian and Tanzania are reported separately.

Results in Table 7.1 show that the root of all above regression functions is in unit circle, so the necessary condition for a series to be stationary is not satisfied. The time series of GDP, public expenditure (PE) and private consumption expenditure (PVCE) are treated as non-stationary. In view of non-stationary nature of all jointly determined variables, Engle-Granger test of residuals linear combination of variables in an equation is applied. It assumes that even if the distribution of values of one or some or all the variables, included in the regression, are non-stationary, the distribution of their linear combination may still be stationary. Results of Engle-Granger test of linear combination of all three variables in regression function will be examined after the analysis of results of basic RWM models of Tanzania.

Table 7.1

Random Walk Model of India

Macro Variable	*Version*	β_0	β_1	β_2	R^2	F	F*
GDP	With Drift	-2.45E+09 (-0.255)	0.07 (5.75)	-	0.611	33.0375	1E-05
	Without Drift	-	0.067 (14.22)	-	0.899	195.922	4E-12
	Stochastic Trend	9.15E+09 (0.8748)	-0.021 (-0.5)	4.5E+09 (2.12)	0.683	21.5053	1E-05
PE	With Drift	1.21E+10 (1.0644)	0.034 (1.08)		0.053	1.16738	0.292
	Without Drift		0.063 (3.96)		0.416	15.6944	7E-04
	Stochastic Trend	4.95E+09 (0.4641)	-0.169 (-1.9)	5.9E+09 (2.43)	0.269	3.6839	0.043
PVCE	With Drift	-1.22E+10 (-1.4332)	0.093 (5.12)		0.555	26.2199	5E-05
	Without Drift		0.068 (10.4)		0.832	108.796	9E-10
	Stochastic Trend	-1.45E+10 (-1.1632)	0.11 (1.54)	-5E+08 (-0.26)	0.557	12.5598	3E-04

Source: Authors' Calculations.

Results of Random Walk Model of Tanzania

OLS estimates of GDP, PE and PVCE of 3 versions of RWM are reported in Table 7.2 for Tanzanian economy.

The table reveals that: (i) slope coefficients of all 3 versions of RWM for GDP are positive and statistically significant. It indicates that the root of these functions is in unit domain. Hence, GDP of Tanzania, like that of India, does not have a stationary series; (ii) Public expenditure also emerges as non-stationary in the same way as GDP; (iii) Slope coefficients of all three versions of PVCE emerge negative; but these coefficients are not significantly different from zero. So the roots of the three equations of PVCE also lie in unit circle.

Table 7.2

Random Walk Model for Tanzania

Variable	*Version*	β_0	β_1	β_2	R^2	F	F*
GDP	No Drift		0.062 (17.308)		0.934	299.6	0.000
	With Drift	-475390833.8 (-5.431)	0.097 (14.019)		0.908	196.5	0.000
	Stochastic Trend	-157576714.7 (-2.186)	0.015 (1.098)	57323749.3 (6.271)	0.970	306.2	0.000
PE	No Drift		0.184 (2.639)		0.014	6.96	0.016
	With Drift	-430212966.4 (-0.503)	0.235 (1.907)		0.154	3.64	0.071
	Stochastic Trend	-1239824620 (-1.242)	0.060 (0.354)	156656849.8 (1.466)	0.240	2.997	0.074
PVCE	No Drift		-0.027 (-0.536)		0.014	0.287	0.598
	With Drift	1812515664.7 (1.580)	-0.247 (-1.674)		0.123	2.803	0.110
	Stochastic Trend	1864688655.4 (1.543)	-0.283 (-1.166)	18244335.5 (0.188)	0.125	1.352	0.283

Note: Not significantly different from zero. **Significant at 0.07 probability level.

Source: Authors' Calculations.

Thus, Dickey-Fuller test reveals time series of all three variables for Tanzania to be non-stationary. It needs to be examined whether linear combinations of the variables, included in three regression functions, are stationary. For this, Engle-Granger Test of stationarity of residuals of the chosen regression models of all three jointly determined variables is applied.

Following functional relations and their residuals are taken into consideration for determining whether the residuals of these regression functions, expressed as linear combinations of variables, are stationary. Results are discussed after the results of growth curves have been explained.

Growth Curves of India and Tanzania

It may be noted that the variables growth of which is estimated by growth function is transformed into logarithm form even if the observed values are non-linear; this is achieved by logarithmic transformation of the variables. This is also likely to remove non-stationarity in most of the cases. Therefore, estimates of growth curves may not need application of Engel-Granger test.

The equation of the growth curve is given below:

$\ln Y_{it} = \alpha_0 + \alpha_1 T$.......................(4)

Y_{it} is the variable growth of which is to be determined, i=1,2,3 and i refers to GDP, PE and Expenditure on Consumption, T stands for time.

OLS estimates of Growth Curves of GDP, PE and PVCE of India and Tanzania are reported in Table 7.3. Calculations are done from data for two countries separately and their year on year sums.

Table 7.3

Growth Curves—India and Tanzania

Country	*Variable*	*Intercept*	*Slope*	*R^2*	*F*	*F**	*CAGR *%*	*CAGR ***	*Relative ACGR% ****
India	GDP	26.435 (1715.96)	0.065 (60.30)	0.99	3636.22	6E-26	6.5	6.717	100.58
Tanzania	GDP	22.533 (775.093)	0.0532 (25.09)	0.97	629.533	4E-17	5.32	5.464	81.807
India	PE	25.298 (657.299)	0.0837 (31.06)	0.98	964.802	1E-19	8.37	8.727	98.78
Tanzania	PE	21.509 (153.989)	0.0724 (7.111)	0.71	50.566	5E-07	7.24	7.513	132.17
India	PVCE	26.07 (1362.26)	0.0565 (42.19)	0.99	1779.57	2E-22	5.65	5.813	102.26
Tanzania	PVCE	22.266 (178.967)	0.031 (3.436)	0.36	11.805	0.002	3.12	3.167	55.707
All	GDP	26.457 (1630.49)	0.0647 (54.63)	0.99	2984.87	0.000	6.47	6.679	100
All	PE	25.311 (634.298)	0.0847 (29.09)	0.98	846.162	0.000	8.47	8.834	100
All	PVCE	26.098 (1517.94)	0.0553 (44.09)	0.99	1943.99	3E-22	5.53	5.684	100

Note * Relative percentage of ACGR is derived from Annual Compound rate of growth of GDP of each country relative to ACGR of both countries taken together.

Source: Authors' Calculation.

Table 7.3 reveals that growth curve fits the data of GDP, PE and private final consumption well for India on all counts: (i) Coefficient of determination is statistically significant for all three variables; (ii) explained proportion of variation of GDP, PE and PVCE is very high, values of the coefficient of determination are as high as 0.99, 0.98 and 0.99 respectively for India; (ii) Systematic factors of growth, whose proxy is time, explain the growth of these variables adequately. Hardly 1 to 2 per cent of total change in growth of these variables over the years is explained by random factors; (iv) But the explained proportion of variation of growth of GDP, Public Expenditure and Private Consumption Expenditure of Tanzania is much lower than the corresponding explained proportion of variation of these variables of India; (v) The intercepts and slope coefficients of all three variables for India and Tanzania both are statistically significant; (v) The significance of intercepts implies that some systematic factors other than the random ones, excluded from growth curves other than time, exercise significant influence on growth of these variables. Policy, private investment, and average propensity to consume are three variables that are theoretically important in the determination of growth of GDP; lead-lag structure of inter-relations between PE and private consumption and influence of excluded variables may not be captured always by temporal changes *per se*. Hence, intercepts turn out to be statistically significant in such cases; (vi) significance of slope coefficients depict the fact that GDP, PE and PVCE have all grown at statistically significant rates, though the rates differ for three variables on the one hand, and between the two countries on the other.

Relative Rates of Growth

Comparative analysis is facilitated better by the evaluation of relative rates rather than the direct comparison of absolute rates of the two countries. Relative rates of growth of these variables are derived as the ratio (percentage) of ACGR of India to ACGR of Tanzania relative to ACGR of combined data of two countries. These values of relative ACGRs display differentials of growth rates of the variables for India and Tanzania. Following interesting inference may be drawn from the results:

- GDP of India has grown more rapidly than that of Tanzania. Though Tanzania had opted for policy of LPG much earlier than India, growth of its GDP has lagged behind that of India. It may be due to the difference in the pace and structure of reforms pursued by both these countries. These differentials may also be partly attributable to the base effect on the one hand, and size and structure of two economies on the other;
- As against GDP, PE has grown much more rapidly in Tanzania than India. The differential may probably be accounted by the lingering effect of regulatory framework in these two countries on the one hand, and accelerated efforts of Tanzanian government to impart impetus to growth of such social sectors as health, education and infrastructure. As against Tanzania, public expenditure on health and education has been left largely to the care of private enterprise in India after 1990-91; private investment has been encouraged to replace public investment in these sectors during the years of reforms. Besides, distribution of electricity, construction and/or maintenance of roads and flyovers are now in the hands of private operators partly, if not wholly, in India;
- ACGR of PE is higher than ACGR of GDP in Tanzania, which points towards the probability of planned economy's norms being still followed. Persistence of high Public Debt in Tanzanian Economy and burden of interest cost on exchequer may be another reason behind this;
- Magnitude of ACGR of PVCE is low both for India and Tanzania i.e. 5.65 and 3.12 respectively in comparison to the growth of PE and GDP. It may be attributed to the fact that income is allocated between consumption and investment/ savings; marginal propensity to spend on consumption out of incremental income is generally less than one except in case of very poor households;

- Private Final Consumption Expenditure has grown almost twice as rapidly in India than in Tanzania. It may be attributed partly to the overall size of Indian market/economy/population and unprecedented growth of middle class in Indian society. It is not that middle class did not exist in India before the commencement of LPG, but during the planning and regime of licenses and controls, demand for convenience and so-called luxury goods was dormant due to suppression by policy. Imports of such goods were either totally prohibited or the imports were very highly taxed. This dormant demand for various commodity groups, especially consumer durables, has been unleashed after the advent of economic reforms in the economy.
- It is noteworthy that the growth of GDP and public expenditure in India has considerably slowed down in the wake of world-wide economic slow-down. Economy of Tanzania could also not remain immune to the global phenomenon of economic slow-down.

Above inferences have important implications for future development of both the countries. These findings are pointers to the policy makers of the economies of both these countries. A lot of distance has still to be covered, if these two economies have to impart impetus to growth in future.

Augmented Engle-Granger (AEG) Test

The pure random walk model (no trend, no intercept; with intercept, no trend; and with intercept and trend) confirmed all the variables to be non-stationary. However, D-F test is weak in power and spread of sample size. So, Augmented Engle-Granger unit root test has been applied to the residuals of the equation given below:

$$Y_t=\beta_0+ \beta_1X+U\text{............} \qquad (5)$$

X and Y are non-stationary variables in absolute values. But their first differences are likely to be stationary of the same order I(1). β_1 captures the long run relation between X and Y. But U, the residual of the equation, captures the degree of divergence of the values of these two variables from their long run equilibrium. But the D-F test does not capture the problem of auto correlation between the residuals. It can be overcome by AEG test. The test is applied on residuals of regression equations of GDP and public expenditure for both India and Tanzania separately. Results are reported in Table 7.4.

Results of application of AEG test reveal that the residuals of GDP and PE of India and Tanzania are stationary of order zero I(0). All variables, included in the equation of GDP and private expenditure on consumption of both India and Tanzania are well co-integrated in their respective regressions. This implies that GDP, PVCE and PE as are shown in model 1 have a long-term equilibrium relationship. Public expenditure is also shown to be co-integrated with current GDP and lagged public expenditure as is shown in model two of Tanzania and India. Thus, the results reveal that the variables on standalone basis are not stationary but the linear combination of GDP and PE makes them stationary in a well co-integrated manner.

Table 7.4

Summary of Augmented Engle-Granger (AEG) Test Results

Models	*Long-run Equations*	*E-G Test Results*
		India
1	$GDP_t=f(GDP_{t-1}, PVCE_{t-1})$	$\Delta\mu_t=-1.0841\mu_{t-1}$, $R^2=0.5697$, d=1.8383 t=5.2795
2	$PE_t=f(GDP_t, PE_{t-1})$	$\Delta\mu_t=-0.6313\mu_{t-1}$, $R^2=0.2574$, d=1.6644 t=2.7011
		Tanzania
1	$GDP_t=f(GDP_{t-1}, PVCE_{t-1})$	$\Delta\mu_t=-0.8738\mu_{t-1}$, $R^2=0.4421$, d=1.7864 t=4.0804
2	$PE_t=f(GDP_t, PE_{t-1})$	$\Delta\mu_t=-0.6173\mu_{t-1}$, $R^2=0.3147$, d=2.0441 t=3.2002

Note: The critical values for AEG are -2.62 and -1.95 at 1 and 5 per cent respectively. Durbin–Watson d- statistic: Significance points of dl and du at 0.01 level of significance are 0.858 and 1.407 for model 1; and 0.938 and 1.291 for model 2.

Source: Authors' Calculations.

Engle-Granger Error Correction Model—GDP

Error correction model (ECM) is also applied in order to evaluate the speed at which the dependent variable adjusts to its long-run equilibrium value after a change in the value of independent variable(s) has disturbed equilibrium by some shock or structural break in the economy. Besides, ECM captures both short-run and long-run effects of change in one variable on another (Mehmood and Sadiq 2010).

The first step of AEG determines whether the residuals (Ut) of model 1 and 2 are stationary I(0) and/or co-integrated. This is followed by estimation of ECM. The ECM uses saved residuals from the estimated equations. The ECM measures short-run dynamic change in economic relationship among the variables. Models 1 and 2 can be rewritten as follows:

$$\Delta \ln GDP_t = \alpha_o + \alpha_1 \Delta \ln GDP_{t-1} + \alpha_2 \Delta \ln PE_{t-1} + \alpha_3 \Delta \ln PVCE_{t-1} + \lambda ECT_{t-1} + \varepsilon_t \quad .....(6)$$

$$\Delta \ln PE^t = \eta_o + \eta_1 \Delta \ln PE_{t-1} + \eta_2 \Delta \ln G\check{D}P_t + \gamma ECT_{t-1} + \mu_t \quad .....(7)$$

ECT_{t-1} is the lagged error correction term or lagged residual which is computed from estimates of co-integrated model 1 and 2; λ and γ depict the speed of adjustment of the dependent variables of model 1 and 2 respectively.

Errors of data of both India and Tanzania have been corrected. The sign of the coefficient of the error correction term (ECT) in the ECM equations is desired to be negative and significant in order to lend empirical evidence to support the prevalence of long-run association among the variables of the regression. Besides, value of the coefficient of error correction should satisfy the following inequality: $-1 \leq \lambda/\gamma \leq 0$ in order to avoid an explosive process of adjustment. It is desirable that the error correction process should be completed within the horizon. Results of ECM of GDP for India and Tanzania are embodied in Equation 1 and two respectively. Besides, outcomes of their respective diagnostic tests are reported in Table 7.5.

$$\underset{t=}{\Delta \ln GDP_t} = \underset{(0.5912)}{0.17} + \underset{(1.3661)}{0.2399 \Delta \ln PE_{t-1}} - \underset{(-0.6037)}{0.268 \Delta \ln PVCE_{t-1}} + \underset{(0.9379)}{0.705 \Delta \ln GDP_{t-1}}$$

$$- \underset{(-1.3960)}{0.8727 ECT_{t-1}}, R^2 = 0.1929, F = 1.016 \quad ....(8)$$

$$\underset{t=}{\Delta \ln GDP_t} = \underset{(0.3358)}{0.0019} - \underset{(1.0102}{0.045 \Delta \ln PE_{t-1}} - \underset{(-1.0898)}{0.064 \Delta \ln PVCE_{t-1}} + \underset{(6.8054)}{1.125 \Delta \ln GDP_{t-1}}$$

$$- \underset{(-2.6335)}{0.761 ECT_{t-1}}, R^2 = 0.891, F = 34.55 \quad ....(9)$$

The estimate of regression equation 7 reveals that even though all variables are shown to be co-integrated (Table 7.4), yet ECM reafirms the non-existence of any long-run relationship in the model. The coefficient of ECT is negative as expected but it is not significant. Therefore, the variables cannot converge to the long-run equilibrium. Besides, all short-run coefficients are not significant. Therefore, preceding period's PE, PVCE and GDP do not affect growth of GDP of India significantly in the long-run as well as in the short-run. But equation 8 reveals the existence of long-run equilibrium relationship between lagged public expenditure, private consumption and GDP because the coefficient of ECT is negative and statistically significant. Above all, speed of adjustment from short-run disequilibrium is as large as 76.1 per cent per annum. However, it is only preceding period's value of GDP that is statistically significant in the short-run at 5 per cent probability.

Residual Diagnostic Checks—GDP

This chapter uses four tests to check robustness of model 1 and 2; description of each test is as follows:

(i) Breusch-Godfrey Lagrange Multiplier (LM) test is used to examine if the residuals are serially correlated or not. This test uses: distribution has s-1 degrees of freedom. The null hypothesis of this test is that the error terms are not correlated;

(ii) Breusch-Pagan-Godfrey test of heteroskedasticity assumes that the residuals have constant variance. The null hypothesis is that the residuals are homoskedastic;

(iii) Jarque-Bera test of Normality assumes that the residuals of the regression equation are normally distributed around zero mean. The Jarque-Bera test statistic is calculated as is shown here:

$JB=n\left[S^2/6+(K-3)^2/24\right]$ where, n=sample size, S and K are coefficients of Skewenes and Kurtosis respectively;

(iv) Durbin-Watson (DW) Test is used to evaluate the seriousness of autocorrelation in the regression model which is commonly experienced in time series models. It assumes that the residuals are correlated like the Breusch-Godfrey Lagrange Multiplier (LM) test. The D-W test statistics are calculated using the following formula:

$$d=2(1-p) \qquad \ldots\ldots\ldots\ldots\ldots(10)$$

The results of Breusch-Godfrey Lagrange Multiplier (LM) test indicate that the model specification has no problem of serial correlation because the null hypothesis of no serial correlation in the residuals in not rejected for both India and Tanzania. These findings are also supported by Durbin-Watson test.

Breusch-Pagan-Godfrey test of heteroskedasticity reveals that the residuals are homoskedastic. Lastly, the Jarque-Bera test of normality points out that the residuals are normally distributed as the probability of Jarque-Bera is greater than 5 per cent level of significance (see Table 7.5).

Table 7.5

Residual Diagnostic Checks—GDP

	India		
Breusch-Godfrey Serial Correlation LM Test			
Obs*R-squared	1.3192	Prob. Chi-Square(2)	0.5171
Heteroskedasticity Test: Breusch-Pagan-Godfrey			
Obs*R-squared	3.2806	Prob. Chi-Square(4)	0.512
Jarque-Bera (JB) Normality Test			
Jarque-Bera	0.8808	Probability	0.6438
Durbin-Watson stat	2.0425	dl=0.777	du=1.534
	Tanzania		
Breusch-Godfrey Serial Correlation LM Test			
Obs*R-squared	1.5627	Prob. Chi-Square	0.4578
Heteroskedasticity Test: Breusch-Pagan-Godfrey			
Obs*R-squared	5.8855	Prob. Chi-Square	0.2079
Durbin Watson statistic	1.7285	dl=0.777	du=1.534

Source: Own Compilation.

Engle-Granger Error Correction Model—PE

Equations 9 and 10 depict empirical findings of ECM of public expenditure of India and Tanzania respectively and residual diagnostic tests of these equations are shown in Table 7.6 below. It is inferred from these equations that there exists no long-run relationship among the variables both for India and Tanzania. The coefficient of error correction term (ECTt-1) is negative but it is not significant. It means that the system does not correct the preceding period's disequilibrium. So, current GDP and lagged public expenditure have no significant impact on the change in current public expenditure in the long-run. Conversely, short-run changes in preceding period's PE and current GDP show significant short-run effect on current public expenditure at 0.1 probability. But in India the current PE has no significant effect on lagged PE and current GDP.

$$\Delta \ln PE_t = 0.0037 + 0.126 \Delta \ln \hat{GDP}_t + 0.7985 \Delta \ln PE_{t-1} - 0.632 ECT_{t-1}, R^2 = 0.103, F = 0.6497$$
$$t = (0.0513) \quad (0.1716) \quad (1.1427) \quad (-0.7938) \qquad ....(11)$$

$$\Delta \ln PE_t = -0.0496 + 1.452 \Delta \ln \hat{GDP}_t + 0.575 \Delta \ln PE_{t-1} - 0.2522 ECT_{t-1}, R^2 = 0.782, F = 21.015$$
$$t = (-1.7947) \quad (1.886) \quad (1.895) \quad (-0.6105) \qquad ....(12)$$

Residual Diagnostic Checks—PE

Diagnostic checks are applied to model 2 of public expenditure. The results are reported in Table 7.6. The table shows that the model specification is robust since the error terms are serially uncorrelated, homoskedastic and normally distributed. It can therefore be concluded that the results reported above are valid and suitable for consistent economic analysis.

Distributed Lag Model (DLM)

Interestingly, DLM shows both short and long-run relationship between the variables of analysis. Besides, it also shows the proportion of total change completed in given number of periods and total time required for short-run equilibrium to reach the warranted level of long-run equilibrium. As theory predicts a prior existence of long-run equilibrium; long-run equilibrium curve is the envelope of short-run equilibrium curves. It is implied that the distance from short to long-run equilibrium represents errors of estimation. This model in authors' view is superior to VECM since it includes lagged as well as concurrent values of determinants and the model incorporates specific theory to back it. This model is therefore different from VAR and VECM models which are not only a theoretical but these models also include only lagged values of the variables of the system.

Table 7.6

Residual Diagnostic Checks

	India		
Breusch-Godfrey Serial Correlation LM Test			
Obs*R-squared	1.5858	Prob. Chi-Square	0.4525
Durbin Watson Statistic	1.7561	dl=0.858	du=1.407
Heteroskedasticity Test: Breusch-Pagan-Godfrey			
Obs*R-squared	1.0519	Prob. Chi-Square	0.7887
Jarque-Bera Normality test			
Jarque-Bera test statistic	1.7112	Probability	0.425
	Tanzania		
Breusch-Godfrey Serial Correlation LM Test:			
Obs*R-squared	0.2607	Prob. Chi-Square	0.8778
Durbin Watson statistic	2.0145	dl=0.858	du=1.407
Heteroskedasticity Test: Breusch-Pagan-Godfrey			
Obs*R-squared	2.1282	Prob. Chi-Square	0.5462
Jarque-Bera Normality Test			
Jarque-Bera test statistic	2.4051	Probability	0.3004

Source: Own Compilation.

Test of Multicollinearity

An important problem which usually affects the results of multiple regression models relates to multicollinearity among the independent variables. Klien (1960) suggested the simple step wise regression modelling to discover not only the presence of multicollinearity but it also helps in locating of the problem. The results are reported in Table 7.7. Besides, the results also help in detecting any predetermined variable which is superfluous and which may be dropped from the regression.

Table 7.7

Results of Step-wise Regression of Current GDP of India and Tanzania

Equations	β_0	β_1	β_2	β_3	R^2	F	F*
			India				
GDPt=GDP_{t-1}	-2.5E+09 (-0.255)	1.07 (88.0)			0.997294	7740.7	1.88E-28
GDP_t=$PVCE_{t-1}$	-1.2E+11 (-4.829)	2.03 (37.7)			0.985449	1422.2	8.89E-21
GDP_t=PE_{t-1}	1.9E+11 (12.027)	1.86 (42.7)			0.988608	1822.3	6.8E-22
GDP_t=GDP_{t-1} +$PVCE_{t-1}$	8.29E+09 (0.469)	1.16 (9.5)	-0.17 (-0.729)		0.997364	3784.2	1.62E-26
GDP_t=GDP_{t-1} +PE_{t-1}	-1.4E+10 (-0.531)	1.14 (8.1)	-0.12 (-0.472)		0.997324	3727.2	1.88E-26
GDP_t=$PVCE_{t-1}$ +PE_{t-1}	4.42E+10 (1.377)	0.92 (4.8)	1.03 (5.945)		0.994741	1891.5	1.62E-23
GDP_t=GDP_{t-1} +$PVCE_{t-1}$+PE_{t-1}	-2E+10 (-0.778)	1.62 (4.8)	-0.51 (-1.577)	-0.500 (-1.47)	0.997634	2670.3	4.08E-25
			Tanzania				
GDP_t=GDP_{t-1}	-4.5E+08 (-5.572)	1.09 (179.5)			0.999349	32234.6	6.01E-35
GDP_t=$PVCE_{t-1}$	-2.4E+08 (-0.734)	1.65 (43.90)			0.989227	1928.4	3.78E-22
GDP_t=PE_{t-1}	3.68E+09 (5.590)	1.69 (16.1)			0.925225	259.8	2.66E-13
GDP_t=GDP_{t-1} +$PVCE_{t-1}$	-4.4E+08 (-6.022)	0.98 (19.9)	0.17 (2.282)		0.999483	19349.2	1.35E-33
GDP_t=GDP_{t-1} +PE_{t-1}	-7E+08 (-9.623)	1.17 (73.0)	-0.13 (-5.161)		0.999721	35802.3	2.88E-36
GDP_t=$PVCE_{t-1}$ +PE_{t-1}	3.21E+08 (1.013)	1.35 (13.9)	0.34 (3.296)		0.99302	1422.7	2.75E-22
GDP_t=GDP_{t-1} +$PVCE_{t-1}$+PE_{t-1}	-6.8E+08 (-8.590)	1.14 (21.7)	0.05 (0.727)	-0.123 (-4.14)	0.999728	23306.5	4.8E-34

Source: Own Compilation.

Application of distributed lag model is preceded by step- wise regression with a view to detect the location and pattern of multi collinearity, if any (Klein 1953, Tinbergen 1974). It also helps in finding the individual contribution of each of the three pre-determined variables to the growth of variable under consideration. Besides, results of step wise regressions also determine if any of the pre-determined variables is superfluous in so far as its relative contribution to the changes in the values of dependent variable is concerned. The OLS estimates of the step-wise and distributed lag regression functions of GDP, PE and PVCE are reported in Table 7.7.

First results of step-wise regression for India are discussed. The following inferences may be drawn from the results reported in the table: (i) First and foremost aspect of regression analysis is the nature of the fit of the chosen model to the data; fit is evaluated in terms of the values of coefficients of determination, intercept and slope and their statistical significance. Value of the coefficient of determination represents the share of contribution of systematic factors included in the regression. Contribution of excluded variables is shown by intercept. Value of (1-R^2) displays the contribution of random factors to the proportion of total changes in the value of the dependent variable of the equation. The coefficients of determination of Step-wise regression have as high values as (a) 0.9973 for auto-regression function of GDP; (b) 0.9886 for GDP as a function of lagged private consumption expenditure; and (c) 0.9855 for GDP as a function of lagged public expenditure. (ii) R^2 is highly significant statistically in all three cases. Thus, the choice of explanatory factors and functional form appears to be correct on this count. (iii) Intercept of all three functions are also statistically significant, which indicates that one or more explanatory variable(s) excluded from above functions exercise significant influence on changes in current values of GDP. However, intercept is positive only in case of GDP as a function of public expenditure as an explanatory factor. Therefore, the excluded variables from functions 1 and 2 influence current values of GDP negatively, while third function indicates that one or some explanatory variable(s), which affects GDP positively, are excluded from this function. Results of step-wise regression also show that (iv) introduction of private consumption as second explanatory factor in auto-regression function of GDP improves explanatory power of the function marginally by 0.0001 percentage point. Though the inclusion of this variable as second explanatory factor improves explanatory power negligibly, yet it is not considered to be superfluous, since this variable individually also depicts high explanatory power. (v) Incorporation of lagged public expenditure in auto regression function of GDP hardly improves explanatory power of auto-regression function and is a bit less than the improvement caused by the inclusion of lagged private consumption expenditure. This variable is also not treated as superfluous. (vi) Dropping of lagged GDP as explanatory variable in order to evaluate the joint influence of lagged private consumption expenditure and public expenditure depicts explanatory power which is slightly less than that of auto-regression function. This suggests that the exclusion of lagged GDP as an explanatory variable may not be right choice. (vii) This takes us to the last function in the series which includes all three explanatory factors. This function has the maximum explanatory power as the R^2 equals 0.997634. But except the positive coefficient of lagged GDP, coefficients of all other explanatory variables are negative and not significant. This is attributed to the presence of serious degree of multicollinearity. (viii) But the coefficient of lagged GDP in this function exceeds unit substantially, which means that the coefficient of partial adjustment is negative and hence, less than zero. This violates the technical condition of distributed lag model. Therefore, the function is not acceptable.

Results of application of step wise regression and distributed lag model of GDP to data of Tanzania also depict the same facets as those displayed by the results for India. Therefore, these results are also not acceptable due to violation of technical condition of distributed lag model.

DLM of Public Expenditure of India and Tanzania

DLM of public expenditure has been estimated by Two Stage Least Squares. Empirical estimates of the functions are reported in Table 7.8

Table 7.8

Step-wise Regression—Public Expenditure

Country	*Equations*	α_0	α_1	α_2	R^2	F	F^*
India	$PE=PE_{t-1}$	1.21E+10 (1.064)	1.034 (32.92)		0.995	1084	1.47E-19
	$PE_t=GDP$	-9.2E+10 (-6.41)	0.553 (32.72)		0.981	1071	1.67E-19
	$PE_t= PE_{t-1}+GDP$	-3.9E+10 (-1.15)	0.531 (1.666)	0.27 (1.58)	0.983	582.1	1.89E-18
Tanzania	$PE_t= PE_{t-1}$	-3.1E+08 (-1.97)	1.136 (44.78)		0.99	2005	2.52E-22
	$PE_t=GDP$	-2.3E+09 (-5.22)	0.634 (20.31)		0.952	412.6	2.75E-15
	$PE_t= PE+GDP$	-9.1E+08 (-4.71)	0.864 (12.14)	0.161 (3.98)	0.994	1717	4.23E-23

Source: Own Compilation.

Following inferences may be drawn from the results reported in Table 7.8: (i) Auto-regression function of public expenditure fits the data of both India and Tanzania very closely as the slope and correlation coefficients are statistically significant; (ii) The function explains 99.5 and 99 per cent of total variation in public expenditure incurred by India and Tanzania respectively; (iii) But all three coefficients of the functions are not significant for India though these coefficients are significant for Tanzania.

Reasons for Non-Acceptance of Results of Linear DLM for India and Tanzania

The following grounds may be adduced for the types of results obtained above for DLM. There may be specific errors involved in the choice of the following: (i) DLM may not be appropriate for analysing the behaviour of Indian GDP and PE; (ii) specification of pre-determined variables may not be appropriate; (iii) specification of the functional form may be inappropriate.

It is note-worthy that the data series of GDP is non-stationary both for India and Tanzania. Volatile changes in the values over the years tend to make the series of a variable non-stationary. This has been observed that Indian economy was in recession during the period from 1998 to 2003, which recurred in 2009 and it still prevails. Tanzanian economy has also not been immune from this facet during the period covered by the study. Analysis of such non-linear changes may need non-linear functional form. Therefore, log-linear function is tried next for both countries and variables under consideration. Besides, annual time series data grosses and averages over different seasons of the year and overlooks differential lengths of lags involved in the production processes of light consumer goods, consumer durables, and heavy producer goods. It may, therefore, require the use of current rather than lagged values of public expenditure.

Log-Linear DLM Functional Relation

Transformation of observed into logarithmic values leads to (i) Change in the scale of measurement; (ii) it smoothens magnitude of change in so far as large magnitudes are replaced by smaller and systematic ones; and (iii) volatile or non-linear functional relation is transformed into log linear functional form.

Results of Log-Linear DLM

Empirical estimates of these functions are reported in Table 7.9. First the results of step wise regression are taken up.

Table 7.9

Log-Linear Regressions—GDP

	Equations	β_0	β_1	β_2	β_3	R^2	*F*	*F**
				India				
1	$\ln GDP_t = \ln GDP_{t-1}$	-0.348 (-1.205)	1.015 95.711			0.99771	9160.5	0.00
2	$\ln GDP_t = \ln PVCE_{t-1}$	-2.679 (-4.976)	1.121 (55.648)			0.99326	3096.7	0.00
3	$\ln GDP_t = \ln PE_{t-1}$	5.826 (19.072)	0.814 (70.231)			0.99576	4932.4	0.00
4	$\ln GDP_t = \ln GDP_{t-1} + \ln PVCE_{t-1}$	0.5707 (1.045)	1.398 (7.068)	-0.424 (-1.94)		0.99807	5183.1	0.00

5	$lnGDP_t = lnGDP_{t-1} + lnPE_{t-1}$	1.0971 (1.035)	0.775 (4.558)	0.193 (1.413)		0.99792	4798.8	0.00
6	$lnGDP_t = lnPVCE_{t-1} + lnPE_{t-1}$	2.694 (2.331)	0.407 (2.785)	0.521 (4.909)		0.99695	3263.3	0.00
7	$lnGDP_t = lnGDP_{t-1} + lnPVCE_{t-1} + lnPE_{t-1}$	1.134 (1.095)	1.211 (3.435)	-0.350 (-1.402)	0.0966 (0.644)	0.99812	3354.4	0.00
	Tanzania							
8	$lnGDP_t = lnGDP_{t-1}$	-1.004 (-5.408)	1.046 (130.48)			0.99877	17023.6	0.00
9	$lnGDP_t = lnPVCE_{t-1}$	1.475 (2.442)	0.954 (35.978)			0.98329	1294.4	0.00
10	$lnGDP_t = lnPE_{t-1}$	5.841 (4.212)	0.779 (12.537)			0.88214	157.2	0.00
11	$lnGDP_t = lnGDP_{t-1} + lnPVCE_{t-1}$	-0.839 (-5.015)	0.900 (18.421)	0.141 (2.998)		0.99915	11753.7	0.00
12	$lnGDP_t = lnGDP_{t-1} + lnPE_{t-1}$	-1.419 (-11.484)	1.137 (78.018)	-0.076 (-6.621)		0.99961	25897.8	0.00
13	$lnGDP_t = lnPVCE_{t-1} + lnPE_{t-1}$	1.060 (2.648)	0.789 (19.542)	0.189 (5.664)		0.99414	1695.0	0.00
14	$lnGDP_t = lnGDP_{t-1} + lnPVCE_{t-1} + lnPE_{t-1}$	-1.603 (-8.677)	1.229 (17.209)	-0.067 (-1.319)	-0.096 (-5.165)	0.99965	17904.5	0.00

Source: Authors' Calculations.

Determination of GDP of India

The following inferences may be drawn from TAble 7.9: (i) Log-linear function fits the data of both India and Tanzania a bit better than the linear function in all cases in terms of explanatory power shown by the magnitudes of coefficient of determination, R^2; (ii) Intercepts are statistically significant at 0.05 or 0.07 (1 case-India) probability; (ii) Coefficient of explanatory variable in every function is statistically significant irrespective of whether it is lagged GDP or PVCE or PE included in the function as an explanatory factor both for India and Tanzania; (ii) Coefficients of explanatory variables in case of inclusion of two explanatory factors in the regression are also significant; (iii) But more importantly distributed lag model in all cases, whether functions of two or three variables are now free from the malady of violation of the technical condition of the coefficient of adjustment being in the range of 0 to 1 for India. As per expectation, log-linear distributed lag model for India furnishes satisfactory results.

The coefficient of adjustment of current to preceding period is 0.63, which is moderately high; therefore, the process of adjustment of current to preceding period's values is not slow and sluggish, though it takes quite some time to complete the adjustment process. Convergence of short to long-run equilibrium is spread over prolonged period. Almost 95 per cent convergence of short to long-run or actual to desired equilibrium value of GDP is completed. Period wise magnitude of completed adjustment is reported below:

Period:	I	II	III
Percent Adjustment completed	63.00	86.31	94.93

Following inferences are drawn from the above results: (i) As much as almost 95 per cent of total adjustment in current values of GDP, warranted by the changes in the values of determinants of GDP of India are completed in three years. Thus, the adjustment process is quite swift; (ii) Corresponding to 100 per cent rise in public expenditure and private consumption expenditure , GDP increases by 49.21 per cent and 44.4 per cent respectively; (iii) Response of GDP to changes in public expenditure is greater than its response to the change in private consumption expenditure. But changes in consumption and public expenditure taken together determine 93 per cent change in GDP in the long run. Thus, both consumption and public expenditure play decisive role in the growth of GDP. Public expenditure is more decisive determinant of GDP than consumption because PE comprises both consumption and investment expenditure of government. Thus, public expenditure activates both multiplier and accelerator process of growth of GDP.

Table 7.10

Residual Diagnostic Tests—GDP

	India		
Breusch-Godfrey Serial Correlation LM Test:			
Obs*R-squared	1.3090	Prob. Chi-Square	0.5197
Heteroskedasticity Test: Breusch-Pagan-Godfrey:			
Obs*R-squared	0.4065	Prob. Chi-Square	0.9389
Normality Test			
Jarque-Bera t-Statistics	1.6561	Probability	0.4369
Durbin-watson Test			
Durbin-Watson t-statistic	2.0470	dl=0.858	du=1.407
	Tanzania		
Breusch-Godfrey Serial Correlation LM Test			
Obs*R-squared	0.7842	Prob. Chi-Square	0.6756
Heteroskedasticity Test: Breusch-Pagan-Godfrey			
Obs*R-squared	6.1988	Prob. Chi-Square	0.1023
Normality Test			
Jarque-Bera	1.1173	Probability	0.57199
Durbin-Watson t-statistic	1.7198	dl=0.858	du=1.407

Source: Own Compilation.

Determination of GDP of Tanzania

Following inferences emanate from the estimates of DLM of GDP of Tanzania: (i) Results furnished by log-linear DL function of GDP for Tanzania are almost similar to those derived from linear DL function; (ii) DLM, having either public expenditure alone as an explanatory variable, or both public expenditure and private consumption as explanatory variables of GDP again transgresses the technical condition required to be satisfied by the coefficient of adjustment. The coefficient of adjustment, μ turns out to be negative: λ=-0.25 (iii) DLM, having private consumption expenditure and lagged GDP as explanatory factors, however, does not transgress this condition; (iii) But addition of private consumption expenditure or public expenditure, or both in the DLM retains more or less the same values of their coefficients as are in the bi-variate function. It implies superfluous nature of these two determinants; (iii) On the available evidence, it seems more plausible to accept either the function 11 or 13; (iv) Acceptance of results of relation 11 will run counter to the results of relation 8 and 9 in view of which the adding of PVCEt to 8 or lagged GDP to 9 does not contribute much to the explained proportion of variation or the value of the slope coefficients. These results indicate that either auto-regression model 11 or model 13 may be accepted for the determination of GDP of Tanzania. Relation 13 is accepted.

Diagnostic Tests—GDP

The diagnostic tests of GDP equation show that the model is well specified since the residuals are not correlated, homoskedastic and are normally distributed. The results are shown in Table 7.10.

Determination of Public Expenditure of India and Tanzania

The empirical estimates of the log-linear regression of PE of India and Tanzania are given in Table 7.11.

The Table 7.11 reveals that (i) log-linear auto regression function of first order difference fits the data of public expenditure of India and Tanzania well so far as the explained proportion of variation and significance of the slope coefficients are concerned; (ii) explanatory power of these auto regression functions is greater than that of the corresponding linear functions examined earlier. Results justify log-linear rather than linear specification of the function; (iii) intercept of auto-regression model of India is not significant. But the intercept for Tanzania is significant which suggests the need for incorporation of some explanatory variable excluded from the function; (iv) the coefficient attached to estimated values of GDP in this equation is highly significant for India and Tanzania; (v) there is no violation of technical condition imposed on the range in which the value of the coefficient of adjustment is expected to fall either for India or Tanzania. Thus, log-transformation of data removes the technical infirmities associated with the linear functional form earlier used in the study; (vi) But the coefficient of lagged public expenditure of India turns from significant to non-significant, suggesting the presence of multi collinearity. There exists no solution to the problem of multi collinearity and one does not throw the baby with the bath-water. As there exists strong theoretical and methodological grounds also for the choice of DLM, already discussed earlier, log linear DLM of public expenditure is accepted both for India and Tanzania.

Table 7.11

Step-wise Regression—Public Expenditure

Equations	β_0	β_1	β_2	R^2	*F*	*F**
		India				
$\ln PE_t = \ln PE_{t-1}$	0.228 (0.471)	0.994* (54.178)		0.99290	2935.3	0.00
$\ln PE_t = \ln GDP$	-6.827* (-10.333)	1.219* (50.317)		0.99177	2531.8	0.00
$\ln PE_t = \ln PE_{t-1} + \ln GDP$	-1.624 (-0.584)	0.735** (1.921)	0.318 (0.677)	0.99306	1430.00	0.00
		Tanzania				
$\ln PE_t = \ln PE_{t-1}$	-1.727* (-2.937)	1.080* (41.004)		0.98766	1681.34	0.00
$\ln PE_t = \ln GDP$	-6.848* (-3.681)	1.259* (15.716)		0.92164	246.99	0.00
$\ln PE_t = \ln PE_{t-1} + \ln GDP$	-3.450* (-5.853)	0.850* (15.011)	0.295* (4.315)	0.99361	1555.44	0.00

Note: In the parentheses () are t-value.
Source: Own Compilation.

The structural form of these functions both for India and Tanzania are reported hereunder:

India: Adjustment accomplished in three periods for India is shown below:

Period	I	II	III
Completed	0.938	0.996	0.9998

The above results shows that the process is swift and almost hundred per cent adjustment to the change in PE in response to changes in GDP is completed in three years.

$$\ln PE_t^* = 7.796 + 1.382 \ln G\hat{D}P_t$$

Adjustment accomplished in three periods for Tanzania is as follows:

Period	I	II	III
Completed	0.144	0.267	0.373

Above results show that the adjustment of PE to the changes in GDP is sluggish and slow in Tanzania. Only 37.3 per cent of total desired change is completed in a period of three years in Tanzania. following is its long run relation:

$$\ln PE_t^* = 23.64 + 23.93 \ln GDP_t$$

Short and long period equilibrium of PE in Tanzania are substantially different from each other. Policy intervention in direction and composition of PE is warranted for the removal of hiatus.

Diagnostic Tests—GDP

The diagnostic checks for public expenditure model of India and Tanzania show the model n to be robust as the residuals are homoskedastic, normally distributed and have no problem of serial correlation. The results of tests, reported in Table 7.12, do not reject null hypotheses, because the p-values are above 5 per cent probability level.

Findings and Conclusions

Following are the major findings of the analysis of results obtained from the applications of different models. Results of linear specifications of functional relations between public expenditure and growth of GDP of India and Tanzania highlight that the below listed errors should be avoided; (i) choice of in-appropriate functional relation; (ii) choice of inappropriate explanatory variable(s); and (iii) choice of inappropriate functional form.

The choice of the function has to be guided both by theory and method of data analysis.

Log Linear specification of functional relations between public expenditure and GDP of India yields satisfactory results, since DLM is found to be an appropriate function both for GDP and Public Expenditure.

Almost 95 per cent of adjustment to total change in GDP, warranted by the change in public expenditure, is achieved in three years.

Table 7.12

Residual Diagnostic Tests—PE

Breusch-Godfrey Serial Correlation LM Test:			
Obs*R-squared	0.3105	Prob. Chi-Square	0.8562
Heteroskedasticity Test: Breusch-Pagan-Godfrey			
Obs*R-squared	2.2749	Prob. Chi-Square	0.3206
Normality Test			
Jarque-bera	3.8326	Probability	0.14715
Durbin-Watson t-statistic	1.4587	dl=0.938	du= 1.291
Tanzania-PE			
Breusch-Godfrey Serial Correlation LM Test:			
Obs*R-squared	3.7517	Prob. Chi-Square	0.1929
Heteroskedasticity Test: Breusch-Pagan-Godfrey			
Obs*R-squared	0.1427	Prob. Chi-Square	0.9311
Normality Test			
Jarque-bera	0.7461	Probability	0.6886
Durbin-Watson stat	1.6720	dl=0.938	du= 1.291

Source: Own Compilation.

Almost 100 per cent of adjustment of public expenditure (PE) of India in response to change in GDP is completed in 3 years.

In the long-run, doubling of public expenditure of India induces its GDP to increase by 49.2 per cent, whereas doubling of its private consumption induces GDP to increase by 44.4 per cent. Corresponding to 100 per cent increases in GDP, Public expenditure increases by 132 per cent.

So far as Tanzania is concerned, DLM is not appropriate, PE and private consumption determine GDP. The GDP of Tanzania is much more responsive to change in private expenditure in consumption (PVCE) than change in PE. This highlights high degree of dormant demand for consumer goods as well as low level of living of the masses. Doubling of private consumption expenditure raises GDP by 72 per cent whereas doubling of public expenditure leads to an increase in GDP by only 23 per cent. It may also probably be accounted by substantial unproductive public expenditure or greater proportion of public expenditure going to long-term growth projects or both.

DLM is valid for regression modelling of public expenditure but adjustment is sluggish and slow. Only 37 per cent of total desirable change, warranted by change in GDP, is completed in three year. This is in consonance with the low and slow response of GDP to change in public expenditure. Above results and findings may be useful for future research and policy.

References

Abramoritz, M. (1962). "Economic Growth in the United States", *American Economic Review* 52.

Adam, J. (2014). "Political and Economic Transition in Tanzania", in G.D. Mjema and G.E. Kaganda (eds.), *Socio-Economic Development in Tanzania: A Multidisciplinary Perspective.* Dar Es Salaam University Press. pp.11-26.

Adleman, Irma (1967). "Political and Economic Transition in Tanzania", in G.D. Mjema and G.E. Kaganda (eds.), *Socio-Economic Development in Tanzania: A Multidisciplinary Perspective.* Dar Es Salaam University Press. pp.11-26.

Almond, Brenda (1996). "John Stuart Mill (1806–1873)", in Adam Kuper and Jessica Kuper (eds.). *The Social Science Encyclopedia.* London: Routledge.

Arrow, Kenneth (2002). *Handbook of Social Choice and Welfare*. Elsevier.

Bagachwa, M.S.D. (1992). "Background, Evolution, Essence and Prospects of Current Economic Reforms in Tanzania", in M.S.D. Bagachwa, A.V.Y. Mbelle and Brian van Arkadie (eds.), *Market Reforms and Parastatal Restructuring in Tanzania.* Economics Research Bureau, University of Dar es Salaam.

Barewald, F. (1969). *History and Structure of Economic Development.* India Book House.

Barnard, Alan (1996). "David Hume, 1711-76", in Adam Kuper and Jessica Kuper (eds.), *The Social Science Encyclopedia.* London: Routledge.

Barro, Robert J. (1990). "Government Spending in a Simple Model of Endogenous Growth", *The Journal of Political Economy* 98(5): 103-25.

———. (1991). "Economic Growth in a Cross Section of Countries", *The Quarterly Journal of Economics* 106(2).

Baumol, W.J. and M.H. Peston and Gerhard Colm (1952). "Fiscal Policy", in S.E. Harris (ed.), *New Economics.* p.143.

Beiner, Ronald (1996). "Jean-Jacques Rousseau (1712-1778)", in Adam Kuper and Jessica Kuper (eds.), *The Social Science Encyclopedia.* London: Routledge.

Bhatia, V.G. (1966). "Measurement of Economic Development and Growth Potential", in P.N. Mathur and R. Bhardwaj (ed.), *Economic Analysis in Input Output Framework with Indian Empirical Explorations.* Vol. 1. Mumbai: Input Output Research Association.

Bigsten, A. and A. Danielson (1999). *Is Tanzania an Emerging Economy?* A Report for OECD Project 'Emerging Africa'.

Bird, R.M. (1971). "Wagner's Law of Expanding State Activity", *Public Finance/Finances Publique* 26(2): 1-26.

Black, Collison (1996). Thomas Malthus (1766–1834)", in Adam Kuper and Jessica Kuper (eds.), *The Social Science Encyclopedia.* London: Routledge.

Black, John, Nigar Hashimzade and Gareth Myles (2013). *Dictionary of Economics.* Oxford.

———. (2012). *Oxford Dictionary of Economics*. Oxford University Press.

Boulding, Kenneth E. (1966). "The Economics of Knowledge and the Knowledge of Economics", *American Economic Review, Papers and Proceedings*. p.11.

Bowen, C.V. (1996). "Taxation", in Adam Kuper and Jessica Kuper (eds.), *The Social Science Encyclopedia*. London: Routledge.

Bowen, M.J. (ed.) (1967). *Economics of Education*. Paris: UNESOCO.

Brahamanand, P.R. (1977). *Determinants of Real National Income and Price Level in India*. Bombay University Press.

Buchanan, J.M. (1975). "Why Does Government Grow?", in T.E. Borcherding and N.C. Durham (eds.), *Budgets and Bureaucrats: The Sources of Government Growth*. Duke University Press

Buchanan, J.M. and G. Tullock (1964). *The Calculus of Consent*. Ann Arbor, MI.

——— (1977). "The Expanding Public Sector: Wagner Squared", *Pubiic Choice* 31 (Fall): 147-50.

Chaligha, A., R. Matters, M. Bratton and Y.D. Davids (2002). "Uncritical Citizens or Patient Trustees? Tanzanians Views of Political and Economic Reforms", *Afro-Barometer Working Paper* No. 18. Retrieved from *http://www.google.co.in/search?hl=en-IN and source=hp&biw=&bih=&q=Uncritical+Citizens+or+Patient+Trustees%3F+Tanzanians+Views+of+Political+and+Economic+Reforms&btnG=Google+Search&gbv=1*

Cliffe, L. (1972). "Democracy in a One Party State: The Tanzania Experience". in L. Cliffe and J. Saul (eds.), *Socialism in Tanzania*. Dar es salaam: East Africa Publishing House.

Colin, Clark (1954). *Conditions of Economic Progress*. Macmillan.

Collisonn Black, R.D. (1996). ""Thomas Robert Malthus (1766-1834)"", in Adam Kuper and Jessica Kuper (eds.), *The Social Science Encyclopedia*. London: Routledge.

Colm, Gerhard (1952). "Fiscal Policy"", in S.E. Harris (ed.), *New Economics*. p.143.

Correa, Hector and Jan Tinbergen (1967). "Modeling Education for Growth", in Mark Blaug (ed.), *Economics of Education*. Vol. II. Penguin.

Cramer, J.C. (1972). *Applied Econometrics*. North Holland: Amesterdam.

Dennison, E.F. (1962). "The Sources of Economic Growth in the United States and the Alternatives before US", *Supplementary Paper* 13. Committee for Economic Development. New York.

Devarajan, Shantayanan, Vinaya Swaroop and Zou Heng-fu (1996). "The Composition of Public Expenditure and Economic Growth", *Journal of Monetary Economics* 37(2): 313-44.

Diamond, J. (1989). "Government Expenditure and Economic Growth: An Empirical Investigation", *IMF Working Paper* No. 89/45. Washington D. C.

Ditimi, Amassoma (2011). "Components of Government Spending and Economic Growth in Nigeria: An Error Correction Modeling", *Journal of Economics and Sustainable Development* 2.

Domar, E.D. (1957). *Essays in the Theory of Economic Growth*. pp.72-73.

Engle, R.F. and C.W. Granger (1987). "Co-integration and Error Correction: Representation, Estimation, and Testing", *Econometrica* 55: 251-76.

Fan, S. and N. Rao (2003). "Public Spending in Developing Countries: Trends, Determination and Impact", *EPTD Discussion Paper* No. 99. USA.

Frankel, S.H. (1952). "Review of the Experts' Report", *Quarterly Journal of Economics:* 309-10, November.

Friedman, Milton (1962). *Capitalism and Freedom*. Chicago: University Press.

———. (1982). "Ideas vs Facts", in M.P. Bhatt and M.S. Trivedi (eds.), *Liberalism and Less Developed Countires*. Ahmedbad: Gujarat University Press.

Friedman, Milton and Simon Kuznets (1946). *Income from Independent Professions in US* .

Galbraith, J.K. (1958). *The Affluent Society.* HougtonMiffin Harcourt

Gregoriou, A. and S. Ghosh (2007). *The Impact of Government Expenditure on Growth: Empirical Evidence from Heterogeneous Panel.*

Grier, K. and G. Tullock (1989). "An Empirical Analysis of Cross-national Economic Growth, 1951-1980", *Journal of Monetary Economics* 24(1): 259-76.

Gujarati, Damodar. N. and Sangeetha (2008). *Basic Econometrics.* Fourth Edition. MCGraw Hill.

Gupta, S., B. Clements, E. Baldacci and C. Mulas-Granados(2005). *Fiscal Policy, Expenditure Composition and Growth in Low-income Countries.*

Hansen, A.H. (1949). *Monetary Theory, Fiscal Policy and Business Cycles.* Indian Edition. p.115.

Harris, C.L. (1958). "Public Finance", in B.F. Haley (ed.), *Survey of Contemporary Economics.* Vol. II.

Harvey, A.C. (1981). *Time Series Models.* Oxford: Phillip Allen.

Hicks, J.R. (1966). *Capital and Growth.* London: Basil Blackbell.

———. (1973). *An Essay on Crisis in Keynesian Economics.* London: Basil Blackbell.

Hicks, Ursual K. (1957). "Learning about Economic Development", *Oxford Economic Papers*, Feburury.

Hirschman, Albert O. (1957). *The Strategy of Economic Development.* New Haven: Yale University Press.

Hirshleifer, Jack (1987). *Economic Behaviour in Adversity.* Chicago University Press.

Humpreys, S.C. (1996). "Aristotle, 384-322 B.C.", in Adam Kuper and Jessica Kuper (eds.), *The Social Science Encyclopedia.* London: Routledge. pp.30-31

———. (1996). "Plato, 428/7-348/7 B.C.", in Adam Kuper and Jessica Kuper (eds.), *The Social Science Encyclopedia.* London: Routledge.

Intriligator, M.D. (1980). *Econometric Models, Techniques and Applications.* New Delhi: Prentice Hall of India.

Jaroensathapornkul, J. (2010). "Spending for Growth: An Empirical Evidence of Thailand", *Applied Economics Journal* 17(2): 27-44,

Kaldor, Nicholas (1955). *An Expenditure Tax.* London: George Allen and Unwin.

———. (1957). "A Model of Economic Growth", *Economic Journal.*

Kendrik, J.W. (1961). *Productivity Trends in the United States.* Princeton University Press.

Keynes, J. M. (1935/1997). *General Theory of Employment Interest and Money.* Paper Back. London: Prometheus Books.

Klein, L. R. (1953). *A Textbook of Econometrics.* Asia Publish House.

———. (1960). *Introduction to Econometrics.* Prentice Hall of India.

———. (1965a). *A Textbook of Econometrics.*

———. (1965b). *An Introduction to Econometrics.*

Kraynak, Robert P. (1996). "Hobbes, Thomas (1588-1679)", in Adam Kuper and Jessica Kuper (eds.), *The Social Science Encyclopedia.* London: Routledge.

Kurihara, Kenneth, K. (1967). *The Keynesian Theory of Economic Development.*

Kuznets, Simon (1973). *Modern Economic Growth, Rate Structure and Spread.* Yale University Press.

Kweka, J.P. and O. Morrissey (1999). "Government Spending and Economic Growth: Empirical Evidence from Tanzania (1965-1996)", *CREDIT and School of Economics* 00(6).

Lasswell, Harold D. (1971). *A Preview of Policy Sciences.* New York: Elsevier.

Lontief, W.W. (1966). *Input Output Economics.* MacMillan.

Learner, Abba P. (1951). *Functional Finance.* London.

Lewis, Arthur (1958). *Economic Backwardness and Economic Growth.* London: George Allen & Unwin.

———. (1963). *The Theory of Economic Growth.* 6th Edition. London: George Allen & Unwin.

Lin, S. (1994). "Government Spending and Economic Growth", *Applied Economics* 26: 83-94.

Lindhal, Erik (1919). Quoted from Jack Hirshleifer (1987), *Price Theory and Applications.* New Delhi: Prenctice Hall of India.

Llewellyn, D.T. (1999). "The Economic Rationale of Financial Regulation", *FSA Occasional Paper* No. 1. London, Financial Services Authority.

Marshall, Alfred (1890/1963). *Principles of Economics, An Introductory Volume.* Macmillan. Reprint 1959/1963.

Mathur, P.N. (1962). "An Efficient Path of Technological Transformation of an Economy", in Tibor Barna (ed.), *Structural Independence and Economic Development.* McMillan.

———. (1967). *Economic Analysis in Input Output Framework.* Vol. I. Poona: Gokhale Institute of Politics and Economics (GPE).

———. (1969). *Economic Analysis in Input output Framework.* Vol.II. Poona: GPE.

———. (1991). *Why Developing Countries Fail to Develop and International Economic Framework and Economic Submission.* London: Macmillan.

———. (1992). *Why Developing Countries Fail to Develop?* London: Macmillan.

———. (1994). *Why Developing Countries Fail to Develop and International Economic Framework and Economic Subordination.* London: MacMillan.

———. (2000) "Embodied Technical Change and Technology Transfer to Developing Countries", in V. V. N Somayajulu and K.N. Prasad (eds.), *Indian Economy in Input Output Framework.* New Delhi: Allied Publishers.

Mathur, P.N. and Shri Prakash (1981). "Inventory Behavior of Agriculture and its Effect on General Prices in Indian Economy", *Elsevere Journal of Engineering and Economics.* Republished in Attila Chikan (ed.), *Economics and Management of Inventories.* Vol. II. Budapest: Hungarian Academy of Sciences.

Mehmood, R. and S. Sadiq (2010). "The Relationship between Government Expenditure and Poverty: A Co-integration Analysis", *Romanian Journal of Fiscal Policy* 1(1): 29-37.

Mill, J.S. (1833/1848). *Principles of Political Economy with Some of their Applications to Social Philosophy.* London: Longmans, Green and Co.

Musgrave, R.A. (1959). *The Theory of Public Finance.* McGraw-Hill Book Co.

Mutalemwa, D., O. Noni and S. Wangwe (1998). "Managing the Transition from Aid dependence: The Case of Tanzania", Paper presented at the *AERC/ODC Aid Dependence Workshop.* Nairobi. December.

Myrdal, Gunnar (1956). *Economic Theory and Underdeveloped Regions.* Mumbai: Vohra.

Nayyar, Deepak (1993). "Indian Economy at Cross Roads: Illusions and Realities", *Economic and Political Weekly,* 10 April.

Ndulu, B. J. (1994). "Tanzania's Economic Development: Lessons from the Experience and Challenges for the Future", L.A. Msambichaka, H.P.B. Moshi and F.P. Mtatifikolo (eds.), *Development Challenges and and Strategies for Tanzania: An Agenda for the 21st Century.* Dar es Salaam.

Neck, R. and M. Getzner (2007). "Austrian Government Expenditures: 'Wagner's Law' or 'Baumol's Cost Disease'?", *International Business and Economics Research Journal* 6 (11): 49-65.

Nurkse, Ragnar (1953). *Problems of Capital Formation in Underdeveloped Countries*. Oxford University Press.

———. (1961). *Problems of Capital Formation in Developing Countries*.

Nord, R., Yuri S., David, D., Alejandro, H., Niko, H., Samar, M. and Stephane, R. (2009). Tanzania: The Story of an African Transition. International Monetary Fund, Washington, D.C.

Peach, Terry (1996). "David Ricardo (1772-1823)", in Adam Kuper and Jessica Kuper (eds.), *The Social Science Encyclopedia*. London: Routledge.

Peakok, A.T. (1979). *The Economic Analysis of Government and Related Themes*. Martin Robertson.

Peacock, A.T. and G.K. Shaw (1971a). *The Economic Theory of Fiscal Policy*.

———. (1971b). "Fiscal Measures to Improve Employment in Developing Countries: A Technical Note", *Public Finance* 3.

Peacock, A.T. and J. Wiseman (1961). "Determinants of Government Expenditure", NBER Chapters, in *The Growth of Public Expenditure in the United Kingdom*. pp.12-34. National Bureau of Economic Research Inc. Available at *http://www.nber.org/chapters/c2302*.

———. (1967). *The Growth of Public Expenditure in the United Kingdom*. New Edition. London: George Allen & Unwin Ltd.

Pigou, A.C. (1920). *The Economics of Welfare*. Fourth edition. London: Macmillan.

Prebisch, Raul (1950). *Economic Development of Latin America and its Principal Problems*. U.N. Commission for Latin America.

Ranis, Gustav and John C.H. Fei (1963). ""The Ranis-Fei Model of Economic Development, *The American Economic Review* 53(3): 448-52.

Ricardo, David (1821). *The Principles of Political Economy and Taxation*. Third Edition. Text files at McMaster

Rosander, A.C. (1951/1965). *Elementary Principles of Statistics and Theory of Probability*. An East-West Edition. New Delhi.

Rosen, H. and T. Gayer (2008). *Public Finance*. NewYork: McGraw-Hill.

Rostow, W.W. (1991). *The Stages of Economic Growth*. Third Edition. Cambridge Books. pp.47-48.

Samuelson, Paul A. (1948). *Foundations of Economic Analysis*. Cambridge, Mssachussets: Harvard University Press.

———. (1962). "Parable and Realism in Capital Theory: The Surrogate Production Function", *Review of Economic Studies* 34.

Schafffer, Bernard (1995). "Policy Making", in Adam Kuper and Jessica Kuper (eds.), *The Social Science Encyclopedia*. London and New York: Routledge.

Schultz, T.W. (1960). "Capital Formation by Education", *Journal of Political Economy* 68: 571-83, December.

Sen, A. (1967). "A Comment on Correa-Tinbergen Model", in Mark Blaug (ed.), *Economics of Education*. Vol. II. Penguin.

Shri Prakash (1976). "Input Output Models of Education with Applications to Indian Data", in P.N. Mathur (ed.), *Economic Analysis in Input Output Framework*. Vol. III. Ahmedabad: S.P. Institute of Social Science Research.

———. (1977). *Educational System of India: An Econometric Study*. Delhi: Concept Publishing Co..

———. (1981). "Cost Based Prices in Indian Economy", *Malayan Economic Review* XXV.

———. (1982). "Industrial Production and its Determinants in India, 1951-76", *The Economic Journal of Nepal* V(4).

———. (1989). "Public Expenditure and Growth of Indian Economy", *Economic Journal of Nepal* X.

———. (1990). "Ecological Implications of Economic Development of Meghalaya (India): A Study of Levels and Patterns of Consumption and Production of Forest-Based Commodities", *Journal of Quantitative Economics* 6(1).

———. (1991). "Generalized Dynamic Linkage Pattern as a Base of Convergence of Unbalanced to Balanced Growth Theory: Some Methodological and Theoretical Issues with Application to Indian Economy", *International Journal of Development Planning Literature* 6(3-4), July-October.

———. (1992a). "Endogenisaiton of Inventory Investment in Harrod Model of Growth", *Singapore Economic Review* 38.

———. (1992b). "Real and Financial Development of Indian Economy", *Key Note Address*. The Indian Economic Journal, 73rd National Conference of Indian Economic Association.

———. (1994), "Liberalization, Privatisation and Globalisation and Relevance of Nehru-Mahalanobis Strategy of Growth", in Ajeet Kumar Sinha (ed.), *New Economic Policy of India-Restructuring and Liberalization of the Economy for 21st Century*. New Delhi: Deep & Deep.

———. (1995). "Liberalization, Privatisation and Globalisation and Relevance of Nehru-Mahalanobis Strategy of Growth", in Ajeet Kumar Sinha (eds.), *New Economic Policy of India-Restructuring and Liberalization of the Economy for 21st Century*. New Delhi: Deep & Deep.

———. (1996). *Cost of Education: Theoretical Explorations & Empirical Prognostication*. Delhi: Anamika Publishers and Distributors.

———. (2000). "Utilization of Human Resources: Concepts and Empirical Illustration", *Business Perspectives* II(2).

———. (2005) *Impact of New Economic Policy on Indian Economy*. Sponsored by ICSSR and supported by BIMTECH.

———. (2006). "Neo-Liberalism of New Economic Policy, Globalisation and Unemployment in India", in K.S. Dhindsa and Anju Sharma (eds.), *Economic Reforms and Development*. New Delhi: Concept Publishing Company.

———. (2010). *Theory of Consumer Behaviour*. Noida: Vikas.

Shri Prakash and Brinda Balakrishnan (2005a). "Managerial Approach to Conceptialization of Development and Growth Convergence of Macro to Micro Theory", *Business Perspective* 8(1).

———. (2005b). "Input Output Modelling of Employment and Productivity as Base of Growth", Presented at *Fifteenth International Conference on Input Output Techniques*. Beijing.

———. (2008). "Input Output Modelling of Labour Productivity and its Human Capital and Technology Components in Indian Economy", *Bulletin of Political Economy* 2(2).

Shri Prakash and Chitra Arora Bhatia (2012). "Determination of Opening Pirces of Equities of the Day", *Journal of Applied Finance, and Banking* III(4): 199-228.

Shri Prakash and Ranita Dutta (1994). "New Economic Policy: Analysis of Actual and Perceived Impact on Indian Economy", in B.M. Jauhari (ed.), *Economic Liberalisation and Globalisation*. Delhi: Commonwealth Publishers.

Shri Prakash and Rekha Sharma (2013a). "Analysis of Indo-lranian Trade", *Iranian Economic Journal*, 17(3): 1-24.

Shri Prakash and Ritu Sharma (2013b). "Multiplier Effect on Growth of Income and Investment: Analysis of Sequential Rounds in Input Output Framework", *The Indian Journal of Economics*.

———. (2015). "Multiplier Effect on Growth of Income and Investment: Analysis of Sequential Rounds in Input Output Framework", *The Indian Journal of Economics* XCV(378), Part III, 2014-15.

Shri Prakash and S.K. Ghosh (1977). "Public Sector in Indian Economy", in K.R. Gupta (ed.), *Organization and Management of Public Enterprises*. New Delhi: Himalya Publishing House.

Shri Prakash and Shalini Sharma (1998). "Endogenisation of Inventory Investment and Generalisation of Mahalanobis Model of Growth", *ArthaVijnana* XL(IV), December.

Shri Prakash and Sudhi Sharma (2013). "Public Expenditure, Public Debt, and Economic Growth of Member Countries of Gulf Cooperation Council", Proceedings of *National Conference on Indian Economic Growth in Regional Framework*, 28-29 September. BIMTECH, Greater Noida.

Shri Prakash and Sumitra Chowdhury (1995). *Expenditure on Education: Theory and Growth*. New Delhi: NIEPA (Now NUEPA).

Shri Prakash and T.J. Buragohani (1990). "Human Capital and Balanced Economic Growth", Proceedings of *Tenth International Conference on Input Output Techniques*.

Shri Prakash and Veena Goel (1987). "Price and Output Movement of Agro-based Industries in Indian Economy", in V.S. Mahajan (ed.), *Studies in Industrial Economy of India*. New Delhi: Deep and Deep.

Shri Prakash, Tarujyoti Buragohain and Abha Gupta (1993). "Literacy and Development: An Analysis of 114 Countries, 26 States and 452 Districts of India", *Journal of Education Planning and Administration, Special Issue of Literacy and Development in Developing Countries*. New Delhi: NIEPA.

Sharma, Shalini (2004). *An Empirical Analysis of Agricultural Prices in Indian Economy*. Ph.D. Thesis. Department of Economics, Aligarh Muslim University. Aligarh.

Sharma, Amit (2012). *Up-gradation of Educational Qualifications in Selected Professional Occupations and Growth of Indian Economy*. Ph.D. Thesis. MLSU Udaipur

Sharma, Amit and S.R. Ajeet (2010). "Productivity, Literacy and Per Capita State Domestic Product of Indian States", in Shri Prakash and H. Chaturvedi (eds.), *Dynamics of Under-Development of Economy of Uttar Pradesh*. New Delhi: Bloomberg.

Sharma, Ritu (2014). *Analysis of Households' Choice between Current and Future Consumption Expenditure: A Study of National Capital Territory of Delhi*. Ph.D. Thesis. Department of Management Studies, Mysore University. Mysore.

Shaw, William H. (1996). "Karl Marx", in Adam Kuper and Jessica Kuper (eds.), *The Social Science Encyclopedia*. London: Routledge.

Simon, H. A. (1981). *The Science of the Artificial*. Second Edition. U.K.: Cambridge.\

Singer H.S. (1989). *Lessons of Post War Development Experiences,1945-1989*. Paper Back

Smith, Adam (1774). *An Essay on the Nature and Significance of Wealth of Nations*.

———. (1776/2003). *The Wealth of Nations*. New York: Bantam Classics (Books).

Solow, R.M. (1957). "Technical Change and the Aggregate Production Function", *Review of Economics and Statistics*: 312-20, August.

———. (1971). "Technical Progress and Productivity Change", in Amartya Sen (ed.), *Growth Economics*. Penguin Books.

Sraffa, Piero (1950). *Production of Commodities by Means of Commodities*. Paper Back. Mumbai: Vora & Co.

Stiglitz, J.E. (1998). *More Instruments and Broader Goals: Moving toward the Post Washington Consensus*. Helsinki: UNU/WIDER.

———. (2002). *Globalization and Discontents*. W.W. Norton & Company.

———. (2008). "Capital-Market Liberalization, Globalization and the IMF", in J.A. Ocampo and J.E. Stiglitz (eds.), *Capital-Market Liberalization and Development.* Oxford University Press. pp.76-100.

Sutcliffe, J.B. (1995). "Theoretical Aspects of the Development of European Community Regional Policy", *Swiss Political Science Review* 1: 1–22.

Swamy, Subramaniam (1973). "Agricultural, Non agricultural and General inflation in India from 1861 -1967", in Maya Shah (ed.), *Essays in Honor of V. N. Kothari.*

Tanzi, V. (2000). "Globalization and the Future of Social Protection", *Working Paper* No. 12. Washington: IMF. Retrieved from *http://www.imf.org/external/pubs/ft/wp/2000/wp0012*

Tinbergen, Jan (1950). *On the Theory of Economic Policy.* North Holland.

———. (1956). *Economic Policy: Principles and Design.* Amesterdam: North Holland.

———. (1974). "Substitution of Graduate by Other Labour", *Kyklos* 27: 217-26.

Tripathy, R.N. (1970). *Fiscal Policy and Economic Development in India.* New Delhi: Deep & Deep.

———. (1985). *Public Finance in Underdeveloped Countries.* New Delhi: Sterling Publishing Private Ltd.

U.N. Expert Group (1951). *Measures for the Economic Development of Under- developed Countries.* p.3.

United Nations (1951). *Measures for International Economic Stability.* Department of Economic Affairs, Taxes and Fiscal Policy in Under-developed Countries. p.14.

———. (1954). *Taxes and Fiscal Policy in Under-developed Countries.* p.11.

United Republic of Tanzania (URT) (2008). *The Economic Survey 2007.* Ministry of Finance and Economic Affairs. Dar es Salaam: Government Printer.

Vakil, C.N. and P.R. Brahmanand (1953). *Planning for an Expanding Economy.* Bombay: Vora.

Vedder, R.K. and L.E. Gallaway (1998). "Government Size and Economic Growth", Paper Prepared for the *Joint Economic Committee of the US Congress.* pp.1-15.

Viner, Jacob (1958). "Stability and Progress: The Poorer Countries' Problem", in D. Hague (ed.), *Stability and Progress in the World Economy.*

Yolton, John (1996). "John Locke (1632-1704)", in Adam Kuper and Jessica Kuper (eds.), *The Social Science Encyclopedia.* London: Routledge.

Waigama, Samuel M.S. (2008). *Privatization Process and Asset Valuation: A Case Study of Tanzania* Doctoral Dissertation. Stockholm, Sweden: School of Architecture and the Built Environment, Royal Institute of Technology.

Wagner, A. (1890). *Finanzwissenschaf.* 3rd Edition. Leipzig; referred from R.M. Bird (1971). "Wagner's Law of Expanding State Activity", *Public Finance* 26: 1-26

Wallis, Kenneth F. (1971). "Wages, Prices and Incomes Policies: Some Comments", *Economica* 38(151): 304-10.

Wenzel and Wiedemann (1989). *Structural Adjustment and Intersectoral Shifts in Tanzania.* Dar Es Salaam

Wiseman, J. and A.T. Peacok (1961). *The Growth of Public Expenditure in United Kingdom.* Princeton University Press.

Wobst, P. (2001). *Structural Adjustment and Inter-sectoral Shifts in Tanzania, A Computable General Equilibrium Analysis.* Dissertation, University of Hohenheim. Retrieved from *http://www.zef.de/module/register/media/1d57_rr117*

World Bank (2000). *Country Report 13: Tanzania.* Washington DC.